STRUGGLING LEARNERS & LANGUAGE IMMERSION EDUCATION

STRUGGLING LEARNERS & LANGUAGE IMMERSION EDUCATION

Research-Based, Practitioner-Informed Responses
to Educators' Top Questions

TARA WILLIAMS FORTUNE
with
MANDY R. MENKE

Struggling Learners & Language Immersion Education:
Research-Based, Practitioner-Informed Responses to Educators' Top Questions

First Edition, First Printing
Printed in the United States of America

Produced by
Center for Advanced Research on Language Acquisition
University of Minnesota
140 University International Center
331 17th Avenue Southeast
Minneapolis, MN 55414
USA
612-626-8600
carla@umn.edu
http://www.carla.umn.edu

Desktop Publishing and Cover Design: The Roberts Group

This book was developed, in part, with input gained from summer institutes sponsored by CARLA, which received support from the U.S. Department of Education, Office of Postsecondary Education, International Education Programs Service, Language Resource Center grant no. P229A020011. The contents of this publication do not necessarily reflect the positions or policies of the U.S. Department of Education.

The University of Minnesota is an equal opportunity educator and employer.

This publication is available in alternative formats upon request. Direct requests to the CARLA office at carla@umn.edu.

Fortune, T. W. with Menke M. R. (2010). *Struggling Learners & Language Immersion Education: Research-Based, Practitioner-Informed Responses to Educators' Top Questions* (CARLA Publication Series). Minneapolis: University of Minnesota, The Center for Advanced Research on Language Acquisition.

ISBN: 978-0-9843996-0-4

TABLE OF CONTENTS

PART ONE: PROGRAM SUITABILITY AND LEARNER DISABILITY

PART TWO: BEST PRACTICE AT THE CLASSROOM- AND PROGRAM-LEVEL

LIST OF FIGURES

ACKNOWLEDGMENTS

In the fall of 2004 a young, bright-eyed graduate student attended the Center for Advanced Research on Language Acquisition's Annual Open House. As a former Spanish immersion teacher in Fairfax County Public Schools, she was drawn to the Immersion Projects display table and it was there that immersion projects coordinator, Tara Fortune, and Mandy Menke first met. That was a very fortuitous encounter. Mandy's interest in becoming actively involved in the Immersion Projects' struggling learner initiative grew into a multi-year commitment to the development of this handbook. I am deeply grateful for Mandy's countless hours invested in reading research, reviewing institute participants' input, and writing draft responses to questions. These initial drafts served as the foundation for the final manuscript.

This project and publication has also benefitted immeasurably from the feedback and insights of project adviser, Kathryn Kohnert, immersion researchers, Merrill Swain and Sharon Lapkin, and CARLA reviewer, Andrew Cohen. Dr. Kohnert's expertise in the area of speech and language development for bilingual children was an invaluable resource. Her informative presentations during the institutes and supportive feedback on early drafts both educated and encouraged. In addition, Drs. Swain and Lapkin of the Ontario Institute of Studies in Education, provided very helpful editing comments and suggested the addition of case narratives to enrich and provide further context for each chapter—an outstanding piece of advice. Finally, Dr. Cohen's careful editing of the manuscript greatly improved its clarity.

I am awed by the generous gifting of time and talent by each of the nine invited case narrative authors: Mary Cazabon (Cambridge Public Schools), Donna Gouin (Sligo Creek Elementary, Montgomery County Public Schools), Denise Joyce (Adams Spanish Immersion Magnet School, Saint Paul Public Schools), Patricia Martínez (Francis Scott Key Elementary, Arlington Public Schools), Marjorie Myers (Francis Scott Key Elementary, Arlington Public Schools), Aline Petzold (L'Etoile Du Nord, Saint Paul Public Schools), Kaari Rodriguez (Lakes International Language Academy, Forest Lake, Minnesota), Jonathon Steinhoff (Rigler Elementary, Portland Public Schools), and the parent author. The "real stories" provide lived context for each chapter, tap the wisdom of each professional and ultimately give this handbook heart. Together they remind me of why this topic matters so much and what a difference educators make in the lives of children and families. Thank you for your work and willingness to share these important stories with the rest of us!

This handbook emerged from work with two groups of dedicated immersion educators and specialists who came to the University of Minnesota to participate in one of CARLA's internationally known summer institutes. Their questions, research summaries and lists of recommendations for practice were the beginning of this handbook. It is at the same time humbling and inspiring to work with such deeply committed, hard-working educators year after year! I offer thanks to each of them who so willingly shared what they have experienced and learned from years of experience educating children in immersion classrooms and programs.

I also thank Emily Alter, Aileen Bach, and Diane Tedick for the careful copy editing of later drafts. I owe a great debt to Sherry Roberts of The Roberts Group whose visually engaging book design and production expertise added the final artistic touches and made this handbook organized and accessible. And finally, I am very grateful for my colleagues and the support staff at CARLA, Elaine Tarone (Director), Karin Larson (Coordinator), Marlene Johnshoy (Technology Support), Liz Hellebuyck (Office Specialist), whose constant, behind-the-scene support has made this work possible.

Tara Williams Fortune

Summer institute participants

Vanessa Alvarez Schröder

Denise Anderson

Aaron Arredondo

Reiko Aya

Michael Bacon

Mary Carmen Bartolini

Mary Fred Bausman-Watkins

Rosa Benavides

Teresa Bohlsen

Heather Briant

Amy Brossart

Andrew Burfeind

Iris Calderon

Elizabeth Chaigne

Bonni Chan

Adria Cohen

Philippe Corbaz

Tracey Crawford

Rosa Cubero-Hurley

Barbara de Gortari

Shannon DeLozier-Yee Yick

Katharina Denny

Annie DePujo

Felicia Eybl

Norma Fernández

Melvelicia Franco

Audrey Gagnaire

Katie George

Dolores Gomez

Graciela Gonzalez

Donna Gouin

Carrie Grabowski

Laura Hanson

Linda Hardman

Tina Haselius

Tamayo Hattori

Andrea Hoehn

Paquita Holland

Nicole Jessen

Denise Joyce

Judy Kostreba

Maren Kramer

Carrie Lawrence

Kathleen Jean Lawrence

Mary Ann Lomack

Aida Luszczynska

Marie Matsinger

John Medina

Jaime Miller

Laura Nelson

Sarah Padilla

Maureen Elwell Peltier

Juanita Pena

Aline Petzold

Sigurd Piwek

Bobbi Jo Rademacher

Victoria Rau

David Reid

Peggy Rigaud

Linda Rivera

Sylvia Seiwert

Miriam Strand

Elaine Tam

LeAnn Taylor

Gayelynn Tunheim

Isabel Patricia Valdivia

Leyda Vasquez-Shotzbarger

Manuel Vega-Hernandez

Beth Villalobos

Maggie Williams

Mei Wong

Annmarie Zoran

FOREWORD
BY KATHRYN KOHNERT

Most young children are quite conversant in the language(s) spoken in their home environment before they enter the formal educational system. That is, they have 'learned to talk' and are able to use language as a tool to meet communicative needs. In the educational setting, school-age children build on this spoken language foundation by talking to learn in a wide variety of content areas. Critically, children also learn to map spoken language skills onto graphic symbols as they learn to read and write, then use these skills in literacy to further their learning in key content areas.

For English proficient children and English learners whose schooling occurs partly or mainly in a language that is different from the one they first learned to speak, as is often the case in immersion education, learning to talk, talking to learn and written language demands interact to present additional challenges on both sides of the learning and teaching equation. As the research clearly indicates, however, these challenges are by no means insurmountable for typically developing children and they are offset by a host of rewards, including proficiency and skill in other languages and cultures, increased metalinguistic knowledge as well as eventual performance at or above grade-level in more than one language. Thus, the case for one-way and two-way immersion education, at least for typical learners, is strong. Yet all learners are not "typical". This handbook addresses a far more complex issue; the possibility and practicality of immersion education for children who are "struggling language learners."

An important subset of children falls significantly below their age and grade peers on language and literacy measures. One in every ten school-age children struggles with language and/or literacy acquisition for no readily apparent reason. Other children who struggle with learning are diagnosed with autism, attention deficit hyperactivity disorder (ADHD) or acquired brain injury. In "Struggling Learners and Language Immersion Education", authors Fortune with Menke tackle the very thorny issue of educational decision-making with atypical learners in the context of immersion education. Decision-making processes are carefully placed within the available research and brought to life with case studies contributed by master immersion educators. The result is not a simple 'one-size fits all' answer to the questions related to who should or should not participate in immersion education. This is a very good thing as a simple response would be inconsistent with the clearly articulated complexities of the multiple factors to be considered. On the other hand, it is also clear in this volume that the presence of a language or learning disability does not, in and of itself, preclude a child's successful participation in immersion education. This volume does not shy away from the toughest questions. Issues including how to assess and intervene with struggling learners as well as how to communicate with parents are addressed head-on, with depth and great compassion.

In "Struggling Learners and Language Immersion Education", the authors provide educators in language immersion settings with practical, empirically-motivated advice on how to best address the needs of students with diverse abilities. This is a massive and timely achievement. This volume also sets the stage for researchers to begin to systematically investigate best practices for struggling learners in a variety of bilingual educational settings.

Kathryn Kohnert

For more than a decade, the Center for Advanced Research on Language Acquisition (CARLA) at the University of Minnesota has sponsored a variety of summer institutes that cater to the needs of language teaching professionals. These institutes serve as one of several outreach venues for the dissemination of CARLA's various projects including the Immersion Research and Professional Development Project. During two consecutive summers, 2003 and 2004, the annual "Meeting the Challenges of Immersion Education" institute focused specifically on one of the field's more complex and persistent challenges—language and learning disorders (LLD) in the dual language and immersion context. Consistent with CARLA's Immersion Projects' professional contributions to this field, this publication targets a variety of dual language settings, including one-way (foreign language) immersion, two-way (bilingual) immersion, and indigenous immersion.

Multiple factors contribute to the enduring nature of this challenge. First, immersion programs are elective programs within the public school system. This means that children and families are able to move to a non-immersion program if they believe it is in the best interest of the child. Thus, individuals who are involved in immersion education can and do ask, "Is immersion the best program for this child?" Most parents ask themselves this question prior to enrolling their child, and if the child begins to show signs of struggling academically, linguistically, or socially, parents and educators are likely to revisit the question time and again.

Secondly, as public schools, immersion programs are open to all children. No prescreening of applicants occurs for initial program entry in K-1 for the vast majority of U.S. programs. Lateral entry in grades 2 and beyond typically requires some kind of language and literacy skill assessment to ensure that the newcomer can be successful learning in two languages. Because immersion programs open their doors to all families, immersion students can be expected to exhibit an incidence of LLD similar to that found in other public schools. The National Center for Learning Disabilities (Cortiella, 2009) reports that in 2007, 9% of all public school students were identified as eligible for additional educational assistance by

INTRODUCTION TO THE PROJECT

2004 institute participants attending to new information from one of the institute presenters.

the Individuals with Disabilities Act (IDEA, 2004); 4% of all children received services under the category of specific learning disabilities (SLD) and 2% were identified for speech or language impairment (SLI). The prevalence of elementary-aged children receiving support for SLI was higher, slightly more than 4%. Eligibility for SLD-related services was even higher among certain ethnic groups; in the category of SLD, for example, 5% of Hispanic children, 6% of African Americans and 7% of Native Americans were eligible.

A third factor that contributes to the persistence of this challenge for immersion educators is the steady rise in program numbers. According to the Center for Applied Linguistics (2006, 2009), there are currently 310 foreign language immersion programs and 346 two-way bilingual

immersion programs. While these numbers may not appear large, as a percentage of the total number of elementary language education programs in the U.S., the number of immersion programs continues to rise. Over the past thirty years, national survey data indicate growth from 2% of all elementary foreign language programs in 1987 to 8% in 1997 to at least 13% as of 2008 (Rhodes & Branaman, 1999; Center for Applied Linguistics, 2008). This upward trend for immersion programming is even more remarkable given the overall decline in elementary-level foreign language program numbers in the past decade from 31% of all elementary schools offering foreign language programming in 1997 to 25% as of 2008 (Center for Applied Linguistics, 2008).

In addition to the topic's persistence, the unique nature of

language and learning differences increases topic complexity. Questions that arise about any given child are highly learner and situation specific and vary a great deal. For example, immersion parents and teachers might ask:

- Are the child's reading struggles due to learning to read in a second language or might there be some other language-based disorder at play?

- Since early intervention is key, how long should teachers and parents engage in "watchful waiting" with a struggling learner before requesting additional learning support?

- Are children who have already been diagnosed with attention deficit disorder or autism able to be successful in the immersion classroom?

While questions are many and varied, answers are few and far between. Pertinent research findings from studies carried out in immersion contexts are limited, and in some cases, inconsistent. Securing funding and designing and carrying out high-quality research studies in this area is a challenge. Moreover, many areas in the U.S. lack a sufficient number of students and programs to create an adequate sample size of struggling learners for certain types of research. As a result, administrators, teachers, parents, and other specialists are frequently asked to make difficult decisions about children who struggle based on incomplete information and relatively few guidelines.

Bilingual school psychologist, Aline Petzold, presents the district's process for distinguishing between a language/learning delay and a disability.

In an effort to meet the challenge of learners who struggle in immersion programs, more than seventy professionals with experience in language immersion education gathered over the course of two summers to engage issues relevant to educating the struggling immersion learner. Together, they examined research, exchanged ideas, and listened to specialists, including researchers, special education teachers, school psychologists, and speech-language pathologists.

The goals of the institutes were:

1. To establish a professional forum for immersion educators and specialists who are interested in this topic to exchange ideas and practices.

2. To examine the research literature on struggling second language learners and discuss implications for teaching and learning in immersion settings.

3. To consider a range of pre-referral procedures and assessment practices that can provide feedback on students' language development and learning.

4. To explore a variety of instructional adaptations known to be effective with under-performing language immersion learners and discuss how to integrate these strategies both at the classroom and program level.

5. To collaboratively create a list of recommended instructional adaptations that address particular language and learning disorders and create a more inclusive learning environment.

The Immersion Projects coordinator, Tara Williams Fortune, facilitated the weeklong event. Various educational specialists from Minnesota's immersion schools presented, as well as Kathryn Kohnert, associate professor in the Department of Speech-Language-Hearing Sciences. All but one Taiwanese participant came from immersion programs located in 16 states representing all continental regions of the U.S. and Alaska. They represented three distinct immersion education contexts: the one-way foreign language immersion context (represented by 71%), the two-way bilingual immersion context (represented by 24%), and the indigenous (heritage) immersion context (represented by 5%). The immersion languages targeted by participants' programs included Spanish, French, German, Japanese (one-way programs), Spanish-English, Cantonese-English (two-way programs), and Yup'ik (an indigenous program).

Collectively, participants brought a wealth of experience in the immersion setting and a wide variety of professional perspectives. On the first day of the institute, participants were invited to complete a survey that requested information about their role and years of immersion experience, as well as the range and frequency of language and learning issues they

2003 institute participants discussing their experiences with struggling immersion learners in small groups.

Introduction Figure 1: Institute Participants' Years of Experience in the Immersion Setting

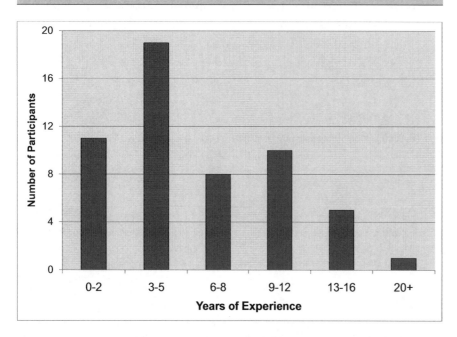

Introduction Table 1:
Number of Survey Respondents by Participant Role

N	Participant Role in the Immersion Setting
35	Classroom Immersion Teacher
3	Immersion Program Coordinator (program-level)
3	Special Education Teacher
2	School Psychologist
2	Speech Language Pathologist
1	Speech-Language-Hearing Sciences Graduate Student
1	Social Worker
1	Gifted/Talented Specialist
1	Reading Specialist
1	Immersion Program Coordinator (district-level)
1	Immersion Administrator
1	Paraprofessional
1	Ph.D. Student
1	Linguistics University Professor

had encountered in their professions. Of the fifty-four participants who responded, the majority of respondents had three or more years working as classroom teachers in an immersion setting (see Introduction Figure 1). In addition, many respondents were educational specialists and program support personnel (see Introduction Table 1).

The "Survey of Exceptionalities and the Immersion Classroom," developed by Dr. Fortune in advance of the institute, was given to all participants at the beginning of the week. It included a list of exceptionality categories recognized by Individuals with Disabilities Education Improvement Act (IDEA) 2004. A brief definition was provided for each category. For example, the label "visual impairment and blindness" was followed by this descriptive text "visual impairment includes any type of sight problem which, even with correction, adversely affects educational performance." Participants were asked to indicate how often they had encountered the particular exceptionality in their immersion practice using a five-point scale that ranged from "never" to "always." See Appendix A on page 115 to review the actual survey.

Results from this informal survey indicated that the most frequently encountered disorders fell under the broad category of SLD, with the exception of two: attention deficit hyperactivity disorder and speech or language impairment. The seven most frequently encountered issues of exceptionality are listed below beginning with the issue cited most often:

1. Reading Comprehension (SLD)

2. Basic Reading Skills (SLD)

3. Attention Deficit Hyperactivity Disorder (ADHD)

4. Listening Comprehension (SLD)

5. Speech or Language Impairment (SLI)

6. Oral Expression (SLD)

7. Math Reasoning and Calculation (SLD)

Appendix B on page 118 displays the survey data totaled for the two institutes.

The following practitioner-oriented document began to take shape during these summers. It is framed by ten questions that were individually identified and mutually agreed upon by institute participants in the summer of 2003. Beginning with these questions the following summer, 2004 summer institute participants broke into groups of four or five and selected one of the already identified questions to examine in greater depth over the course of the institute. As various presenters shared information and research, participants were invited to apply what they were learning from one another to their group's question. They were also encouraged to avail themselves of the rich array of research articles in the institute's Struggling Learners' Lending Library. Based on institute presentations, discussions, and readings, each group put together a list of relevant research findings. On the final day of the weeklong institute, the groups brainstormed implications and offered recommendations for immersion classroom and program practices.

The work presented here expands on this initial collaboration. Over the past few years, Tara Fortune and Mandy Menke, a Ph.D. candidate in Hispanic Linguistics at the University of Minnesota, have reviewed and refined the practitioner contributions from the summer institutes. The ten original questions were reduced to nine chapters because questions 5 and 6 were combined into one. These nine chapters have been organized into two sections: Part One: Program Suitability and Learner Disability, and Part Two: Best Practice at the Classroom- and Program-Level. Part One addresses educators' uncertainties about the appropriateness of immersion schooling for various learner profiles and learning needs, initial literacy challenges, and the subtleties involved in differentiating delay vs. disability, including the development of assessment practices to determine eligibility for special education services. Part Two focuses on classroom-based and program-level responses to language and learning struggles. It discusses ways that teachers, reading specialists and special education teachers can modify and adapt instruction; presents a variety of early support programs and services developed by immersion educators; provides guidance for the "In which language?" conundrum; and addresses the important role of home-school communication.

To provide a more meaningful reading experience, a number of veteran educators who work in immersion programs were invited

Group photo of 2004 summer institute participants.

to share a personal case story that relates to the question at hand. Their lived experiences offer readers a forum for reflecting on the issues at a deeper level. Each chapter then begins with questions. The questions in chapters 1-8 are followed by an immersion educator's narrated experience with the particular challenge introduced by the questions. Next, background information on the topic precedes a brief discussion of relevant research and literature from the field of language and culture education. Depending on topic complexity, these discussions may be on occasion further organized into sub-topics. After the presentation of research, there is a list of research and practitioner-informed recommendations intended to guide program

and classroom practice. Finally, a number of online and print resources are listed that can serve to provide further information and support best practice. More complete citations for print resources can be found in the reference section. References and a master list of resources for each of the nine chapters are also accessible on the CARLA website at www.carla. umn.edu/immersion.

This document was designed with practicing immersion educators in mind. We hope that those who work in immersion contexts are able to use this document as a resource as well as a tool for professional development. It has been our intent to bridge the research-practice divide by synthesizing research findings in the context of practitioners' lived

experiences and the questions that stem from these experiences. We have sought to present this information in a format that is readily accessible to Child Study Teams within the immersion setting, including teachers, administrators, special educators, school psychologists, social workers, speech language pathologists, and other educational specialists. This resource can also be used as a course textbook for language teacher education programs, and other post-secondary programs that offer professional development for allied professionals (e.g., school administrators, special educators, school psychologists, social workers, speech language pathologists, etc.) who work in bilingual and immersion environments.

Dual language education/learners. These terms are increasingly used in the U.S. in lieu of "bilingual education/learners" to describe a set of educational programs and their participants. These programs are committed to additive bilingualism and biliteracy through sheltered subject matter instruction in a minority language for at least 50% of the school day. The four programs are: one-way (foreign language) immersion, two-way (bilingual) immersion, maintenance (developmental) bilingual, and indigenous immersion (Howard, Olague and Rogers, 2003).

First language. First language (L1) refers to the language that an individual learns first; this is sometimes known as a native language or mother tongue. An individual's L1 may not be his/her dominant language throughout the course of his/her entire life.

Impairment/disability/handicap. In 1980, the World Health Organization (WHO) introduced definitions for impairment, disability, and handicap. The American Speech-Language-Hearing Association (ASHA) summarizes WHO definitions on the web:

- *Impairment* is defined as an abnormality of a structure or function (e.g., an abnormality of the ear or auditory system);

- *Disability* is the functional consequence of impairment (e.g., inability to hear certain sounds or inability to speak clearly);

- *Handicap* is the social consequence of impairment (e.g., isolation, loss of job, or having to make career changes as a result of communication difficulties).

(ASHA, 2008)

The terms learning disabled, impaired, and disordered are not consistently differentiated in the literature, and different authors use these terms in different ways at different times. The meanings of these terms have also changed over time. Consequently, these words are used interchangeably throughout this document.

Indigenous immersion. Indigenous immersion can take the form of either a one-way or two-way dual language model (see definitions on pages xix-xx); the student population is comprised primarily of students with ethnic ties to the language of instruction. The primary goal is language and culture revitalization.

Language disabled/impaired/disordered. As with *learning disabled*, the terms language disabled (LD), impaired, and disordered are regularly interchanged. Kohnert (2008) characterizes language disorders as

... deficits in the production and/or comprehension of any aspect of language as compared to chronological age peers. By definition, this relatively poor ability in language cannot be attributed to differences in the child's cultural, linguistic, or educational experiences. That is, language disorders are not the same as differences in communicative performance which result from naturally occurring diverse circumstances. (p. 84)

Language immersion education. Language immersion education refers to a school-based educational model, which uses an integrated approach to language and content instruction. As outlined in Fortune and Tedick (2008), defining characteristics are:

- A goal of additive bilingualism. This is accomplished by means of sustained and enriched instruction through the minority language while promoting development of the majority language.

- Subject area or content instruction occurs in the minority language for minimally 50% of the school day during the elementary school years and two year-long courses per grade level at the secondary level.

- Programs are content-driven and content-accountable.

- Teachers are fully proficient in the language(s) of instruction.

- Support for the majority language is present in the community at large.

- The separation of languages during instructional time is clear and sustained.

Three main program strands exist: one-way (foreign language) immersion, two-way (bilingual) immersion, and indigenous immersion. Within this document, attention is given to students in one-way and two-way programs because the majority of studies on struggling immersion learners has been conducted in these contexts. The needs of the indigenous group are nonetheless tangentially addressed since indigenous immersion learners exhibit characteristics similar to those of the other groups; issues such as dialect, ethnic diversity, and socioeconomic status, are faced by all three strands, albeit in different ways.

Language majority learner. Language majority learner is a term that refers to a learner's language background. The language majority learner speaks the language of the majority of people in a given regional or national context; in the U.S. context, this is English; in Germany, German, and in Japan, Japanese.

Language minority learner. Language minority learner is a term that refers to a learner's language background. The language minority learner, in contrast, is from a home where a language other than the dominant language of the majority is spoken; for example, a Spanish speaker in the U.S. or a speaker of English in Japan or Germany.

Non-immersion. *Non-immersion* is used in this document to describe educational settings that do not meet the criteria defined for an immersion program. Such settings are also referred to as traditional, English-medium, English-only, or all English programs in the literature. They may include use of language(s) other than English for more limited periods of time, e.g., transitional bilingual programs for language minority children or foreign language programs in the elementary or secondary school.

One-way (foreign language) immersion. One-way (foreign language) immersion targets language majority speakers with limited to no proficiency in the immersion language prior to beginning the program; because students share a common language background, they are all moving in one direction, toward bilingualism in the immersion language and the majority language of their community. Student exposure to the immersion language occurs primarily in the classroom and school. One-way (foreign language) programs are often further classified by factors such as the amount of time spent in the immersion language during the initial years (partial vs. full/total) and when immersion begins (early, mid, or late).

Second language. Second language (L2) refers to the language that an individual acquires after having already learned a first. This term is often used to refer not only to the L2 learned but also any subsequent languages; that is to say, any language that an individual learns after the first can be considered an L2.

Second and foreign language learners are sometimes differentiated in the foreign language literature base. An L2 learner is one who learns another language in a context in which it is a majority language; a native Spanish speaker learning English in the U.S. is considered an L2 learner. In contrast, a foreign language learner learns the L2 in a context where it is not a majority language. For example, a native Spanish speaker learning English in Mexico is considered a foreign language learner.

Specific learning disability. A specific learning disability is defined in federal law as:

> . . . a disorder in one or more of the basic psychological processes involved in understanding or in using language, spoken or written, that may manifest itself in an imperfect ability to listen, think, speak, read, write, spell, or to do mathematical calculations, including conditions such as perceptual disabilities, brain injury, minimal brain dysfunction, dyslexia, and developmental aphasia. (Institute for Education Sciences/ U.S. Department of Education, n.d.)

ABBREVIATIONS AND ACRONYMS

ADD	Attention Deficit Disorder
ADHD	Attention Deficit/Hyperactivity Disorder
EA	Educational Assistant
ELL	English Language Learner
ESL	English as a Second Language
CBM	Curriculum-Based Measurement
DA	Dynamic Assessment
FL	Foreign Language
L1	First Language
L2	Second Language
LCDH	Linguistic Coding Differences Hypothesis
LD	Learning Disability
LLD	Language Learning Disability/Disorder
RTI	Response to Intervention
SLD	Specific Learning Disability
SLI	Specific Language Impairment
SpEd	Special Education
TWI	Two-way Immersion

"The term does not include learning problems that are primarily the result of visual, hearing, or motor disabilities, of mental retardation, of emotional disturbance, or of environmental, cultural, or economic disadvantage" (Massachusetts Department of Elementary and Secondary Education, 2008, n.p.). Learning-disabled students can have difficulty with basic reading skills, reading comprehension, written expression, mathematics calculation, listening comprehension, and/or oral expression.

Struggling learner. A struggling learner, for the purposes of this document, is a student who has attracted the attention of teacher(s) for an extended period of time, approximately 6 weeks to a few months, depending on the grade level. This student struggles relative to the average performance of classroom peers, and the struggles may involve academic, linguistic, social-emotional, and/or behavioral issues. The primary emphasis within the arena of exceptionalities has been on those individuals who experience challenges with language and learning.

Two-way (bilingual) immersion. Two-way (bilingual) immersion (TWI) targets two distinct learner groups: language majority students and language minority students, who are dominant in their first language and have support for this language at home. The ideal ratio between the two groups is 1:1, but minimally each group comprises one-third of the student population (i.e., a 2:1 ratio). Although the goal for the two groups is the same— bilingualism and biliteracy in both the majority language and the immersion (minority) language— the groups move in opposite directions, with each acquiring the dominant language of the other. In other words, the language majority student group acquires proficiency in the minority language while continuing to develop their majority language skills, and the language minority group acquires proficiency in the majority language while continuing to develop their minority language skills. In order for the two learner groups to effectively learn from and with each other in an integrated setting, it is essential that instruction through the minority language be viewed as an enriching experience for all and that an academically challenging, highly collaborative learning environment is provided.

PART ONE

Program Suitability and Learner Disability

CHAPTER

KEY QUESTIONS

- For whom might immersion not be appropriate?

- For whom might immersion be appropriate?

- Who is likely to struggle and stay in the immersion program?

- Who is likely to struggle and leave the immersion program?

Between 1986 and 1995, Key School in Arlington, Virginia housed an immersion program as a separate program within the school. In the 1995-1996 school year, the program became a "full school" program, turning Key into a 50:50 two-way elementary (K-5) Spanish immersion school. Although Key School was to be an immersion school, it would still host other separate and distinct programs within the building:

- an English to Speakers of Other Languages/High Intensity Language Training (ESOL/HILT) program,

- a Special Education (SpEd) program, and

- an early childhood Montessori program.

Only children who were not found to be best served by participation in one of the school's other programs could participate in the immersion program. This resulted in separate programming for students with limited English proficiency, students eligible for special education services, and preschoolers.

To transition Key School to a full school program, a second neighborhood school was established to accept the students who did not want to attend Key or who were too old to begin in immersion.

REAL STORIES

Marjorie L. Myers, Ed.D.

Principal

Francis Scott Key Elementary

Arlington, Virginia

Program Model: Two-way bilingual immersion, 50:50, K- Gr. 5

Program Environment: Whole school, Urban

Language(s): Spanish, English

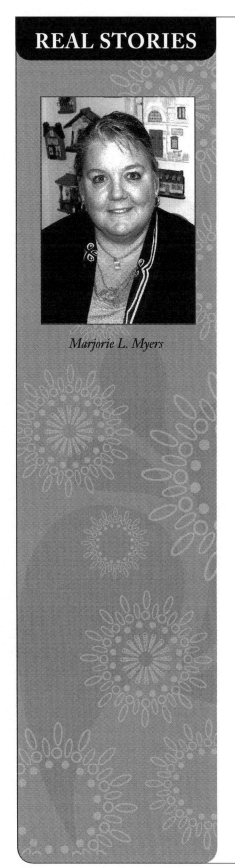

REAL STORIES

Marjorie L. Myers

In the fall of 1995 when the doors opened as a full school, many of Key's former non-immersion students were relocated to the new neighborhood school. All of the children who had already enrolled in the immersion program at Key remained. All of the native Spanish-speaking ESOL/HILT and Spanish-speaking SpEd students also remained, as did the Montessori students. For the first year, the ESOL/HILT and SpEd children remained in their small "self-contained" settings around the building. All pre-existing staff assured the new administrator that that was the best educational setting for these children. The administrator's feelings were different, and beginning in 1996-1997 all ESOL/HILT and SpEd students were included in the regular (immersion) classrooms. There was great concern expressed among the immersion teachers as well as the SpEd and ESOL/HILT staff; neither group felt that ESOL/HILT or SpEd children could be successful in the immersion classroom and they believed these children would bring down the level of academic rigor in the classroom.

Initially, the Spanish-speaking SpEd and ESOL students in the upper grades (4 and 5) had a great deal of difficulty with this new model. They had never had formal instruction in Spanish, and found it difficult to read and write in that language. For many of them, separate classes were maintained until they completed their time at the school. The resource staff and teachers expressed a great deal of enthusiasm and excitement for the younger students entering immersion. Children who in the past had been viewed as unable to participate were participating in the Spanish side of the day. Children who had trouble demonstrating their reading skills in English demonstrated considerably better reading skills in Spanish. It was quite a success. Since the 1996-1997 change in practice, full inclusion has existed at Key School for all students.

One of the highlights of Key's history was the student performance in the second year of state testing. The Standards of Learning (SOLs) are the state's objectives for learning as well as the name for the tests used to meet the assessment requirements for No Child Left Behind (NCLB). In the spring of each year, all students must take the SOLs. The first year the tests were administered in the state, only two of the 22 elementary schools in the county had their students meet the proficiency benchmarks for the tests. Key Elementary was not one of them, but the second year it was.

Passing the SOLs that year changed the way everyone felt about the school. It was no longer a school that parents hesitated to send their children to, but rather became the preferred school to attend. It

had diversity, two languages, the same curriculum as other schools, and inclusion. The demand for immersion became so great that the district had to build a second school in 2003 on the other side of the county to meet the demand. Between the two schools, over 1,100 children a year were participating in immersion schooling during the 2008-09 school year.

Through these experiences, educators at Key have come to believe that immersion can be appropriate for every child. An important aspect of deciding if immersion is appropriate for a child is having expectations for an individual child's learning outcomes. For example, occasionally native Spanish-speaking children with low mental abilities become part of the program. In one instance, Analisa, a child who started at Key in second grade, could speak in two word phrases both in English and Spanish, respond to commands in both languages, and write a few words in both languages by the time she was a fifth grader. For Analisa, this was progress. In her own very limited way, she was bilingual and this could only have happened through a program like that at Key.

Educators at Key School believe that immersion can be appropriate for children even when language and learning are a struggle. In their own way, all immersion children struggle. Language immersion education is an academically rigorous program and even the most able children must work hard to be successful. Many high performing English-speaking children will beg their parents to let them attend their neighborhood school so that they can do all of their homework in English and have less of a work load. Some English language learners struggle, some special needs children struggle, very few have no difficulties, but despite the challenges, they all walk away with a second language, and for that, educators at Key School feel the efforts are worth the struggles.

Over the years, educators at Key have encountered students with particular backgrounds and situations for whom immersion has not proven to be a worthwhile match for their needs. For this two-way immersion program, they include (1) monolingual English speakers who enter the program after second grade, (2) English L2 learners with varying degrees of oral proficiency in Spanish who enter after third grade and bring no formal schooling or literacy experiences in Spanish, and (3) children with severe issues with transitions and change. Key School has experienced limited success "catching up" native English speakers who have been in a monolingual environment since birth. Similarly, the English language learner from a Spanish home language environment who has studied in English only until grade 3 or 4 has found it difficult to read and understand

REAL STORIES

academic Spanish since none of their prior instruction has been in Spanish. Finally, struggles with transitions and change, more than the language, have presented a difficult situation for a few children over the years. It is not so much the degree of disability, but the type. Key School has found emotionally difficult students who have severe problems with transitions and change often need to be placed in a self-contained situation in another school.

Key elementary students who struggle and then leave the program have been few and variable in their reasons for leaving. Reasons for opting out of the program include lack of parent commitment to regular school attendance, severe emotional difficulties and lack of school-based services for deaf children. Following are some examples of children who have opted out.

A mother of twin daughters pulled both children out after first grade because one twin was behind her peers academically. In this situation, the twin had fallen behind her peers in part due to irregular attendance during kindergarten.

Another child, Toby, a native English speaker, screamed, cried and huddled under the desk from the day he started school. His older siblings had attended Key, including his profoundly gifted and autistic older brother, who, despite the fact that he never turned in one assignment or participated in a classroom other than by sitting and reading books, could understand and respond to everything in Spanish. Key School set up a self-contained situation for Toby: he stayed in the room and five special education teachers took turns throughout the day working with him. He was eventually found eligible for Interlude, a behavior modification program with limited access in another school, where he spent his elementary school years. He is now in private placement in a school for difficult children. Toby's problems were bigger than second language learning; no regular elementary school setting was appropriate for him. The older brother continued in the middle school immersion program where he received very low grades (D's), since he still wasn't turning in homework, but won the state championship in mathematics scoring the highest score ever on the competition.

Three young deaf students have also left the immersion program because there were teachers trained in teaching the deaf in other neighborhood schools. One of these children, an African American special needs child, stayed until the end of third grade before he moved to the other neighborhood school. In this case, his immersion struggles seemed to stem from being deaf; he missed so much language in the classroom, both English and Spanish, that it was easier for his English-only parents to help him in an English-only school.

REAL STORIES

While a few struggling learners have left Key School to find a better program match, the vast majority of students who struggle end up staying. To help make this possible, the school makes many kinds of support programs available within the school. To assist with this priority, the school employs between four and six bilingual special education teachers and assistants. The school works very hard to meet the needs of all children and except for a few extreme cases, it has managed to do so and do it well. A critical component to Key's success is the administration and staff's firm belief that all barriers are bumps in the road that can be overcome.

Two-way immersion at Key School has made a very significant difference in the lives of students who have come through the doors as kindergarten students and left after six years. Every year former students contact me with success stories about being admitted to the best universities in the country as well as some amazing programs and universities around the world. Parents all credit Key School with setting the stage for a rigorous and academic career for the children. Today, there are students who once studied at Key and were students identified with special needs and are now productive members of society. One particularly difficult student is currently employed as an after-school, "Extended Day" employee. He loves the school and is proud of still being bilingual . . . and I am happy to have him back as a working adult contributing to his own wellbeing and that of the current students.

BACKGROUND INFORMATION

Because immersion programs function as choice-based educational alternatives within the public school system, immersion educators are often asked to respond to questions of program suitability. Even after a child is enrolled in the school, questions about program-learner match-ups persist. Both academic and non-academic factors influence a learner's degree of success in an immersion program. Boschung and Roy (1996) accurately illustrated the challenges of isolating and identifying the causes and predictors of a learner's success when they stated that there are "no magic formulae, no clearly defined categories" (p. A9).

In response to the questions for this chapter, we consider the literature from two vantage points: (1) possible predictors of success, and (2) possible predictors of difficulty.

RELEVANT DISCUSSIONS AND RESEARCH FINDINGS

POSSIBLE PREDICTORS OF SUCCESS

Demers (1994) identified traits that tend to be common among successful immersion learners based on his years of experience as a French immersion teacher, resource room teacher, administrator, teacher educator, and parent of two gifted LD sons (see Figure 1.1 on page 11). According to Demers, the successful immersion learner is verbal, imitates easily, self-corrects, experiments without fear of making mistakes, is exposed to many good models, readily accepts challenges, has strengths in the first language (L1), trusts, is attentive and focused, is willing, possesses good auditory discrimination, has good memory and metacognitive awareness, and receives parental support.

Demers (1994) also recommended that students who score low only in the verbal performance areas of the WISC-R (Wechsler, 1981) and the Stanford-Binet (Roid, 2003) standardized tests stay in immersion programs, as these learners are equally likely to struggle in an immersion or unilingual program. Additionally, he proposed that students with strengths in short-term memory, auditory, and reasoning skills but weaknesses in visual perception and comprehension could succeed in immersion programs with some modifications. His complete list of characteristics of successful and unsuccessful immersion learners can be found in Figure 1.1 on page 11. It is important to note that this list was not designed to be used as a prescreening tool or to discourage admission into an immersion program. In fact, Demers (1994, 2001) has admonished teachers, administrators, and parents that decisions about program suitability need to be thoughtfully considered on a case-by-case basis.

Teacher expectations of students have been found by various researchers to be a factor influencing student success (Boschung & Roy, 1996; Cummins, 1984; Demers, 1994; Krueger, 2001). To demonstrate the importance of high teacher expectations, Cummins (1984) cited achievement test results of a Milwaukee German/French immersion school in which learners of low socioeconomic status who typically struggled in traditional programs excelled in immersion programs as a result of increased academic self-esteem. Cummins attributed this increase to a sense of pride developing from their new proficiency in a second language as well as increased teacher expectations. Some two decades later, Krueger (2001) found similarly positive achievement outcomes for German immersion students regardless of ethnic and socioeconomic backgrounds. Based on student surveys and one-on-one interview data, she too acknowledged the effect that supportive relationships with teachers had on students' success.

Milian and Pearson (2005) conducted a case study of two visually impaired students who participated in a two-way bilingual immersion program. Based on data gathered during semi-structured interviews of the students, their parents, and twelve teachers (two of whom specialized in teaching students with visual impairment), researchers found that the dual language setting was possible for these students given strong collaboration among home and school support systems, use of written materials (i.e., materials in English and Spanish Braille), and unyielding commitment to the goal of bilingualism and biliteracy. They also noted that parents and staff perceived an additional benefit for the two students due to the school environment's promotion of acceptance of diverse characteristics among all students.

POSSIBLE PREDICTORS OF DIFFICULTIES

Trites (1976) argued that immersion students should be screened for auditory processing challenges prior to admittance into an immersion program. In this initial study, Trites found that 32 struggling French immersion students, of average or above-average ability, did not perform as well as the same number of students in seven other "problem" groups on the Tactual Performance Test (TPT) (Halstead, 1947), a psychomotor problem-solving task which involved block manipulation with blindfolded subjects. All students under study were experiencing difficulties at school; however, only the French immersion student group displayed underperformance on the TPT task which Trites attributed to an underdeveloped primary auditory cortex located in the temporal lobe of the brain. Because of this evidence, Trites concluded that there was a maturational lag for this French immersion group in this area of the brain, which is important for language, memory, and auditory perceptual functions.

In this initial research study, Trites (1976) also found that many educators were not willing to deal with the wide range of learning abilities within the context of the immersion program; students who were considered less bright or of low socioeconomic status were sometimes discouraged from entering the program or recommended for transfer out of the program by teachers who viewed them as academically weak as a result of being below the extremely high average of their classmates. Inappropriate teacher expectations are still cited as a challenge for immersion programs today (Fortune, 2003; Woelber, 2003).

In a follow up study of 32 French immersion students (Trites & Price, 1977), half of whom had transferred out of the program into an English-medium learning environment and half of whom remained in the program, Trites administered the same battery of tests as above. After matching students for age and sex, those who had transferred out performed very differently on the TPT than those who stayed in French immersion. These findings provided Trites with additional support for his recommendation to transfer children who experience difficulty in immersion to an English-medium learning environment.

Convinced by this empirical evidence, Trites (1986) set out to identify a battery of tests that could be administered to prospective immersion students to predict success or failure in the French immersion program. Over a multi-year period of time, he followed some 200 English speakers attending French immersion from the time they were 4 years old until they were in Grade 4. In contrast to his earlier findings, immersion students who were having difficulties in the program performed significantly lower than those who were not on all 14 test measures. This outcome made it challenging for Trites to pinpoint the appropriate tests for a predictive battery and seemed to call his earlier conclusions into question as well.

Trites' research methodology has been repeatedly taken to task by research peers and these findings are now largely discredited (Carroll, 1976; Cummins, 1979, 1984; Genesee, 1983, 1987). Notably, questions have been raised as to the nature of the relationship between a test involving spatial and tactual processing abilities and difficulties in a language immersion setting. Subsequent field advances in understanding auditory processing disorders (today known as Central Auditory Processing Disorders) and their relationship to learning also call his findings into question (Bellis, 2004).

In her comparison study on learning-disabled vs. non-learning-disabled immersion students, and learning-disabled students in immersion vs. unilingual classrooms, Bruck (1982) found that psycholinguistic abilities and language of instruction did not predict underachievement. In other words, a learner's language processing abilities and the language of instruction (L1 or L2) were not in themselves determining factors of poor language acquisition and poor academic performance. Rather, social psychological factors, such as lack of adequate support outside of school for the language of instruction, negatively impacted a learner's achievement.

In a follow-up study, Bruck (1985) concluded along a similar vein that a learner's attitude and motivation towards the immersion language and program were better predictors of eventual transfer out of the program than language and learning ability. As evidence for this, she identified student discomfort speaking the immersion language in front of class, fewer details given on an oral production task, and teacher ratings on three dimensions of student behavior (conduct problems, hyperactivity, and inattention-passivity) on the Conners' Behavior Rating Scale (Goyette, Conners, & Ulrich, 1978) as three of the four factors most predictive of struggling students who decide to leave the immersion program. The fourth predictive factor, the immersion teachers' ratings of student reading skills, was related to language and/or learning abilities, while the other three factors were not.

Stern (1991) compared characteristics of ten learners who were considered for transfer to a monolingual program but remained in the immersion program with learners who were considered for transfer and did transfer. She noted that those students who transferred tended to have weaknesses in the areas of auditory discrimination, memory, and expressive skills in addition to difficulties with phonics, receptive language, and auditory-visual association. They had notably lower verbal IQ scores and conversely higher performance IQ scores suggesting an information processing difficulty. Demers (1994) has also suggested that students who struggle with auditory discrimination might be good candidates for transfer since immersion students are expected to make sense of a great deal of auditory input.

Stern's study (1991) also found that struggling learners who remained in the immersion program tended to exhibit a different profile. As a group, these students were about a year older, demonstrated a more even development in verbal and visual/perceptual performance skills, had some visual processing difficulties and overall exhibited less pronounced academic weakness in French. In addition, the parents of children who stayed strongly supported the immersion program and expressed an unwillingness to move their children to the English-only program.

Students who struggle with their L1 are likely to find the immersion setting difficult. Boschung and Roy (1996) and Demers (1994) cited poor L1 acquisition as a risk factor for low achievement in the immersion setting. Bruck (1982) also noted that L1 and pre-literacy skills could predict L2 or immersion language achievement. However, Wiss (1989) argued that language-based learning difficulties alone were not sufficient conditions for struggling in an immersion program; rather it was the combined demands of a setting that was linguistically challenging *and* academic in nature that appeared to overburden the learner.

Boschung and Roy (1996) included maturity development as a risk factor. Wiss (1989), however, argued that cognitive or linguistic immaturity did not inhibit language acquisition as Trites implied, citing the fact that many preschool-aged children (much less linguistically and cognitively mature than school-aged children) successfully communicate in and (some) even learn in two languages.

GUIDING PRINCIPLES

Based on the research reviewed above, and on the collective experiences of veteran immersion educators, we offer the following principles to guide practice.

Consider the learner as a unique individual. The personality, strengths, weaknesses, and educational needs of each student differ and thus influence an individual's success in an immersion program in varied ways (Boschung & Roy, 1996; Milian & Pearson, 2005). Researchers have emphasized the importance of deciding each case on an individual basis, taking into consideration the many facets of a learner's make-up (Bruck, 1985; Cummins 1979, 1984; Demers, 1994; Gouin, 1998; Kohnert & Derr, 2004; Mannavarayan, 2002; Wiss, 1987).

Establish realistic achievement and proficiency standards. Boschung and Roy (1996) recommended setting reasonable standards for each immersion program, in other words, defining realistic levels of proficiency and academic achievement to be attained by students in order to have a common standard for evaluation and comparison.

Elicit expectations from parents. What counts as success for one family will be different from educational success for another. Educators need to assist parents in identifying appropriate expectations for their child and the immersion program.

Secure specialist staffing and appropriate materials to address language and learning difficulties within the program itself. Transfer into a non-immersion program may be the only solution available to learners who struggle when there is a lack of intervention resources and remediation services available in the immersion program. By ensuring access to language and learning support services and materials within the program, educators may enable learners to stay and continue learning through the immersion language.

Put student needs first. It is imperative that the decisions made be based upon the best interests of the student (Demers, 1994). While this may seem evident, the struggling learner's needs must be put before those of the parent, teacher, and/or the program. Decisions should not be based solely upon what a parent wants for his/her child, the desires of a teacher to not have any struggling learners in his/her class, nor the needs of the program to maintain high numbers.

Hold high expectations for your learners. Paramount to student success is high teacher expectations. Students need to be encouraged and challenged to do their best.

Believe in and remain committed to the philosophy of the immersion program. Only when all who are involved with immersion students recognize, value, and work to uphold the philosophy of the program is success for all students promoted (Milian & Pearson,

2005). Specialists, resource teachers, psychologists, administrators, teachers, and parents all play an important role. A level of trust and support needs to be developed between the school and the home, which requires that schools not only educate parents about options and resources but also provide them with quality ones.

Trust the universal human capacity for language learning. When discussing issues of program-learner suitability, keep in mind that under the right circumstances, all children, even those with language impairment, are able to acquire and learn in two languages (Genesee, Paradis & Crago, 2004; Gutierrez-Clellen, Simon-Cereijido, & Wagner, 2008). Language-impaired learners educated in immersion settings will still exhibit impairment and function below normal, and they will do so in all languages, not just one.

Figure 1.1: Characteristics of a "Successful" vs. an "Unsuccessful" French Immersion Student (Demers, 1994)

"Successful" French Immersion Student	"Unsuccessful" French Immersion Student
• Is verbal, likes to talk	• Is often a reluctant speaker
• Imitates easily	• Imitates with difficulty
• Self corrects	• Doesn't notice errors
• Experiments without fear of making mistakes	• Often fears making mistakes
• Is exposed to many models of good modeling (at home, in the community, and in school)	• Poor modeling environment (at home, in the community and in school)
• Readily accepts challenges	• Has a defeatist attitude
• Shows strengths in first language	• Often has poor first language skills
• Trusts	• Mistrusts
• Is usually attentive and focused	• Is often inattentive and unfocused
• Is willing	• Is often unwilling
• Has good auditory discrimination	• Has poor auditory discrimination
• Has good memory and metacognitive awareness	• Has poor memory and poor metacognitive awareness
• Has determined parental support and convinced parents	• Often has unconvinced parents who are unprepared or unwilling to help

Note: This checklist was not designed to be used as a prescreening tool or to discourage admission into an immersion program. Such use would be inappropriate and likely increase public perception of immersion education as elitist. We recommend using this tool, instead, as a guide for behaviors to actively promote (in the case of the successful student descriptors) and transform (in the case of the unsuccessful student descriptors).

USEFUL RESOURCES

Below are selected online and print resources that pertain to issues discussed in this chapter.

1. *Characteristics of a "Successful" vs. an "Unsuccessful" French Immersion Student*
D. Demers, 1994, pp. 1-2

Based on his research and experience, Demers outlined a list of what he considered to be the main characteristics of successful and unsuccessful learners of French immersion. We recommend using this tool as a guide for behaviors to actively promote (in the case of the successful student descriptions) and transform (in the case of the unsuccessful student descriptions).

2. *Possible Factors Influencing Student Performance in French Immersion*
N. Roy, 1997b

http://www.carla.umn.edu/immersion/acie/vol7/May2004_Student_Performance_Factors.html

This document arose out of district wide concerns for students who were experiencing difficulties in French immersion. This profile was therefore developed to facilitate discussion among the classroom teacher(s), learning assistance teacher(s), and other School-Based Team members. In addition, the profile could be used when working with parents during educational planning for their children.

For more information contact:
Iria Knyazyeva, Vancouver Public Schools Media, Library Services, & Technology
Email: iknyazyeva@vsb.bc.ca
Fax: 604-713-5078

3. *Auditory Processing Disorder in Children*
National Institute on Deafness and Other Communication Disorders, 2004

http://www.ldonline.org/article/8056

In this article, the following questions about auditory processing are addressed:

- What is auditory processing?
- What causes auditory processing difficulty?
- What are the symptoms?
- How is it diagnosed?
- What research is being conducted?
- What treatments are available?
- Where can I learn more?

4. *Accessing Foreign Language Materials as a Blind or Low Vision Student*
M. Scheib, 2008

http://www.miusa.org/ncde/tipsheets/foreignlanguageandblind/infoguide/?searchterm=Accessing%20foreign%20language%20materials

This informational guide, published by the National Clearinghouse on Disability and Exchange, is designed to support blind and low vision students studying foreign languages, specifically addressing access to course materials. The guide emphasizes the reading and writing components of critical languages, but the information provided can be applied to more commonly taught languages. Some of the topics addressed include:

- adaptive technologies and software,
- locating audio, Braille, and large print materials in foreign languages, and
- transcribing foreign language textbooks into Braille.

5. *Autism and Foreign Language Learning*
V. Wire

http://www.hilarymccoll.co.uk/autismMFL.html

Wire provides evidence on this website to support her conviction that all children, including those with autism, should be provided the same opportunities to develop cultural awareness and a second language. Included are the findings from her research into the foreign language learning experiences of autistic students in Scotland.

6. *Autistic Spectrum Disorders (ASD)—Guidance from the Autism Working Group*
Teachernet

http://www.teachernet.gov.uk/wholeschool/sen/teacherlearningassistant/asd/

These documents, developed by an Autism Working Group, provide educators with advice and pointers for best practice with students with autistic spectrum disorders.

7. *Developing Deficit-Specific Intervention Plans for Individuals With Auditory Processing Disorders*
T. J. Bellis. 2002. Developing deficit-specific intervention plans for individuals with auditory processing disorders. *Seminars in Hearing, 23*(4), 287-295.

Table 1 on page 293 of the Seminars in Hearing article (referenced above and reproduced below) summarizes three specific auditory deficit profiles and affected processes followed by profile-specific management and intervention techniques developed with monolingual learners in mind.

Table 1: Selected Management and Intervention Techniques for Specific Auditory Deficit Profiles and Dysfunctional Processes

Deficit Profile	Process(es) Affected	Environmental Modifications	Compensatory Strategies	Direct Remediation Activities
Auditory decoding deficit	MSC* Speech-sound discrimination[†] Temporal processes[†] BS/BI*	Preferential seating, assistive listening device, preteach new information, repetition, visual augmentation	Auditory closure, vocabulary building, problem-solving, active listening, schema induction	Phoneme discrimination, temporal resolution and/or integration, phonological awareness, word attack (speech-to-print) skills
Prosodic deficit	APTO* Nonspeech-sound discrimination[†]	Placement with "animated" teacher, acoustic clarity less critical	Memory enhancement, schema induction, use of prosody and social judgment	Perception of prosody, temporal patterning, pragmatics
Integration deficit	BS/BI* Localization[†]	Acoustic enhancements, avoid use of multi-modality cues	Metalinguistic and metacognitive strategies as needed	Interhemispheric transfer, binaural skills using dichotic stimuli, sound localization

*Primary deficit area; †secondary or possible deficit area.
MSC, monaural separation/closure; BS, binaural separation; BI, binaural integration; APTO, auditory pattern/temporal ordering.

Table 1. Selected Management and Intervention Techniques for Specific Auditory Deficit Profiles and Dysfunctional Processes. Reprinted with permission from "Developing deficit-specific intervention plans for individuals with auditory processing disorders," by T.J. Bellis, 2002, Seminars in Hearing, 23, p. 293. Copyright 2002 by the Thieme Medical Publishers, Inc.

CHAPTER

KEY QUESTIONS

- How do you differentiate between typical delays experienced by children who are learning through a second language and a language and/or learning disability?

Thomas was an eight-year-old one-way Spanish immersion third grader who was referred for a special education evaluation by his second grade teacher due to concerns with his general academic performance in both English and Spanish. In particular his reading skills, writing skills and oral expression in both languages were of concern. He attended an English-only kindergarten program, and transferred to this urban, Midwestern, one-way full immersion school in first grade. In his kindergarten year, instruction was 100% in English, while instruction in first grade was at least 90% in Spanish. As a toddler, Thomas lived in Mexico for two and a half years and his ethnic background was Hispanic and Native American. Both English and Spanish were used in his home, but English was the language used most often in the home, and it was the only language used by Thomas's mother. Thomas was the oldest of five siblings, ages 6, 2, 17 months and 6 months. His mother did not feel that she could compare his academic skills to his siblings, but she did note that Thomas began speaking when he was between two and-a-half years old, which was the same as his siblings.

Although Thomas was exposed to Spanish at home (sometimes with Dad), his teacher had noted that he had great difficulty understanding and using Spanish in the classroom. Thomas could sometimes understand single vocabulary words when listening to

REAL STORIES

Denise Joyce, MST, CCC-SLP

Bilingual Speech Language Pathologist

Adams Spanish Immersion Magnet School

St. Paul, Minnesota

Program Model: One-way foreign language immersion, total, K- Gr. 6

Program Environment: Whole school, Urban

Language(s): Spanish

REAL STORIES

Denise Joyce

instruction, but he did not understand what was specifically said about that word. For example, if the teacher said, "Saquen los libros y ábranlos a la página 123 [Take out your books and open them to page 123]," Thomas knew that he was supposed to do *something* with a book, but he would have to ask a classmate or watch what others were doing in order to follow the direction. Thomas also had difficulty constructing simple sentences in Spanish. Examples included: "porque es nice [because it's nice]," "en el barn [in the barn]," "porque es un tiene un perro [because it's a has a dog]." At times, he switched to English when he didn't know the word in Spanish and/or he used two different verbs to say one thing.

In line with the practitioner recommendation that students be assessed comprehensively with a variety of measures, we administered many different standardized and non-standardized tests to determine if underlying difficulties with language might have been affecting Thomas' academic performance. Assessments were given in both English and Spanish to compare language development in his L1 and L2 since his education and home background involved both languages. Results varied dramatically in English: he scored in the average range on a few tests and scored significantly below average on others. On the Spanish assessments, however, he consistently scored very low.

None of the tests we used to assess Thomas's performance were normed or designed for immersion students, so when interpreting the results, his teacher focused more on how his performance on various language tasks compared with one another. For instance, Thomas scored below average on all subtests of the Clinical Evaluation of Language Fundamentals (CELF)-4, an English language test that helps to detect language disorders, strengths and weaknesses in children by testing a large range of language abilities. However, he performed considerably better on subtests involving language comprehension tasks (understanding grammar, understanding that words are related, understanding some stories read to him in English) than on language production tasks (expressive vocabulary, grammar, ability to formulate complete/logical/correct sentences, ability to talk about relationships between words). I also gave Thomas the Receptive One-Word Picture Vocabulary Test: Spanish-Bilingual Edition (ROWPVT-SBE), which tests receptive vocabulary and allows for use of both English and Spanish. On this test, I showed Thomas four pictures and said, "Show me the . . ." I first gave the word in English, his stronger language. If he did not answer correctly, I offered another opportunity with the word given in

Spanish. Thomas's receptive vocabulary was within the average range on this test; however, he often seemed to find the English cues more helpful than the Spanish cues.

In contrast to his relatively poor performance on the CELF-4, on an English language test called the Oral and Written Language Scales (OWLS), Thomas's overall English language scores were in the average range for monolingual speakers of English. He again scored better in language comprehension and lower in language production. His teacher noted that this test was administered on a morning when Thomas was feeling very happy because his dad had just bought him some new clothes. He was confident and smiling. This indicated that in optimal conditions, Thomas was able to understand English like his typical English-speaking non-immersion peers (the norming group).

The Del Rio Language Screening Test gives information related to a large variety of receptive and expressive language skills in English and Spanish. As part of Thomas's comprehensive evaluation, we found it useful to sample his abilities in both languages to see if the scores in each language supported the test results and language sampling carried out by his teachers. These results could also have been used to show his parents how different or how similar his skills were in his two languages. Thomas consistently performed better in English than in Spanish, with his English scores ranging from average to about a grade level below average in story comprehension. His Spanish scores were all low enough to warrant concern, and his story comprehension score in Spanish was two grade levels below average.

One test that spoke to Thomas's general classroom performance was the Boehm Basic Concepts, a standard measure of concept development. This tool was developed to measure a young child's understanding of basic positional concepts, such as "over," "least," "left," and so on. At the end of second grade, most children know 49 or 50 of the 50 Boehm Basic Concepts. As a midyear third grader, Thomas was given the opportunity to hear each of these basic concept vocabulary words in both English and Spanish (e.g., "Show me the cat at the top. Enséñame el gato arriba."). Thomas's low performance on this measure indicated to his teacher that part of his difficulty following directions in the classroom might stem from the fact that he was struggling with some of these basic positional concepts, regardless of the language used for communication.

Overall, while Thomas scored very low on some language tests, he scored well on others. This is not typical of a child with a true language disability. Language-disabled children will usually score

REAL STORIES

below expectations on similar items across testing situations and using multiple testing materials. For example, if one test indicates that sentence formulation is an area of weakness, another test will generally support those findings. Language-disabled children will also score low on tests in all of their languages.

In addition to Thomas's uneven language testing performance, his receptive abilities were stronger than his expressive abilities, which is common for most people. When happy and in an English-only environment, Thomas's receptive language scores on the OWLS fell within the average range overall, and his expressive language was only slightly lower than expectations. However, on another measure of language, Thomas scored significantly below age expectations. In interpreting these results, we considered Durgunoglu and Öney's (2000) findings that learner attitude could affect students' performance and willingness to use language.

In summary, test results showed that Thomas had some strong English skills that he was not able to use at Adams, where his day was conducted in Spanish. At the same time, his abilities in Spanish were not what would be expected of a third grader in immersion with some exposure to Spanish at home. We felt that, although Thomas did not have a language disability per se, he would benefit from language support services. Consequently, I work with him twice a week. Once a week, I teach a lesson to his entire class, in Spanish, supporting vocabulary development and language in the area of science. The other session is an English pull-out therapy session in which two students meet with me to talk about the science lessons in English and discuss learner behaviors and strategies that support academics all day long, regardless of the language of instruction. Language support services were found to be critical for Thomas if he was to remain in a Spanish immersion setting, but they would also have been recommended if Thomas were to have moved to an English-only school because of his inconsistent performance in English.

BACKGROUND INFORMATION

Conversational speech among adult speakers of English takes place at a rate of 180-225 words per minute. While working at this speed, speakers construct the meanings that they want to convey, select words from a set of approximately 40,000 alternatives, sequence each item according to language specific rules, assign appropriate inflections, and coordinate more than 100 muscles to produce the whole string smoothly, while following the appropriate rules of social interactions. On the receiving end, listeners must first perceive the signal then retrieve the speaker's intended meaning from a stream of sounds that are exceedingly fast (i.e., 5-8 syllables and 25-30 phonetic segments per second) with overlapping borders between meaningful units. (Kohnert, 2004b)

Clearly, language is one of the most complex skills an individual human being learns to use, and acquiring language is a developmental process that occurs throughout one's lifetime.

Developing high levels of language and literacy is a complicated process for all students. When the process appears to be atypical and questions surface about a possible disability, confirming the existence of a disorder is difficult. Even more daunting, however, is the process of identifying a language disorder and/or learning disability in bilingual learners or those learning through a second language.

The amount of instructional time spent in the L2 will impact the process. For example, educators working in partial one-way immersion programs [referred to as 50/50 programs in the two-way immersion (TWI) literature] may have a slight advantage in teasing difference apart from disorder. Because students in these programs are developing language (and sometimes literacy) skills in both the L1 and the L2 from the outset, educators have the opportunity to observe whether the difficulty occurs in the L2 only or in both languages, a helpful indicator used to rule in a language-based disability. In contrast, educators in 90/10 TWI programs and early total one-way immersion programs may be more challenged in differentiating between a language/learning difference and a language/learning disorder since they tend to observe literacy development in one language only.

A clear guideline states that if atypical language development is exhibited in all languages, then language impairment may be a possibility (Genesee, Paradis, & Crago, 2004; Kohnert, 2008). Besides that guideline, few defining behaviors exist to assist educators in sorting out difference and disability. Fradd and McGee (1994) and others have noted a strong similarity between characteristics exhibited by second language learners and those found in children with language disorders and learning disabilities. For example, Petzold (2004), a bilingual school psychologist with experience in immersion settings, referenced a number of general behaviors in students with a language disorder and/or learning disability that are also typically exhibited by non-disordered learners still acquiring the language of instruction. These behaviors may include a short attention span, shyness or timidity, nervousness/anxiousness, speaking infrequently, not volunteering information, appearing confused, low levels of comprehension, and inappropriate comments.

Other traits shared by language and/or learning-disabled and second language learners include but are not limited to difficulties in expression (including articulation), low vocabulary and comprehension, difficulty following oral directions, reading below grade level, confusion in sound/symbol associations, reversing words and letters, and poor recall of sequences of syllables (Kohnert, 2008). Delays and disorders may manifest themselves in multiple academic areas for older learners as language proficiency is closely tied to measures of academic achievement, intelligence and general cognitive abilities. Developing language skills can impact a student's ability to think, organize and structure ideas as well as generate meaning from language (Fradd & McGee, 1994).

Recent research corroborates the observations of many practitioners about the language use similarities between second language learners and language-impaired monolinguals. Gutiérrez-Clellan, Simon-Cereijido and Wagner (2008) examined the performance of English L1 children with and without language impairment (LI), Spanish-English bilinguals with and without LI, and typical English as a second language (ESL) speakers on accurate use of verb morphemes and use of subject pronouns. Of their many findings, one important finding was that the accuracy rate of Spanish-dominant children for whom English was a second language was similar to that of language-impaired children, both English L1 and Spanish-English bilinguals (who were English-dominant). Researchers concluded that, "children whose English is the weaker language have the potential to be misdiagnosed as impaired in that language" (p. 16).

The research literature distinguishes between two main types of language that L2 learners encounter in schools, social-interactional and academic-trans-actional (Brown & Yule, 1983; Collier, 1987, 1992; Cummins, 1981). Social-interactional language is developed most quickly, generally within six months to two years. Academic-transactional language and literacy skills, however, are *fundamental* for long-term school success and take longer to develop, usually between five and seven years. Because of the period of time necessary for developing academic-transactional language skills, many L2 learners are unable to demonstrate grade-level achievement on standardized tests given in the L2 once the language and literacy demands of the curriculum have outpaced their language and literacy skills in that language. Thus, when L2 and immersion learners are given normed assessments in their second language, individual student performance cannot be reliably used as a valid measure of delay or disorder.

We present literature that can shed light on this question by first addressing the question of delay versus disorder. Then we continue the discussion while making a distinction between two specific vantage points, within-the-learner and outside-the-learner. Before we begin these sections, it is important to acknowledge the limitation of binary categories (e.g., delay/disorder, within-the-learner/outside-the-learner). In reality, the human condition is much more complex than these suggest and behavior is best viewed as existing along a continuum where interaction is possible between these two extremes. Thus, we qualify use of these more extreme endpoints by first recognizing that they are an oversimplification of complex developmental phenomena that can and do interact.

RELEVANT DISCUSSIONS AND RESEARCH FINDINGS

DELAY OR DISORDER?

Each state's interpretation of the federally mandated Individuals with Disabilities Education Improvement Act (IDEA) 1999 outlines specific criteria for determining eligibility for special education services. For example, in Minnesota, there are three requirements that must be met. Qualifying students must exhibit:

- a severe discrepancy (-1.75 standard deviations below the mean using the state's regression table) in ability (IQ) and academic achievement,

- evidence of severe underachievement in the classroom setting, and

- a noted information processing condition.

(Minnesota Department of Children, Families & Learning, 1998)

More recent federal legislation on learning disabilities, IDEA, 2004 (Public Law 108-446), began implementation during the 2005-2006 academic year. One of the most significant changes is the national mandate of additional procedures (i.e., not simply the ability-achievement discrepancy criterion described above) for identifying children with specific learning disability (SLD). Now the identification process must include data evidencing a child's response to scientific, research-based intervention, frequently referred to as Response to Intervention (RTI).

According to the National Center for Learning Disabilities (2006), the recently updated determining factors for eligibility include:

- inadequate achievement measured against expectations for a child's age or the grade-level standards set by the state;

- insufficient progress when using a process based on RTI;

- evidence of a pattern of strengths and weaknesses in performance, achievement, or both, relative to age, grade-level standards or intellectual development.

Unchanged is the stipulation that the child's learning difficulties are not primarily the result of a visual, hearing or motor disability, mental retardation, emotional disturbance, cultural factors, environmental or economic disadvantage, limited English proficiency or lack of appropriate instruction in reading or math.

An important distinction between delay and disorder is that the former is largely the result of external factors such as a lack of sufficient linguistic input for the student while the latter is innate to the learner (Kohnert, 2004b, 2008). According to the American Speech-Language-Hearing Association (2008), language and/or learning disabilities are rooted in a biological deficit in the brain that manifests itself in an inability to receive, send, process, or comprehend concepts of verbal, nonverbal, or graphic symbol systems. Struggling learners are considered learning disabled when their achievement is not at a level that matches their age and ability level even though suitable learning experiences and documented interventions have been provided (National Center for Learning Disabilities, 2006), making it a measurable information processing condition. Delays, in contrast, primarily result from a mismatch between a student's experiences and environmental expectations.

Researchers guesstimate that between 5 and 10% of dual language learners are likely to struggle with language disorders (Kohnert, 2008). This guesstimate is based on findings from monolingual children.

Gutiérrez-Clellen and Peña (2001) advocated Dynamic Assessment (DA) as one type of assessment for determining language delay versus disorder with linguistically diverse children. DA is an alternative approach to traditional language development assessments, which focuses on determining a student's potential language-learning skills and/or ability. Based upon Vygotsky's model of the zone of proximal development (ZPD), it can help speech language pathologists make inferences about underlying learning processes and determine appropriate intervention strategies. DA employs three main approaches to the language assessment process: 1. testing the limits, 2. graduated prompting, and 3. test-teach-retest. (For more information about these methods, see Gutiérrez-Clellen & Peña, 2001; Lantolf & Poehner, 2004; Poehner & Lantolf, 2005).

Gutiérrez-Clellan and Peña (2001) suggested that while all three DA methods are effective, the **test-teach-retest method** is best suited for differentiating between language disorders and differences. In this approach, the evaluator first identifies a weak skill (test) and then provides the student with intervention (teach) before retesting the student. The idea is that students who are "typical" language learners will make significant changes with meaningful language experiences that take place in the learner's ZPD, whereas students with language impairment will show few quantitative changes during post-testing.

Kohnert (2008) discussed two different types of measurement used to shed light on a child's language development, experience-dependent and processing-dependent measures. **Experience-dependent language measures** can provide a snapshot of an aspect of language development such as grammatical accuracy or vocabulary size, and this snapshot is strongly tied to prior knowledge and experience with language. In contrast, processing-dependent measures aim to limit the impact of prior language experiences by measuring the speed of processing high-frequency words (that are more than likely known by all) and/or nonsense words (that are more than likely known by none). Because **processing-oriented measures** reduce the role of prior knowledge, they may be particularly appropriate for linguistically and culturally diverse learners such as those found in dual language classrooms.

Using experience-dependent measures, researchers have examined and compared specific grammatical features (e.g., Håkansson and Nettelbladt, 1996) and vocabulary development (e.g., Peña, Iglesias, & Lidz, 2001) in the language produced by L2 learners and L1 learners with language disorders. Findings show a strong similarity between the language abilities demonstrated by these two groups of children. More recent research provides clear evidence that these misleading similarities exits (Gutiérrez-Clellan, Simon-Cerejido Wagner, 2008).

Research has also sought to determine the added value of processing-dependent measurement in distinguishing between monolingual children with language disorders and typically developing bilingual children. Across a series of studies (e.g., Kohnert, 2004a; Windsor & Kohnert, 2004, Windsor, Kohnert, Rowe & Kah, 2008), researchers concluded the following:

- The non-word repetition task [for example, repeating nonsense words in a language using sound combinations that could exist (*wug* or *simaput* in English] can help differentiate between monolinguals with a language disability from those without for speakers of certain languages.

- The non-word repetition task does *not* successfully separate typical bilinguals functioning in their L2 from monolinguals with a language disorder.

- Testing in a child's L2 only is insufficient for determining the existence of a language disorder whether one uses experience- or processing-dependent measures.

- Non-linguistic comparisons using visual and sound detection tasks (e.g., push one button when you see a red shape/high-pitched tone and another for a blue shape/low-pitched tone) may hold potential for sorting out delay and disorder with linguistically diverse learners.

Measuring the speed, efficiency, or ability of a child to respond to a stimulus with non-language tasks may provide useful evidence of a less efficient information processing capacity. This, in turn, may play a fundamental role in atypical language development.

In addition to federal and state requirements, Petzold (2006) has recommended that immersion programs quantify the degree of difference or discrepancy necessary to be considered learning-disabled using curriculum-based measurements established over time within the program itself. She proposed that for learners to qualify as disabled (significantly discrepant) they must attain correct answers at a rate that is half or less than half of the rate of their peers in both the immersion language and their L1. Kohnert (2008) also emphasizes the importance of using appropriate comparison groups in testing, that is, groups of learners whose language and learning experiences are similar, which, for this group, would be the learners' immersion peers.

WITHIN-THE-LEARNER CONSIDERATIONS

Ganschow and Sparks (2000) concluded that most struggles in foreign language learning result from difficulties with the rule systems of language in general, not with one specific language system. This conclusion is based upon the work of researchers who have found that foreign language students who struggle with a second language have difficulties at the phonological/orthographic (sound-symbol), syntactic (grammar and word order) and semantic (word meaning) level (Ganschow & Sparks, 2000; Schwarz, 1997; Sparks, Ganschow & Patton, 1995). The Linguistic Coding Differences Hypothesis (LCDH) accounts for this phenomenon, proposing that this learner's first language skills (phonological, syntactic, and semantic) provide the basis for L2 learning. If a foreign language learner has language impairment in the L1, this will transfer to the L2; the LCDH does not account for why these phonological, syntactic and/or semantic deficits exist in the L1. (For a discussion of the LCDH, see Sparks, 1995.)

Similarly, researchers and practitioners in immersion settings have observed that impairment impacts all languages of bilingual learners. Howard and Sugarman (2007) make reference to a two-way immersion teacher who noted an advantage to being the observer of a learner's language development and literacy acquisition in both languages because she could directly compare the learning process in both L1 and L2.

In 1980, the World Health Organization (WHO) introduced a distinction between impairment, which is organic to the learner, and disabilities or handicaps which are direct consequences stemming from the impairment. The disability that may result will impact an individual's day-to-day functioning; subsequent handicaps, on the other hand, affect a person's interface with society. For example, a child born with a restricted lingual fraenum (the tissue that attaches the tongue to the floor of the mouth, commonly referred as "being tongue-tied") has a physical impairment. This impairment may cause imprecise articulation, especially when speaking quickly as a consequence of reduced mobility of the tongue (the disability). Embarrassment about the disability or impairment may further impact a child's self esteem and willingness to respond orally when addressed, especially in public settings like the classroom (the handicap).

It is possible for an individual to have an impairment yet not have a disability because he/she has learned to accommodate it using self and social supports (Kohnert, 2008). It follows then that the impairment was never observed nor did it become problematic in the L1 for these learners. With the added linguistic and cognitive demands of an L2, however, learners who have an impairment yet have learned to compensate for it in their L1 may demonstrate a disability in the L2. What may look like a delay in the acquisition of the immersion language may actually be a language learning disability that has been overcome in the L1, and can similarly be overcome in the L2.

A student's attitude can impact his/her acquisition of language skills. A learner's negative attitude toward a language, which results in unwillingness to use and/or learn that language, is often mistaken for a delay in language acquisition (Durgunoglu & Öney, 2000). When a learner sees a particular language as making demands that he/she cannot meet, he/she may move away from that language, identifying more with one in which he/she finds success (Fradd & McGee, 1994). In the immersion setting, this situation is further compounded as a learner's attitude toward the subject matter can also be reflected in limited, if any, language use. It is important to note that learner attitudes are not constructed in a vacuum; rather they are socially constructed beliefs that develop over time.

In bilingual individuals, language knowledge is distributed across the two languages and both languages interact with the cognitive and social development of the learner. Oft-encountered characteristics such as code-mixing (speech that draws from both the L1 and L2), gaps in word knowledge in one language or the other, and other cross-linguistic influences on language production are typical. Interaction among these developmental systems and the resultant behaviors do not evidence or *cause* impairment or disability (Genesee et al., 2004; Kohnert, 2008; Paradis, 2005).

OUTSIDE-THE-LEARNER CONSIDERATIONS

Language differences and language delays are often the result of sociocultural influences on the development of a learner's language. They result in a lower language level than what is typically expected because of a mismatch between a student's actual background and the background presumed by the schooling environment (Durgunoglu & Öney, 2000).

Durgunoglu and Öney (2000) argued that political, economic, and social forces can affect literacy development given that the majority of a student's language experiences take place outside of the academic setting, normally in the home environment, making it a critical environment for language development. Research has shown, for example, that students from homes that receive welfare benefits are exposed to 10,000,000 words by age 3. This pales in comparison to the 20,000,000 words heard by working-class children and the 30,000,000 by children of professional parents (Hart & Risley, 1995). It is not only the quantity of input that distinguishes the pre-schooling language experiences of children but also the nature of the language input. For example, professional parents' children receive eight times as many encouragements as children of parents on welfare by age two (Hart & Risley, 1995).

Language learning differences can also be language-dependent. For example, Escamilla (2000) called attention to the fact that Spanish speakers learning to read in Spanish will learn about the vowel system earlier than children developing literacy skills in English. Because Spanish-language vowel sounds are far more transparent than vowel sounds in English, they tend to be introduced and learned earlier. Likewise, consonant sounds are typically acquired later when learning to read in Spanish, and earlier when learning to read in English. Thus, an observed difference may be linked to the language and/or the learning experiences, not to the learner.

GUIDING PRINCIPLES

Based on the research reviewed above, and on the collective experiences of veteran immersion educators, we offer the following principles to guide practice.

Respond proactively if delay is perceived. Once teachers and family members have communicated concern about a possible language or learning delay, immersion teachers are best advised to begin gathering samples of student work, keeping anecdotal records, and monitoring student progress at specific intervals. If the program already implements a variety of assessment tools to measure learner progress, these may suffice. If not, it is vital to begin collecting supportive evidence of student progress, which can later be used as part of a more comprehensive assessment process.

Consider all potential sources of difficulty. It is important to look at the whole child, taking into account his/her language learning background and experiences. Growing up bilingual does affect language development and does not predict disability. Diagnosis of a language-learning disability in bilinguals, as in monolinguals, requires multifaceted assessment including nonverbal measures of intelligence, achievement, language and literacy development, and basic psychological (information) processing abilities. Whether bilingual or monolingual, the source of a learner's struggles with language must be identified, be it environmental, instructional, inherent to the learner, or some combination of the above (Fradd & McGee, 1994).

Compare, compare, compare! Kohnert (2004b, 2008) has recommended comparing students not only to *standardized norms* but also to *other students with similar experiences*. Language learning experiences can vary because of within-the-learner (endogenous) as well as outside-the-learner (exogenous) factors. Thus, when making comparisons, it is necessary to take both types of influences into consideration, seeking out comparison groups for each of the different factors. Kohnert suggests comparing

siblings as one possible way to control for some of the exogenous factors that may have an impact, as siblings may have had comparable home language experiences.

As mentioned, making comparisons with other *students who have had similar educational experiences* is useful; establishing developmental benchmarks as well as achievement norms for learners in immersion programs is beneficial in the assessment process as bilingually schooled learners have educational experiences that differ greatly from their monolingual peers. It is advantageous for individual school districts and schools to develop their own norms in order to account for common academic language experiences as well as the interaction of bilingualism with cognitive and social development. Petzold (2006) has recommended collecting data every three years in order to reevaluate and more accurately reflect students' current language experiences, given inevitable curricular changes.

Woelber (2004) also included comparisons amongst *other struggling immersion learners*. For example, in one Midwest immersion school, struggling learners participated in a "Foundations of Learning" class, an academic support program, independent of the district's special education services, that was made available during the school day for primary students identified as needing additional support in the areas of Math and/or Language Arts. Comparing student progress to other students participating in this support program helped staff distinguish between delayed language and skill development, and severe underachievement that could indicate a disability.

Compare the struggling learner to *him/herself across time*. Students who begin schooling with lower than average performance yet make a relatively similar amount of progress as peers over time, are more likely to have a delay based on their prior learning experiences and limited language input as opposed to a language disorder.

Compare the struggling learner's *language and literacy development in L1 and L2*. Observed developmental delays that indicate a possible language-based disorder for either the L1 or L2 warrant closer examination. Language-based disabilities impact the development and use of any language, not only the L2. However, keep in mind that it is possible that a child in the primary grades learning to read in an L2 has learned to compensate for the language disability in their L1, thus masking its existence in that language as well. This implies a need to gather information on the early language development experiences of the learner from family members and others who may help in reconstructing this history. It also suggests that with appropriate supports in place, compensatory mechanisms may be successfully developed for the L2 as well.

Expand beyond the standardized, norm-referenced assessment. To account for exogenous and endogenous influences on a learner's language development as well as those that reflect interaction between these two influences, educators should be wary of relying too heavily on formal evaluations, such as nonverbal IQ tests and standardized assessments. Also, because student performance will vary across tasks, it helps to include a broad range of assessment types.

For school psychologists, a curriculum-based measurement (CBM) tool was developed in the early 1980s at the University of Minnesota to measure reading ability as an alternative to standardized testing; its emphasis is on the direct observation of a student's academic skills and on fluency (both rate and accuracy of performance), measuring performance repeatedly over a period of time to show progress.

For speech language pathologists, a recommended alternative to traditional assessments to assist in distinguishing between a language delay and a language disorder is Dynamic Assessment (Gutiérrez-Clellen & Peña, 2001). Such assessments provide an important link to actual teaching and learning in the classroom.

Finally, as Kohnert (2008) argues, complementing *language experience-dependent measures* with *language and non-language processing-dependent* measures holds great promise in current efforts to differentiate between bilinguals with and without a language disorder.

Assess comprehensively. The assessment process should not consist solely of student language evaluation. Nonverbal intellectual functioning, classroom

behavior, academic performance, student's language development and family history are also important components. Reviewing the learner's cumulative file and interviewing parents (with trained interpreters, if necessary) are some effective ways to gather information about these and other factors necessary for more comprehensive assessment (Petzold, 2004).

Adhere to Kohnert's (2008) Guiding Principles for Language Assessments with Bilingual Learners.

- Identify and reduce sources of bias.
- Individualize the timing of assessment.
- Consider L1 and L2 abilities and needs—past, present and future.
- Look beyond the obvious.
- Gather data using multiple measures at different points in time.

(Kohnert, 2008, pp. 115-126)

Involve the perspectives of multiple teaching professionals and specialists. In addition to employing a wide variety of formal and informal assessments, it is essential to involve the perspectives of multiple teaching professionals and specialists when deciding between difference and disorder or disability. Input from specialists such as the school psychologist, principal, classroom teacher, school nurse, music/art/media/physical education specialist, speech language pathologist, etc. in the school should be included in the comprehensive assessment of a student (Woelber, 2003). Conflicts between a student's learning style and a teacher's instructional style can be revealed in this manner; a student's attitude and personality may also be exposed through this multifaceted input. In this way, a team approach guards against premature decision-making based on partial information and an overly simplistic view of the learner and the learning process, and a comprehensive assessment is ensured.

Become familiar with typical L1 development for immersion students. For example, research shows that early total foreign language immersion learners may experience a lag in English language arts until instruction has occurred in English for 1-2 years (Genesee, 1987; Swain & Lapkin, 1982).

Take advantage of pre-referral activities. Pre-referral activities, such as assessment and evaluation of the learning ecology, language proficiency, learning opportunities, and any educationally relevant cultural and linguistic factors, are a must in order to eliminate or add factors external to the learner (Ortiz, 2003; Petzold, 2001; Woelber, 2003). They are also helpful in that they guide appropriate instructional interventions and subsequent assessment activities (Ortiz, 2003).

USEFUL RESOURCES

Below are selected online and print resources that pertain to issues discussed in this chapter.

1. *Legal Information in Special Education*
   National Association of Special Education Teachers, 2006/2007

   http://www.naset.org/specialedlaw01.0.html

   This comprehensive website provides links to special education legislation and government agencies in order to keep practitioners in the field up to date. Some of the included links are: Americans with Disabilities Act, Individuals with Disabilities Education Act (IDEA 1997 and IDEA 2004), No Child Left Behind, state education departments, and government resources.

2. *Legislation on Special Education and Rehabilitative Services*
   U.S. Department of Education

   http://www.ed.gov/policy/speced/leg/edpicks.jhtml?src=ln

   On this web page, you can find links with detailed information about special education and rehabilitative services legislation including IDEA (2004) and The Rehabilitation Act.

3. *LD Online: IDEA 2004*
   WETA, 2008

   http://www.ldonline.org/features/idea2004

This web page provides an understandable review of the history, purpose and various components of the IDEA 2004 legislation. It specifically addresses the key differences between IDEA 1997 and IDEA 2004.

4. *Child Speech and Language*
   American Speech-Language-Hearing Association (ASHA) website

   http://www.asha.org/public/speech/disorders/ChildSandL.htm

   This resource provides links to information on speech disorders, language disorders, medical and developmental conditions, and communication options. There is also a section dedicated to frequently asked questions that addresses how to help children with communication disorders in schools. Finally, the ASHA website hosts a page on learning more than one language, a reference for educators and parents alike.

5. *Dynamic Assessment (DA)*
   http://dynamicassessment.com/_wsn/page2.html

   This website describes the primary characteristics and procedures for DA. It additionally provides information about who to contact for procedural materials in a variety of languages, including Chinese, Danish, English, French, Hebrew, Italian, Norwegian, and Spanish.

   http://calper.la.psu.edu/dyna_assess.php

   This Center for Advanced Language Proficiency Education and Research (CALPER) at Pennsylvania State University counts DA among its many projects. This particular website highlights professional development materials, websites, and other references for articles on DA.

   http://www.etni.org.il/etnirag/issue2/erica_garb.htm

   Dynamic Assessment is presented within the larger context of summative and formative assessments in this resource. The document explores both how to use DA and how it has impacted learning.

6. *Cultural and Linguistic Diversity Resource Guide for Speech-Language Pathologists*
B. Goldstein, 2000

This comprehensive guide is designed to help speech-language pathologists meet the needs of culturally and linguistically diverse students. Information is included about a number of varieties of English (for example, African American English, Spanish-influenced English, and Asian-influenced English) as well as assessment and intervention techniques.

7. *Encyclopedia of Language and Literacy Development*
Canadian Language and Literacy Research Network

http://literacyencyclopedia.ca/?switchlanguage=EN

Launched in 2007, this online resource is being developed by the Canadian Language and Literacy Research Network to provide in-depth, research-based information about topics such as language, numeracy, reading and writing development. Submissions are written by internationally recognized experts and address unilingual and multilingual development for typical and atypical learners.

CHAPTER

3

KEY QUESTIONS

- In an immersion program, how much of a reading lag still falls into the normal range when learners are acquiring initial literacy?

- What initial literacy challenges should constitute a cause for concern?

Rigler School is a K-8 school in a high poverty neighborhood in Portland, Oregon with more than 500 students. Rigler houses a 90:10 two-way (Spanish-English) immersion (TWI) program; the program started in 2005 with only one kindergarten class. I began as full-time program coordinator/Spanish reading coach that same year. Since then, the TWI program has grown to comprise four classes, K-3, in the otherwise English-medium school, and plans are in place to expand the program each year until it becomes a full K-8 program in 2013.

Cynthia, a native Spanish speaker, began her schooling in an English-only kindergarten classroom at Rigler in 2005. After her initial year of schooling, her kindergarten teacher recommended that she be evaluated for special education services because she had made no progress in English reading. The following year, during Cynthia's first month in the English-only first grade, she became increasingly discouraged by her experiences at school. She insisted that she could not learn to read, was terrified of the teacher, and refused to go to school. She screamed when her mother brought her to school and when it finally got to a point where she began to desperately grab at the classroom's doorframe as her mother tried to get her to enter the classroom, her mother had had enough. She insisted on meeting with the principal and me to discuss admitting

REAL STORIES

Jonathan Steinhoff

Program Coordinator/Reading Coach

Rigler Elementary

Portland, Oregon

Program Model: Two-way bilingual immersion, 90:10, K- Gr. 8

Program Environment: Strand program, Urban

Language(s): Spanish, English

REAL STORIES

Jonathan Steinhoff

Cynthia into the immersion program even though the first-grade class in that program was already at capacity. The first-grade TWI teacher was willing to accept an additional student, so the arrangements were made. All involved understood that Cynthia would be switching from 100% English to 100% Spanish as her language of literacy instruction. An appointment was made to meet again with Cynthia's mother once Spanish reading assessments were completed and an initial instructional plan was designed.

Cynthia's performance on English literacy assessments coming into the TWI first grade was troubling. She knew three letter names, had scored at an early kindergarten level in a phonemic awareness measure, and could only identify four English letter sounds. Her scores on these measures in Spanish were not much better: she demonstrated an early kindergarten level on the phonemic awareness measure, knew five letter names, and seven Spanish letter sounds—three vowels plus /m/, /p/, /s/ and /t/ (the consonants she knew in English).

Cynthia's literacy support plan consisted of three short daily practice sessions on learning the letter sounds in Spanish (letter names were ignored). One session took place with a small group of struggling readers during the 90-minute Spanish literacy block. The other two sessions were one-on-one with the teacher or an educational assistant (EA). All Spanish literacy sessions were held in the immersion classroom. I met frequently with the instructors to refine the lessons and chart Cynthia's progress based on the snapshot assessments we administered every two to three weeks.

As Cynthia mastered the sounds, open-syllable blending was introduced. Together we coached her mother on how to drill the sounds with Cynthia and play a syllable bingo game to practice new sound combinations after they were introduced in her lessons at school. The year-end goal set for Cynthia was for her to be able to read two and three open syllable words with consonant blends by reading the syllables and then recoding them into a word. This was an ambitious goal. Cynthia took so long to read the separated syllables in a word that when she went back to recode, she had forgotten the initial syllable and would make up a word that began with the final syllable. Often this word was not even an actual word (e.g., The word is "camisa" [shirt]. Cynthia slowly reads: /ca/ /mi/ /sa/, then utters "sati"—or some such nonsensical word).

During this extended period of intensified support, Cynthia continued to participate in whole class interactive read-alouds and study Houghton Mifflin anthology selection readings. Lessons focused primarily on developing comprehension skills. One of Cynthia's

REAL STORIES

remarkable talents emerged during these lessons. Because she was determined not to be seen as a non-reader, she became adept at memorizing texts. She could say the words and turn the pages making it look to a casual observer that she was reading the words. But, when asked to point to a word on the page, she could not find it. Nor could she read words or phrases from the text when they were written on a separate piece of paper.

By the end of first grade, Cynthia was still a year below grade level on the Spanish phonemic awareness measure. However, she knew all the Spanish letter sounds, could blend two open syllables into words consistently and had acquired about twelve sight words in her repertoire. English reading assessments showed similar gains in the phonemic awareness measures and phonics but not in word recognition.

The first grade teacher and I met with Cynthia's second grade teacher in the fall of 2007 to discuss her reading goals and develop the instructional plan for meeting these goals. We all felt it reasonable to expect Cynthia to be able to read texts leveled for the end of first grade (Developmental Reading Assessment (DRA) level 18) with at least word-by-word fluency, a rate of 40 words per minute, 95% accuracy, and an adequate comprehension score of 18 on the DRA retelling rubric. To get there, we planned to have Cynthia working mostly on syllable blending early in the year and shifting to text fluency as she mastered blending routines. Again she received this instruction in extra reading sessions during the day with either her teacher or an EA. These sessions always took place in the classroom using a push-in model, in which support specialists were invited into the regular classroom to provide services. At times that meant the EA gave her intensive instruction and other times the EA monitored independent work sessions while the teacher met with Cynthia and, on occasion, other struggling readers.

I continued to meet with the teaching team to check on how the instruction was being organized and whether progress indicators were being met. By the end of second grade Cynthia had made significant progress in Spanish reading. She could read at a DRA level 16 (mid to late first grade text) often with fluent reading of short phrases, at 40 words per minute, 97% accuracy with a comprehension/retell score of 17 (adequate comprehension). Her reading was still below grade level, but she had made significant gains. Most importantly, from our perspective, was her newly found belief in her reading ability and pride in the progress she had made.

Now, in the winter of her third grade year, Cynthia is reading at a DRA level 20 (mid second grade text) with better than adequate

REAL STORIES

comprehension, and she is beginning to find and read books independently. In a retell situation, she still only offers minimal information but with prompting it becomes apparent that she is attending to meaning and following the storyline fairly well. Her next challenge is to transfer her reading skills from Spanish to English and to apply the instruction of non-transferable skills as she works on English reading. Additionally, writing represents a major challenge to Cynthia. Writing and English reading are the areas where her third grade teacher and I will focus our planning efforts to build towards the next stages of effective dual language instruction for Cynthia.

A reasonable question after reading this case study would be: Why wasn't Cynthia referred for special education services? The simple answer to that question is: because intervention services were not available in Spanish at Rigler school. My experience with Spanish-speaking children like Cynthia who struggle to acquire literacy in an alphabetic language has indicated the importance of focusing initial literacy efforts on one language at a time. In the case of Spanish speakers that language is Spanish. For Cynthia, this meant providing intensive Spanish language and literacy support to further Spanish literacy development in the primary years. While the ultimate goal for all TWI students is biliteracy, we at Rigler believe that the best way for students like Cynthia to achieve this is intensive concentration on native language literacy first.

Now that Cynthia is reading competently in Spanish and a greater percentage of her instructional day is taking place in English, staff has begun the process of making a referral to the Special Education Department. As the focus on English literacy skills increases, we will continue to work with Cynthia to further develop her Spanish literacy with the hopes of seeing her reach grade level by the end of third grade.

BACKGROUND INFORMATION

Reading is a language-based skill, yet it is not a simple skill derived merely from learning to talk (Kahmi & Catts, 1999); in fact, it is one of the most cognitively challenging tasks that humans learn as it "involves neuropsychological functions, cognitive abilities, and linguistic abilities" (Maldonado, 1994, p. 3). Literacy development in an alphabetic language has at its foundation two sets of skills: word-level skills (e.g., decoding, word recognition, etc.) and text-level skills (e.g, reading comprehension and writing) (August & Shanahan, 2006; Durgunoglu & Öney, 2000; Fradd & McGee, 1994; Kahmi & Catts, 1999).

Literacy development begins early. During the preschool years, most children from language- and literacy-rich home environments begin to recognize familiar letters and words as well as the structure and elements that make up stories (Snow, 1983). Children who come from low-language home environments with minimal access to print materials will likely need additional support to develop foundational pre-literacy concepts, such as an understanding of the various uses of literacy, and the abstract knowledge of sounds and symbols used to create language (August & Hakuta, 1997).

There are several research studies that provide relevant information for this question. We have limited this discussion of the literature. However, to alphabetic languages and present these findings by language learning context and target audience: (1) ESL contexts for language minority students (English learners) and traditional foreign language programs for language majority (English proficient) learners, (2) one-way (foreign language) immersion learners who begin the program as English proficient, and (3) two-way bilingual immersion learners including both English learners and English proficient students.

RELEVANT DISCUSSIONS AND RESEARCH FINDINGS

RESEARCH CARRIED OUT IN ESL CONTEXTS FOR LANGUAGE MINORITY STUDENTS (ENGLISH LEARNERS) AND TRADITIONAL FOREIGN LANGUAGE PROGRAMS FOR LANGUAGE MAJORITY (ENGLISH PROFICIENT) LEARNERS

Monolingual students learning to read their native language draw on knowledge of the three main cuing systems: semantics, syntax, and phonics. Typical literacy benchmarks for monolingual students include:

- By the end of kindergarten, most monolingual students read upper and lower case letters as well as some words and simple books.

- In first grade, the majority of students begin to decode words that they do not know by sight; by the end of first grade, they can read simple books smoothly, albeit word-by-word.

- Second and third grade students begin to make meaning when reading, relating new information to what they already know; reading typically becomes smoother, more efficient, and more fluent for them.

In contrast to students learning to read in their L1, students learning to read through a language they are just acquiring must simultaneously develop oral proficiency in the second language, each of the three aforementioned cuing systems *and* the reading process (August & Shanahan, 2006; Fisher, 2004). For this reason, teachers can anticipate that learning to read in a language still being acquired will take longer. Additionally, delays or difficulties with L1 development are predictive of language learning and literacy development challenges in L2 (Ganshow & Sparks, 2000).

Reading challenges change as students move through the grade levels. Primary-grade learners struggling to develop initial literacy skills encounter difficulties acquiring skills at the word level; whereas struggling readers in upper elementary more often face text-level comprehension difficulties, which may in part result from the slow processing rates of labored word decoding. Research has clearly indicated that children who learn to read in a second language master the skills of decoding much more quickly than those of text comprehension (Bernhardt, 1991).

In their comprehensive review of extant literature on language minority students in the U.S., August and Shanahan (2006) emphasize the key role of oral language proficiency in literacy development. They identify, however, an important difference in the relationship between oral proficiency in English and *initial word-level skills*, as compared to oral proficiency in English and *reading comprehension and writing skills*. Whereas a child's oral proficiency level may positively correlate with some word-level reading skills (e.g., rapid naming of words, letter-sound awareness); studies also found that oral proficiency skills such as vocabulary and grammatical knowledge did not predict word-level reading skills in English. In contrast, research clearly points to a strong link between oral proficiency in English and text-level skills (e.g. such as word knowledge, listening comprehension, and ability to provide definitions).

Research has found that vocabulary knowledge serves as a consistent and reliable measure of reading ability for monolingual children (Stanovich, 1986) as well as English language learners (Fitzgerald, 1995). Fitzgerald noted that children who speak languages that have a large number of English cognates may have an advantage with word recognition skills. Importantly, many children need to have this cognate-meaning connection explicitly taught, especially during the early elementary years.

Because studies on languages with alphabetical scripts clearly point to a strong relationship between developing phonological awareness skills and reading achievement, some research suggests that poor phonological awareness is cause for concern (Catts, Fey, Zhang, & Tomblin, 1999; Durgunoglu & Öney, 2000; Ganschow & Sparks, 2000). Phonological awareness is the understanding that oral language can be divided into smaller sound units (e.g., words can be separated into syllables) and skillfully manipulated (e.g., initial rhyming—*c*an, *m*an, *f*an, *r*an). It implies a level of metalinguistic awareness, which is consciousness about specific linguistic forms and structures and how the parts of language relate to the whole of making meaning with language. In contrast, phonological processing is the more encompassing perception, storage, retrieval, and manipulation of sounds during both comprehension and production of spoken and written codes (Catts, Fey, Zhang, & Tomblin, 1999).

After reviewing several studies on oral language development of L2 learners, Genesee et al. (2004) challenge the "children soak up language like a sponge" myth, concluding that, "one striking facet of children's acquisition rates in their L2 is the degree of variation among individuals" (p. 136). They further state that such findings are consistent across all child L2 research. Specific studies have found that children's rate of acquisition of phonology (Snow & Hoefnagel-Höhle, 1977) and grammatical morphology (Wong-Fillmore, 1983) can take between one and two years of schooling. Durgunoglu and Verhoeven (1998) also showed that children's achievement and rate of learning to read and write vary to a much greater degree among L2 learners when compared with native-speakers. Given the strong link between oral language and initial literacy development, teachers should expect greater variability among L2 children, as well as a *minimum* of 1-2 years for language and reading to develop.

The relative percentage of poor readers among children learning to read in their L1 as opposed to their L2 is quite similar. Both groups of learners struggle with phonological awareness skills and working memory. August and Shanahan (2006) point out that individual learner differences (e.g., general language proficiency, oral proficiency in the L2, cognitive abilities, prior knowledge and experience) and the degree of difference between the child's first and second language, likely play a much greater role in literacy development than language minority status per se. They also note that while language minority families demonstrate an ability and willingness to support their child's achievement in school, educators frequently misgauge and underuse this important resource (August & Shanahan, 2006).

RESEARCH CARRIED OUT IN ONE-WAY (FOREIGN LANGUAGE) IMMERSION CONTEXTS WITH LEARNERS WHO BEGIN THE PROGRAM AS ENGLISH PROFICIENT

Research carried out in early total foreign language immersion programs has consistently shown that a diverse range of students can successfully acquire initial literacy in a second language (Genesee, 1987, 2007b; Swain & Lapkin, 1982; Turnbull, Hart, & Lapkin, 2003). A limited number of studies find similar results with languages such as Mohawk and Hebrew, where the writing scripts, while still alphabetic, are very different from the L1, in this case English (Genesee, 2007b).

Certain studies carried out in early total immersion settings[1] point to a limited period of time in which an immersion learner's first language and literacy skills may test lower than same-age peers who have received all literacy instruction in their native language. Specific skills found to evidence lower test scores include word knowledge, word discrimination, spelling, capitalization, and punctuation (e.g., Barik & Swain, 1975; Polich, 1974; Swain & Barik, 1976). However, this lag is found to disappear within one to two years after the immersion learner begins receiving literacy instruction in their first language, typically between grades 4 and 5.

---

1. Early total immersion programs typically do not introduce instruction in students' first language until grade 2 or 3, and sometimes not until grades 4 and 5.

Research from partial foreign language immersion contexts, where children are usually taught to read in their L1, does not indicate this lag. At the same time, there is no research-evidenced advantage to introducing English earlier. By grades 5-6, the English language development of partial immersion students is found to be no different from that of total immersion students, despite the greater number of instructional hours in English (Swain & Lapkin, 1982; Turnbull, Lapkin, & Hart, 2001). Importantly, however, the immersion language proficiency of partial immersion students is found to be less developed.

Students who have internalized a sense of failure and/or demonstrate distaste for reading are a cause for concern. Students who struggle and develop a sense of failure become less motivated and often face even more difficulties as a result (Demers, 1994; Mannavarayan, 2002). This may lead to a permanent disdain for reading and result in severe academic difficulties as reading provides the foundation for academic success.

Very few studies have looked specifically at struggling immersion readers and no studies to date have been carried out on reading-impaired immersion learners. However, in a recent review of the literature on reading difficulties and French immersion learners, Genesee (2007a) concluded that

- immersion students who read well in L2 are very likely to read well in L1, just as those who read poorly in one language are apt to read poorly in the other;

- whereas immersion students learning to read first in French exhibit similar reading profiles as non-immersion students who learn to read first in English, English-only students were found to read faster and with greater fluency than their French immersion counterparts, suggesting a need for more practice in this area among immersion learners;

- tests that predict good readers in English (e.g., word-level skills such as phonological awareness, phonological decoding, verbal memory) also predict good readers in French, a finding that points to a strong similarity

between foundational skills for learning to read in French as an L2 and English as an L1.

These findings provide immersion educators with an initial research base that suggests early primary learners can be tested in English when concerns are raised about a possible reading disorder in a closely related language such as French.

During a November 2007 conference presentation, Montgomery County Public Schools (MCPS) reported on the reading performance of students in French and Spanish immersion. Over several years, MCPS has collected data on reading achievement in French and Spanish, the language of initial literacy for their immersion students. With these data, French and Spanish reading benchmarks have been established to measure student progress. These benchmarks align with English reading benchmarks used with non-immersion students in the district. Data from K-2 reading benchmark assessments indicated that

- French immersion program benchmarks are lower than English language program benchmarks in all but the final quarter of K-2;

- by the final quarter of K-2, French immersion students as a group perform at the same benchmark *in French* as grade-level peers schooled in English only do *in English*;

- during the K-2 time period the number of French immersion students performing below grade level diminishes, as, correspondingly, the number of students achieving at or above grade level increases;

- French immersion students that do not perform at grade-level by the last quarter of grade 2 receive additional reading support in grade 3;

- Spanish immersion program benchmarks are the same as English language program benchmarks during the K-2 years. The difference in reading performance between French and Spanish immersion students is thought to be linked to the high degree of sound-symbol transparency in Spanish.

(D. Gouin, personal communication, October 9, 2008; Klimpl, Amin, Gouin & Sacks, 2007)

Large-scale studies on reading achievement of immersion learners in the U.S. are few. Nonetheless, evidence from U.S. immersion programs points to similar levels of English reading achievement as have been found in the Canadian context. In other words, U.S. immersion students are reading at a level that meets or exceeds state and district standards. Most of these assessments measure English reading (e.g., Anderson, with Lindholm-Leary, Wilhelm, Boudreaux, & Zeigler, 2005; Arthur, 2004; Essama, 2007; Jones, 2005; Krueger, 2008; Lindholm-Leary, 2001); some also consider reading in the student's second language (e.g., Fortune & Arabbo, 2005; Klimpl, Amin, Gouin & Sacks, 2007; Lindholm-Leary, 2001).

RESEARCH CARRIED OUT IN TWO-WAY BILINGUAL IMMERSION CONTEXTS INCLUDING BOTH ENGLISH LEARNERS AND ENGLISH PROFICIENT STUDENTS

Collier (1992) and Cummins (1991) both reported that it can take between 5-7 years for children being schooled in a second language to acquire the academic language and literacy skills necessary for success in schools. These authors also stated that literacy instruction and formal schooling in one's first language are two critical aspects in furthering this process and ensuring success for language minority children.

Thomas and Collier (1997, 2002) find that English language learners in two-way immersion programs, in which students receive sustained and intensive support for both language and literacy development in L1 and L2, achieve higher levels of academic success when compared to other educational programs targeting L2 learners in U.S. schools. Collier and Thomas (2004) also showed that English language learners in two-way immersion programs take longer to demonstrate achievement on English standardized tests when these programs segregate Spanish-dominant from English-proficient learners during initial literacy instruction in English (i.e. Spanish-dominant learners receive English language arts instruction in one group and English-dominant learners are taught English language arts in another).

Research in two-way immersion has found that, regardless of first language background, it can take language minority students until grades 7 or 8 to achieve performance at or above the 50th percentile on standardized tests given in their L2 (Lindholm-Leary, 2001; Lindholm-Leary & Howard, 2008).

August and Shanahan (2006) examined English reading proficiency for language minority learners in two-way bilingual immersion versus English-only settings. On average, the comparison revealed higher levels of reading proficiency in dual language programs. In other words, language minority students who learn to read first in their L1 typically outperform those who do not on English (L2) reading assessments over the long term.

GUIDING PRINCIPLES

Based on the research reviewed above, and on the collective experiences of veteran immersion educators, we offer the following principles to guide practice.

Do not panic. Stay the course. All of the factors mentioned above interact to make learning to read in an immersion language a highly individual process; every student will have his/her own unique experiences. Some students will read faster than others, and for some students it will be a lengthy process.

Remember, reading is fun! Reading is not merely decoding words but rather gathering information, experiencing other's stories, and sharing an enjoyable exercise; students who take longer to master reading processes need to feel supported and not threatened. By emphasizing the more joyful elements of reading, literate individuals can counterbalance a child's potential withdrawal and resistance.

Involve parents. Parents need to be involved in literacy development from home and regularly invited into the school. Schools can develop outreach programs to teach parents about what they are able to do at home to encourage reading for pleasure. Parents should also be informed of what learning to read looks like in an immersion language to help them develop reasonable expectations of their children.

Attend explicitly and consistently to oral language proficiency development. Given the strong connection between oral proficiency and text-level literacy skills, programs that offer targeted support for oral language skill development in addition to high-quality literacy development will benefit second language learners.

Implement an interactive, guided model of reading. To extend the literacy skills of all readers, not just those that struggle, adopting an interactive approach to teaching reading is valuable. A guided reading approach within this notion of an interactive model has been found to be effective in the immersion classroom (Fisher, 2004). Guided reading requires that the text match the reading level of the student; within a classroom, students read different texts based upon their literacy skills and interests. Ensuring that vocabulary is at an appropriate level can aid the decoding and comprehension processes; when vocabulary is too difficult, students tend not to be able to form "a coherent and ordered set of propositions representing the ideas in the text" (Stahl, Jacobson, Davis, & Davis, 1989, p. 40). Within this interactive, guided reading model, students can begin to identify words, phrases, and meaningful groups of words quickly and accurately, as the text is suited for their individual level (Fradd & McGee, 1994). Grammar and vocabulary skills should also be developed through discussing reading texts and their practical applications. Developing student background knowledge about the topic prior to reading can also help them to identify the important information (Stahl et al., 1989).

Use Reciprocal Teaching (Palincsar & Brown, 1984) for text-level reading skill development. One teaching technique that is well established as promoting reading comprehension development along with oral language development is Reciprocal Teaching. In the Reciprocal Teaching classroom, teachers repeatedly model and then scaffold students' questioning as teachers and students take turns leading the dialogue about expository text. Incorporated into this technique are four key reading strategies: predicting, questioning, summarizing and clarifying difficult-to-understand parts of the text. These strategies help all students learn to monitor their own learning and thinking as they interact with and dialogue about a text.

Compare, compare, compare! Students should also be compared to other students within their guided reading group to monitor growth. Those students who are not making progress in comparison to peers are a cause for concern.

Assess struggling L2 readers earlier in their L1. While most programs have opted to put off testing early primary immersion students who exhibit difficulty acquiring word-level reading skills in their L2, research suggests that early assessment of foundational skills in a child's L1 can help to identify students who will need additional reading support services, and give the teacher a head start on focusing on the students' specific needs (e.g., phonological awareness).

Collaborate with the speech language pathologist at your school. These specialists have a knowledge base in language development and an understanding of oral language development as well as the development of the sound-symbol relationship in young students. Tapping into this important resource specialist's skill set is an essential part of offering support for struggling readers.

USEFUL RESOURCES

Below are selected online and print resources that pertain to issues discussed in this chapter.

1. *Parents Guide to Reading and Language*
   Public Broadcasting Systems (PBS), 2008

   http://www.pbs.org/parents/readinglanguage/

   This online guide is available in English and Spanish and describes how children become readers and writers and how others can help them develop by talking, reading, and writing together every day.

2. *Launching into Literacy: Early Childhood Professionals' Developmental Language and Literacy Milestones*
Kehl and Ballweg, 2007

www.madison.k12.wi.us/tnl/lilm/early_literacy/infants&toddlers/milestones0-3.html

This web page describes various research-based language and pre-literacy behaviors that typically developing children (ages 0-3) display.

3. *Learning to Read/Reading to Learn Campaign: Helping Children with Learning Disabilities to Succeed*
http://idea.uoregon.edu/~ncite/programs/read.html

The National Center to Improve the Tools of Educators, based at the University of Oregon, sponsored a *Learning to Read/Reading to Learn* campaign in 1996. This web page presents 10 prerequisite skills necessary for building a solid reading foundation. It also contains links to other resources that address developing reading skills in children with learning disabilities as well as tips for parents.

4. *Recognizing Reading Problems*
Colorín Colorado, 2007

http://colorincolorado.org/article/14541

This bilingual site provides useful information about reading for parents and educators. This particular article identifies specific behaviors to look for when a child is struggling with learning to read and ways to respond.

5. *Dyslexia and the Brain: What Does Current Research Tell Us?*
R. F. Hudson, L. High, and S. Al Otaiba, 2007

http://www.ldonline.org/article/14907

This online article defines dyslexia and dispels some common myths about this neurological disability. It includes resources and recommendations for teachers and parents of dyslexic children who struggle with reading.

6. *Reciprocal Teaching*
Florida Online Reading Professional Development (FOR-PD), 2005

http://forpd.ucf.edu/strategies/stratreciprocalteaching1.html (Predicting and Questioning)

http://forpd.ucf.edu/strategies/stratreciprocalteaching2.html (Clarifying and Summarizing)

http://forpd.ucf.edu/strategies/stratreciprocalteaching3.html (Reciprocal Teaching and Whole-Class Instruction)

These websites developed by the FOR-PD Program describe the rationale behind Reciprocal Teaching and explain how to implement it in the reading classroom. The first two pages focus on the four reading strategies, what they are and how to instruct students on their use. The third page considers how reciprocal teaching can be used with a whole class and assessment options. These FOR-PD pages also provide links to additional resources and references.

7. *Encyclopedia of Language and Literacy Development*
Canadian Language and Literacy Research Network

http://literacyencyclopedia.ca/?switchlanguage=EN

Launched in 2007, this online resource is being developed by the Canadian Language and Literacy Research Network to provide in-depth, research-based information about topics such as language, numeracy, reading and writing development. Submissions are written by internationally recognized experts and address unilingual and multilingual development for typical and atypical learners.

CHAPTER

KEY QUESTIONS

- What kind of assessments can be given to language immersion students who are not progressing in the target language and may not be developing cognitively at an appropriate rate? Who are not yet reading and writing?

- What languages should be used to assess an immersion learner?

Martha is an eight-year-old enrolled in the second grade at an early total French immersion school in a large city in the upper Midwest. Her parents are White, English-speaking and work as full-time professionals in the service sector. The school's 450 students are multilingual and multicultural with a sizeable number of students coming from French-speaking countries. However, the majority (68%) of students are White from monolingual English home backgrounds like Martha's. She has attended this program since kindergarten.

In February of her second grade year, a referral was completed by her classroom teacher due to her lack of progress in reading, written language and math. The teacher identified retention of information, concepts and words as the primary concern. The second grade teacher tried some classroom-based interventions. For example, Martha had one-to-one instruction for phonics and sight word recognition in French; however, her retention was poor and her growth was uneven.

A cumulative file review indicated that in kindergarten, Martha had great difficulty staying on task to complete her work independently; by the end of the year her kindergarten teacher noted that she was better able to participate in instructional activities and had shown some academic growth. At the end of first grade, Martha

REAL STORIES

Aline S. Petzold, M.Ps., NCSP

School Psychologist

L'Etoile du Nord

St. Paul, Minnesota

Program Model: One-way foreign language immersion, total, K- Gr. 6

Program Environment: Whole school, Urban

Language(s): French

REAL STORIES

Aline S. Petzold

was showing good consonant recognition but had difficulty reading words in French. Writing in French was also a struggle. She seldom finished writing assignments and was not getting more than one spelling word correct, even after reviewing words several times during the week. Martha was also frequently tuning out and consequently missed many opportunities to practice and learn.

At the end of second grade, her second grade teacher reported that Martha could express herself well, and was very social in French. She felt that Martha's spoken French was similar to that of her peers. She judged Martha's reading in French to be at a beginning first-grade level, which was also true of her reading comprehension; her retention of learned information was inconsistent. Martha was verbally able to share ideas but struggled to put her thoughts on paper. She wrote only two to three words rather than sentences and what she wrote was very hard to understand.

As part of the referral process, a comprehensive assessment was conducted. The referral team employed a variety of measures based upon the recommendations that traditional norm-referenced tests of ability and achievement be interpreted carefully when used with students whose history of instruction is different from the population on which the test is normed (Cummins, 1984; Kohnert, 2008; Ortiz & Ochoa, 2003). The following measures were used as part of the assessment process:

- *Comprehensive Test of Nonverbal Intelligence (CTONI)*, a nonverbal reasoning test useful for individuals with difficulties in language or fine-motor skills, given in English;

- *Nonverbal subtests of the Wechsler Intelligence Scale for Children, 4th ed. (WISC-IV)*, an individually administered instrument used to assess the intellectual ability of children, ages 6-16, given in English;

- *Similarities and Digit Span subtests from the WISC-IV*, an indicator of short-term memory and verbal reasoning in English, given in English;

- *Curriculum-Based Measurements (CBMs)*, reading probes and mixed math computation tests taken from French language texts comparable to those used in the immersion classroom, reading probes in French and English, math tests given in English.

It is the view of educators in our district that if a student does not have the same experience as those in the norming sample of a

standardized test that test should not be used to make decisions regarding that student's schooling. Therefore, we have developed and implemented an assessment process to reduce bias by (1) using tools to assess Martha's academic progress that are created from the curriculum, and (2) comparing her progress to that of her French immersion peers. Further, since cognitive testing is limited to abstract reasoning tasks, we can be assured that the results obtained are not influenced by lack of exposure to vocabulary, and the practice of using two nonverbal test batteries rather than just one increases the reliability of our test results.

Testing was completed one-on-one. Martha was able to understand and to engage in general conversation in French about familiar topics such as her family, and likes and dislikes, but often hesitated or tended to switch languages and substitute English words. She stated that being at the French immersion school was her parents' choice and that she would rather be learning at an English school. When given the choice, she preferred to complete the testing in English.

On the CTONI, Martha's overall ability fell in the average range for her age of 8 years old. She did slightly better on items that required her to complete a sequence or pattern based on geometric shapes as opposed to familiar objects. She had the greatest difficulty with a task that required her to pay attention to details in order to choose an item that completed a story sequence, scoring in the mildly delayed range, at an age equivalency of 6 years. In contrast, she scored well above peers, at an age equivalency of 11 years, on a task that required her to find similarities across groups of geometric shapes.

Martha's results on a series of nonverbal reasoning tasks reiterated the findings of the motor-free task. She scored in the broadly average range for her age on a test of spatial/perceptual reasoning. In contrast, Martha struggled with a test that required her to pay attention to details in order to pair groups of familiar objects. She scored well above peers, at an age equivalency of 10 years, in auditory memory. She scored in the average range on a test of visual scanning but struggled with a paper/pencil test of visual memory, scoring well below the base of 8 years. She scored in the average range for her age on a test of verbal reasoning.

In order to formulate a complete picture of how well Martha had profited from instruction, academic testing using CBMs for reading and writing was carried out in both French and English, directions for testing math skills, on the other hand, were given in English only. Testing in both languages lowers the possibility that

REAL STORIES

an academic strength or weakness will be overlooked (Kohnert, 2008). Martha's performance in reading, written expression and math was compared to that of her peers, other second graders at her school. On CBM results, differences in performance are considered significant when a student's performance is half the rate of peers or less. The following are the CBMs administered and Martha's results.

To assess her abilities in math, Martha was given a mix of math facts to solve in one minute ("Mad Minute"); directions for this task were in English. Martha's math skills fell into the late second to early third grade level.

To determine Martha's French and English reading levels, her teachers asked her to read from several levels of a controlled vocabulary reading curriculum in order to determine her instructional level[2] in French and English reading. Martha's oral reading fluency rate in English on second grade passages was 8 correct words per minute while peers read a median of 94 correct words per minute, and in French, Martha read 9 words correctly in one minute on grade level probes while peers read 60 words. She was able to read 5 words per minute at the first grade level, with 5 errors per minute; in comparison, first graders at her school are able to read 18 words with an average of 6 errors per minute. It is interesting to note that before beginning the reading task (and Martha and I had been working in French for some time) Martha looked at the passage and asked if it was in French or in English. From these measures, it was determined that Martha's instructional level in oral reading was at an ending first grade level in French.

For written expression, Martha was given three minutes to write a story using a sentence starter. In English, Martha's story was very difficult to read; spelling errors affected text comprehension. Moreover, correctly spelled words were out of sequence with the story's context. In English, Martha wrote a total of 22 words and when the sample was scored for correct spelling, grammar, punctuation and capitalization, her score was 6 correct word sequences. Peers wrote 34 total words with 16 correct word sequences.

Martha struggled to write in French. She made no attempt to write a story; after repeated prompting, she just wrote a list of pronouns. When writing in French, Martha wrote 4 total words in three minutes with 0 correct word sequences; her peers wrote 36 total words with 6.5 correct sequences.

---

2. The definition of instructional level used here is the highest level at which the student can read 40-60 correct words per minute for pre-primer to second grade level materials (Mark Shinn, CBM research, AIMSWEB).

REAL STORIES

Results of this evaluation placed Martha in the broadly average range of nonverbal reasoning ability as compared to peers. She did best on tasks that contained fewer confusing details or had contextual supports to help with problem solving. Curriculum-based test results showed that she has grade-appropriate math skills. Her skills in reading, spelling and written language fell at the first grade level or below. Martha's slower rate of reading grade-level texts impacts her ability to learn at a pace similar to peers. Her poor decoding and word recognition skills also impede adequate progress. Martha therefore meets eligibility for Specific Learning Disabilities in Reading and Written Language.

BACKGROUND INFORMATION

THE CHALLENGE OF OVER- AND UNDER-IDENTIFICATION

The purpose of assessing students is to determine students' instructional needs and provide them with instruction corresponding to those identified needs (Fradd & McGee, 1994). Linguistically and culturally diverse learners present special challenges to this process as evidenced by the many groups of culturally and/or linguistically diverse children that are either over- or under-represented in special education programs. For example:

- In Minnesota, 20.58% of American Indian and 18.77% of African Americans from English-speaking homes were identified as needing special education. In contrast, only 7.1% of Asian students from non-English speaking homes were so identified in 2001-2. (Minnesota Department of Education, 2003).

- During the 1991-1992 school year, approximately 25% of English language learners in Massachusetts, South Dakota and New Mexico participated in special education programs, whereas less than 1% of English language learners received special education services in Colorado, Maryland and North Carolina (Henderson, Abbot, & Strang, 1993).

- Between 1993-1994 and 1998-1999 the Latino English language learner population in one California school district increased by 12%. However, during that same time, the percentage of Latino English language learners in special education increased by 345% (Rueda, Artiles, Salazar, & Higareda, 2002).

Such statistics point to the complexity of accurately assessing linguistically and culturally diverse learners. How diverse are language immersion programs? This appears to vary a great deal by program type. In the U.S., there are three distinct branches of immersion: one-way (foreign language), two-way (bilingual immersion), and indigenous (language and culture revitalization). Each of these programs targets a specific learner audience. One-way foreign language immersion programs adopt the prototypical Canadian immersion model and are designed for English-speaking students regardless of their ethnic and socioeconomic background. Two-way immersion, in contrast, sets out to integrate two linguistically diverse groups of learners, one English-dominant and one dominant in the partner immersion language, typically Spanish. Indigenous immersion programs are developed for native cultural groups, for example, Native Hawaiian or Native Ojibwe children. All of these program varieties are open to all ethnic groups and students from every socioeconomic background. As a rule, immersion programs do not screen for admission, although there have been individual cases where this does occur.

The student make-up of one-way foreign language immersion programs has historically been

Caucasian from middle to upper-middle income families (Burns, 1983; Swain & Johnson, 1997). Charges of elitism have long plagued these programs and continue to do so even today (Freeman, Freeman, & Mercuri, 2005; G. Lukaska, personal communication, January 8, 2010; Lindholm-Leary, 2001). However, while this lack of diversity was likely the case in many immersion programs in the 70s and 80s both nationally and internationally (see Cadez, 2006 for a review of this issue in Canadian French immersion), today's one-way immersion classrooms, though generally less ethnically and socioeconomically diverse than two-way and indigenous models, include a broader array of learner characteristics (e.g., Caldas & Boudreaux, 1999).

Because demographic data on immersion programs as a whole are lacking, with the exception of Howard and Sugarman's (2001) *Two-Way Immersion Programs: Features and Statistics*, we provide information on the Minnesota immersion context as an example of the more diverse nature of today's immersion classrooms. Minnesota is a particularly compelling context to review for two reasons: (1) all three types of immersion exist in Minnesota, and (2) as of the 2007-2008 school year, Minnesota had more one-way foreign language immersion programs than any other state in the U.S. The data presented below are taken from a review of demographic information available on the Minnesota Department of Education website and supplemented by individually reported program data as necessary.

THE MINNESOTA ELEMENTARY IMMERSION CONTEXT

Minnesota's elementary-level immersion programs include all program varieties: one-way, two-way and indigenous. When we compare student data from all 27 elementary immersion programs (23 one-way, 4 two-way) and 4 indigenous preschool programs to data for all K-6 students in the state of Minnesota (Table 2), we find greater linguistic and ethnic diversity in immersion programs. In contrast, there are relatively fewer immersion students receiving special education services and/or participating in the school's free and reduced lunch programs, an indicator of socioeconomic background. This said, one of four elementary immersion students in Minnesota comes from a low-income household.

Table 2: Comparison of Student Data in Minnesota: Elementary Immersion Programs vs. All Elementary Programs in the State

| | Total N | Ethnic Background** | | | | | LEP | SpEd | Fr/Reduced Lunch |
		AmIn	As	Bi	Hisp	Wh			
Minnesota Immersion Programs	6,756	2%	4%	6%	21%	67%	11%	8%	25%
Minnesota Elementary Programs	420,228	2%	6%	10%	7%	75%	10%	13%	35%

Sources: Minnesota Department of Education School Report Card for 2006-2007 School Year and 2007-2008 data obtained from administrative personnel for 11 new immersion programs and 3 programs that are housed within an elementary school.

* Immersion program data include all elementary immersion programs and 4 indigenous preschool programs; state data on all elementary programs include elementary immersion programs.

**Abbreviations stand for the following ethnic descriptors: AmIn—American Indian; As—Asian; BI—Black; Hisp—Hispanic; Wh—White.

Figure 4.1: Student Ethnicity in Minnesota Elementary Immersion vs. K-6 State Schools, 2006-2007 and 2007-2008

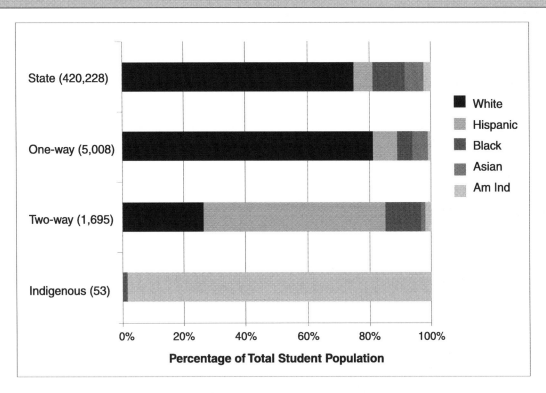

Percentage of Total Student Population

Figure 4.2: Students Receiving Special Services in Minnesota Elementary Immersion vs. K-6 State Schools, 2006-2007 and 2007-2008

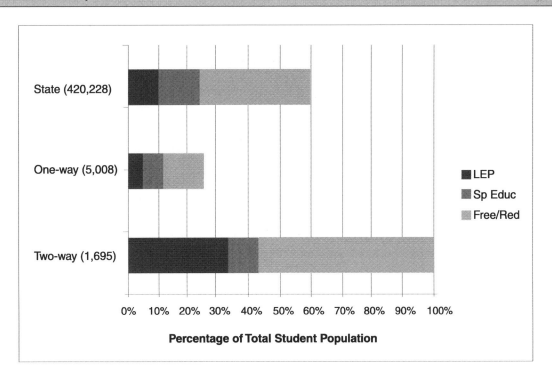

Percentage of Total Student Population

In an effort to better understand the breakdown of student demographics by immersion program model, we disaggregated data from Table 2 to compare numbers of students in each program model to state elementary student totals. Figures 4.1 and 4.2 on page 45 display this information. Minnesota's one-way elementary immersion programs as a whole are less ethnically and socioeconomically diverse when compared to the state's K-6 student population. Slightly less than three-fourths (75%) of K-6 students in the state come from European Americans families, while 81% of one-way elementary students are from European American backgrounds. Similarly, fewer one-way elementary students receive special education services relative to the state average, 7 and 13 percent respectively. Finally, 4% of students in one-way programs versus the state's 10% are English learners, even though this program model is not designed to address the linguistic needs of this population. While these programs are clearly less diverse than state schools overall, nearly one in five one-way elementary students does come from an ethnic minority background and 13% come from low-income families.

There is a common perception that TWI programs are predominantly made up of a mix of low-income, Spanish-dominant Latino learners and white, middle- to upper-income English speakers. Survey data on two-way immersion programs in the U.S., however, indicate that the English-speaking student population is far more diverse. Culturally, in over half of TWI programs there is ethnic balance among English speakers such that no one ethnicity predominates. With respect to socioeconomic diversity, in nearly one-third (32%) of TWI programs over half of students from both linguistic backgrounds qualify for free and reduced lunch (Howard & Sugarman, 2001). Minnesota data show a similar trend as found throughout the nation.

Finally, the make up of indigenous immersion programs whose goal it is to revitalize an endangered language and create a strong sense of cultural identity and ethnic pride, is almost exclusively Native American/Pacific Islanders. The majority of indigenous immersion students come from low-income families

and often speak a non-standard (i.e., indigenous language influenced) variety of English (Harrison & Papa, 2005; Wilson & Kamanā, 2008; N. McKay, personal communication, November 12, 2007).

We are unaware of survey data that has examined the immersion student population in terms of over- or under-representation in special education. This is the case both in the U.S. and abroad. Nonetheless, anecdotal reports indicate that some schools postpone referring a struggling learner until grade 2 or 3, which could result in under-representation in the early grades. The demographic information presented above may reflect this possible under-representation as a slightly smaller proportion of students receive special education services in both one-way and two-way immersion programs relative to the Minnesota state average.

While survey data on the percentage of immersion learners identified as eligible for special education services are unavailable, Canadian researchers report a high percentage of students who opt to transfer out of French immersion, especially at the secondary level. In the Canadian province Alberta, for example, 174 schools offered French immersion programs to nearly 27,500 students as of 1991. However, while many students enter French immersion at the elementary level, far fewer remain in the program through grade 12. According to Alberta Education (1990) data, between 1983 and1991 attrition rates ranged from 43 to 68 percent by grade 6, 58 to 83 percent by grade 9, and 88-97 percent by grade 12. Reasons for this dramatic attrition are many, including a perception that secondary students will perform better if schooled in English, the lack of course offerings and high-quality teachers at secondary levels and the highly mobile French immersion student population (Cadez, 2006). Some Canadian researchers have also identified academic and learning difficulties as the primary reason for elementary students leaving French immersion (Halsall, 1991; Hayden, 1988;Lemire, 1989; Obadia & Thériault, 1995).

U.S. studies detailing student attrition trends in immersion are scant. Rigaud (2005) reported results from her analysis of student withdrawal data from four elementary immersion schools over a ten-year period. Three of the elementary programs were K-6; one was K-5. This study is interesting in that she compared individual immersion school transfer rates to those of a demographically similar, non-immersion elementary school in the same district. Results indicated that immersion transfer rates were either the same as or lower than non-immersion. Rigaud noted, however, that the more complete data came from two of the four schools, both suburban, and suggests caution in extending her findings to urban immersion settings. She also found that in one of the suburban schools the average attrition rate for six cohorts of K-5 immersion students was 24.7%, indicating that nearly one in four students who began had left the program before grade 5. The reasons for students leaving the immersion program were not a focus of this study. While more U.S. studies are clearly needed, this first look at attrition in U.S. immersion presents a somewhat more positive picture than elementary-level findings in Canada for K-6 students.

OUT WITH THE OLD, IN WITH THE NEW: THE RESPONSE TO INTERVENTION (RTI) MODEL

Before presenting literature and research relevant to this chapter, it is necessary to review recent federal legislative changes in the guidelines used to determine eligibility for special education services. As mentioned in chapter 2 (page 20), the former discrepancy-based measure emphasized the role of standardized tests in eligibility determinations. To qualify for special education services students typically needed to display "normal intelligence" *and* severe underachievement on standardized tests and in classroom settings, as well as evidence of an information-processing problem.

As a result of recent federal special education legislation (IDEA, 2004), use of Response (or Responsiveness) to Intervention (RTI) acts as an alternative to or as a supplement for the IQ-achievement discrepancy measure in the identification of a specific learning disability. Shifting the focus away from IQ and achievement testing, measures found to be particularly challenging for increasing numbers of culturally and linguistically diverse learners, RTI is a multi-tiered method that requires quality, differentiated instruction for all learners and early intervention and continual monitoring of at-risk learners. The many variations on this model tend to appear as elaborations or modifications on the following three-tiered model for deciding whether or not a child has a language/learning disability:

Figure 4.3: Response to Intervention Model (National Joint Committee on Learning Disabilities, 2005)

Tier 1: High quality instructional and behavioral supports are provided for all students in general education.

- School personnel conduct universal screening of literacy skills, academics, and behavior.

- Teachers implement a variety of research-supported teaching strategies and approaches.

- Ongoing, curriculum-based assessment and continuous progress monitoring are used to guide high-quality instruction.

- Students receive differentiated instruction based on data from ongoing assessments.

Tier 2: Students whose performance and rate of progress lags behind those of peers in their classroom, school, or district receive more specialized prevention or remediation within general education.

- Curriculum-based measures are used to identify which students continue to need assistance, and with what specific kinds of skills.

- Collaborative problem solving is used to design and implement instructional support for students that may consist of a standard protocol or more individualized strategies and interventions.

- Identified students receive more intensive scientific, research-based instruction targeted to their individual needs.

- Student progress is monitored frequently to determine intervention effectiveness and needed modifications.

Figure 4.3: Response to Intervention Model (continued)

- Systematic assessment is conducted to determine the fidelity or integrity with which instruction and interventions are implemented.

- Parents are informed and included in the planning and monitoring of their child's progress in Tier 2 specialized interventions.

- General education teachers receive support (e.g., training, consultation, direct services for students), as needed, from other qualified educators in implementing interventions and monitoring student progress.

Tier 3: Comprehensive evaluation is conducted by a multidisciplinary team to determine eligibility for special education and related services.

- Parents are informed of their due process rights and consent is obtained for the comprehensive evaluation needed to determine whether the student has a disability and is eligible for special education and related services.

- Evaluation uses multiple sources of assessment data, which may include data from standardized and norm-referenced measures; observations made by parents, students, and teachers; and data collected in Tiers 1 and 2.

- Intensive, systematic, specialized instruction is provided and additional RTI data are collected, as needed, in accordance with special education timelines and other mandates.

- Procedural safeguards concerning evaluations and eligibility determinations apply, as required by IDEA 2004 mandates.

Tier 1 tends to be the responsibility of the classroom teacher; tier 2, on the other hand, is a shared responsibility between classroom teachers and special education teachers. Tier 3 as mentioned in the descriptor is the responsibility of a multidisciplinary team (Fuchs & Fuchs, 2005). It is essential that programs clearly identify support professionals, who will participate as members of the multidisciplinary team, and their respective roles. The following support professionals (see Figure 4.4 on page 49), presented in alphabetical order, all have an important role to play in this process: administrators, art/music/physical education/technology specialists, immersion classroom teachers, health care providers, non-immersion classroom teachers, school psychologists, social workers, special educators and speech language pathologists. Figure 4.4 suggests some of the unique perspectives each of these professionals can contribute.

Figure 4.4: Roles and Contributions of Support Professionals

Administrators—school and district policy, team meeting facilitation, home-school connection, parent communications

Art/Music/Physical Education/Technology Specialists—observations of child's interaction in additional school contexts

Immersion Classroom Teachers—observations of child's interactions in immersion classroom, during recess; language development concerns specific to the immersion language, child responses to various instructional adaptations, parent communications

Health Care Providers—information on physical and emotional development and well-being

Non-Immersion Classroom Teachers—observations of child's interactions in non-immersion classroom, during recess; child responses to various instructional adaptations, parent communications

School Psychologists—intellectual reasoning and curriculum-based assessment performance data, test bias implications and other data interpretation challenges, compilation of program-level achievement data for immersion students in the district

Social Workers—social and emotional well-being, home-school connection

Special Educators—observation of child's interactions in classroom, small group and one-on-one settings, observation of teacher's instructional practice, instructional adaptation recommendations, child responses to various instructional adaptations, parent communications, compilation of program-level achievement data for immersion students in the district

Speech language pathologists—typical vs. atypical language development, history of child's language development, L1 and L2 assessment data, norming groups and other data interpretation challenges, unique language-specific markers of language disorder

---

THE MULTI-FACETED NATURE OF LANGUAGE AND LANGUAGE LEARNING

Collier (1995) identified four interdependent components for understanding the K-12 learner's second language acquisition process: language development, academic development, cognitive development, and social and cultural processes. A variety of assessment tools are available for evaluating each of these components, which influence a learner's performance. It is essential that educators be aware of who and what they are assessing and use assessment tools that align with their intended purpose.

Because of the many factors that influence a learner, best practice indicates that assessments need to be *developmentally, linguistically and culturally appropriate,* i.e., the assessments chosen need to be learner-dependent. "Every child is an individual, and what may apply to one child in a certain linguistic and ethnic context may not apply to another child in that same context" (Genesee et al., 2004, p. 195).

The call for a case-by-case response to struggling immersion learners has resulted in a decision to re-organize and address practitioner questions as four sub-questions:

1. When a learner is not yet reading and writing in the language of assessment, is it appropriate to assess cognitive development using verbal or nonverbal tools?

2. Are standardized measures sufficient to determine eligibility for special education services?

3. How can educators minimize the linguistic and cultural bias of standardized tests?

4. Is it appropriate to assess students with diverse language backgrounds and language learning experiences in one of their languages or both/all?

Each sub-question considers two distinct groups of U.S. immersion learners, those who come from a linguistic and cultural minority background (language minority learners) and those who speak the majority language (English) and represent the cultural majority (language majority learners).

RELEVANT DISCUSSIONS AND RESEARCH FINDINGS

SUB-QUESTION 1: When a learner is not yet reading and writing in the language of assessment, is it appropriate to assess cognitive development using verbal or nonverbal tools?

Language minority learners

Nonverbal assessments of intelligence such as the Performance Scale of the Wechsler Scales (WISC-III) (Wechsler, 1991) are generally preferred over the Verbal Scale to safeguard against the interference of language and culture issues on tests of cognitive ability. However, many researchers express dissatisfaction with standardized cognitive ability tools due to language and culture bias, mismatched backgrounds of norming populations, among other concerns (Cummins, 1984; Holtzman & Wilkinson, 1991; McCloskey & Athanasiou, 2000; Petzold, 2001).

Kohnert (2008) discusses use of some newer nonverbal IQ measures, for example, the Test of Nonverbal Information-R (TONI-R), that were developed to reduce linguistic and cultural bias. Still, as Kohnert argues, because these nonverbal IQ tests are

experience-dependent, it is very difficult for them to circumvent bias completely.

As an alternative to nonverbal IQ tests, researchers at the University of Minnesota have been investigating the speed, efficiency, or capacity to act on a nonverbal stimulus such as a pure tone (sound stimulus) or a shape that cannot be named (visual stimulus). With **dynamic nonverbal processing tasks** children are invited "to detect, choose or sequence individual or patterns of nonlinguistic stimuli" (Kohnert, 2008, p. 99). The rationale for this line of research lies in findings that indicate the existence of slight differences in the nonverbal processing abilities of monolingual children with vs. without language impairment. Researchers hypothesize that similar processing differences may also exist in bilinguals and second language learners, thus providing an additional tool for differentiating children who struggle because of a language delay and those that have a disorder.

Gutiérrez-Clellen, Simon-Cereijido and Wagner's (2008) study compared the use of specific grammatical features of 71 Hispanic children from three diverse language backgrounds: English as a first language, Spanish-English bilinguals (English-dominant), and English as a second language (Spanish-dominant). The English as L1 children and bilinguals were further separated into two groups: those with language impairment and without. Researchers predicted cross-linguistic influence on language production for bilinguals and English as L2 children such that these children might exhibit greater rates of ungrammaticality in English due to interference from Spanish.

English-dominant bilingual children's language use does not show a higher number of grammatical errors than the monolingual English as L1 group. In contrast, the language of Spanish-dominant English as L2 learners did indicate significantly more verb-ending errors (on one of two measures examined), a finding that pinpoints similarities between their language development and that of language-impaired children. Based on these findings and other research support discussed in the article, researchers argue that when measuring the language performance of bilingual groups, it is important to address language dominance. Specifically, they state "applied research with affected [i.e., language-impaired] children who are bilingual should consider dominance in the identification of the disorder. Children, whose English is the weaker language, have the potential to be misdiagnosed as impaired in that language" (p. 16).

Language majority learners

While language majority learners as a group may not exhibit the same degree of cultural and linguistic diversity as language minority learners, it is clear that their linguistic development is different from peers schooled in English only. In response to this difference, one school psychologist whose caseload included an early total immersion school in the Midwest reported use of nonverbal cognitive testing measures such as the Wechsler Intelligence Scale for Children—Revised (WISC-R) (Wechsler, 1981). She had found over years of testing native English-speaking immersion children that such measures were less susceptible to language-based challenges because they focused more on problem-solving than the more linguistically influenced academic skills (Woelber, 2003).

Fewer assessments are available for young learners who are not yet reading and writing. Joyce and Bushey (2004) suggested building rhyming skills with nonreaders as a non-traditional means of assessing them: poems, finger plays, bean bag games, and picture bingo.

> **SUB-QUESTION 2:** Are standardized measures sufficient to determine eligibility for special education services?

Language minority learners

Educators frequently use standardized tests when assessing students for possible learning disabilities. These normed measures provide required information to qualify a learner for special education services. Some tests assess academic achievement, others intellectual ability. Gathering information on the individual learner's cognitive ability and academic performance allows school psychologists to compare what a learner *should* be able to do cognitively with what he/she *does* on achievement tests. Several researchers, however, caution against the use of standardized tools because they may not be appropriate information sources for all children, especially culturally and linguistically diverse learners (Cummins, 2001; Escamilla, 2000; Flanagan & Ortiz, 2002; Genesee et al., 2004; Kohnert, 2008; Wiss, 1987).

Bentz and Pavri (2000) review the literature and highlight the need for alternative approaches to monitoring reading development, particularly for English language learners coming from Latino backgrounds. These authors argue for use of nontraditional assessments, including portfolios, interviews, and curriculum-based measurements. They view such assessments as beneficial because they are generally inexpensive, require few materials, and are easily carried out over time and across contexts.

Even though the inclusion of nontraditional assessment techniques is widely embraced as best practice, McCloskey and Athanasiou (2000) report that the majority of school psychologists in their study made more extensive use of standardized tests. They do so primarily because of the lack of professional development and materials to support alternative approaches, and district/state/federal policies that do not require it.

Genesee et al. (2004) express concern about using English-language standardized tests because none exist whose norms are based on bilingual children specifically. They note that bilingual children may test slightly below monolingual norms at certain stages and on certain components of language and subject matter learning, even when a language disorder is not present. These authors also contend that preliminary testing of bilinguals needs to account for the learner's dominance in one language over another.

Elizabeth Watkins, Limited English Proficient and Minority Consultant for the Division of Special Education at the Minnesota Department of Education, suggests both informal and formal measures as a means of carrying out a comprehensive assessment of linguistically and culturally diverse students (personal communication, August 14, 2004). Some measures recommended by Watkins include language preference surveys, home language background questionnaires, an informal language assessment developed by Damico (1991), as well as tools to assess student language acquisition.

Language majority learners

Genesee et al. (2004) do not view use of standardized tests in the majority language as a concern for language majority children enrolled in immersion programs. They argue that especially the younger learners (K-1) have not yet achieved sufficient proficiency in the immersion language to warrant concern about use of existing norms. However, they also state the need for a variety of data in both or all languages and that a child's language should be observed in several contexts, not simply clinical or classroom settings.

Increasingly, immersion educators are adopting the use of alternatives to traditional tests such as site-specific CBM. Such tools have been used for many years with English language learners and can be developed for other students with linguistically different instructional experiences. CBM provides a way to establish within-program "norms" in particular skill areas, typically reading fluency and math computation. Language immersion students' educational experience is different from that of monolingual students learning through the medium of English. Once immersion program norms for average reading fluency and math computation are in place, CBM offers particularly useful comparative information when determining a struggling learner's eligibility for special education (for more information about this process for immersion programs in one school district, see Petzold, 2006).

SUB-QUESTION 3: How can educators minimize the linguistic and cultural bias of standardized tests?

Language minority learners

First and foremost, all assessment tools contain some level of bias. To minimize bias, using a variety of measures (formal and informal; standardized and alternative; within and outside of the classroom; oral and written; cognitive, linguistic, and academic, etc.) is important.

Beyond this, Samuel Ortiz, a bilingual researcher and former school psychologist, proposes a system for identifying the impact of language and culture bias in standardized tools used to measure cognitive abilities (Ortiz, 2003). He argues that because all tests vary in terms of linguistic and cultural knowledge demands, it is important to determine how much linguistic and culturally based information is being assumed on any given test. To do so, Ortiz begins by using a continuum as a way to describe the degree (low, moderate, high) of both cultural loading and linguistic demand. He then creates a matrix to show the ways language demand and cultural bias may interact and influence test performance (Figure 4.5).

The matrix can be used as a tool by trained specialists to analyze any cognitive ability assessment by categorizing each subtest according to its language and cultural bias. Subtest placement within the matrix is based on identification of targeted cognitive abilities using the integrated Cattell-Horn-Carroll (CHC) theoretical model of broad and narrow cognitive abilities (Carroll, 1993). For example, subtests targeting visual processing abilities (including such skills as visual memory, spatial relations, and length estimation) are classified as "low language, low culture." In contrast, those that target crystallized intelligence (including skills such as lexical knowledge, general information, grammar sensitivity) are seen as "moderate/high language, high culture."

An individual's score on each subtest is placed in the corresponding cell. All scores in each of nine possible cells are then averaged and this mean score is displayed. If a pattern emerges across the matrix indicating higher performance in the "low language-low culture" cells and progressively lower scores in the high language-high culture" cells, then the evaluator has evidence to argue that there may be cultural and linguistic difference influencing performance. Ortiz' approach promotes nondiscriminatory assessment practices by allowing for an interpretation of cognitive ability data that take into account the role of linguistic demand and cultural load. Ortiz cautions that classifications of subtests are subjective, insufficient if used alone, and need to be viewed as supplemental to a more comprehensive assessment process. For practicing school psychologists to become proficient at classifying subtests, professional development is critical.

SUB-QUESTION 4: Is it appropriate to assess students with diverse language backgrounds and language learning experiences in one of their languages or both/all?

Language minority learners

Cummins (2001) and Ortiz (2002) point out that to date no truly bilingual standardized assessment exists. That is to say, learners may be given a standardized test in both of their developing languages at separate times, but they are not able to show what they know drawing upon both of their languages with one tool at the same time. More recent developments, however, provide combined or composite scoring on a limited number of standardized assessments of lexical skills, for instance, the Spanish and English versions of the Expressive One-Word Picture Vocabulary Test (Brownell, 2000; 2001).

Muñoz-Sandoval, Cummins, Alvarado, and Ruef (2001) also set out to address the lack of assessment tools for bilingual learners by developing the Bilingual Verbal Abilities Test (BVAT) in order to estimate the combined linguistic knowledge of a bilingual student. This assessment combines verbal-cognitive L1 and L2 assessment in the same instrument. Students are given the opportunity to respond first in English, but secondarily in their L1. In the end, their combined scores (correct responses in English *and* correct responses in the L1) are used to determine individual learner performance relative to the norm. This measure provides teachers with information on a student's verbal academic ability in addition to a more accurate picture of a student's academic potential. It is currently available

Figure 4.5: Matrix of Cultural Loading and Linguistic Demand (L/C IMPACT) and Pattern of Expected Performance of Culturally and Linguistically Diverse Children

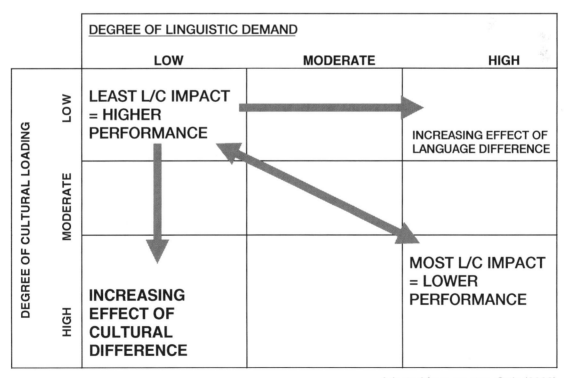

Adapted from source: Ortiz (2003)

53

in fifteen languages including Spanish, Arabic, Chinese (two forms), Japanese, French, German, Korean, Hmong, and Russian. In 2005, BVAT norms were introduced in the Normative Update edition, called BVAT-NU (Muñoz-Sandoval, Cummins, Alvarado, & Ruef, 2005).

Kohnert (2008) cites two standardized tests that offer normative data *in Spanish* for Spanish-speakers in the U.S.: the Spanish Preschool Language Scales-4, (Zimmerman, Steiner, & Pond, 2002), and the Clinical Evaluation of Language Fundamentals-4 (Spanish version) (Semel, Wiig, & Secord, 2003). A few other standardized tools exist in Spanish but Kohnert cautions against overuse and misinterpretation since test scores, while a necessary part of the assessment process, are insufficient measures of ability when considered on their own.

Recommendations from those who provide professional development for school psychologists regarding the appropriate language(s) of assessment are influenced by the individual's level of competence in L1 and L2 (Ortiz, 2003). For example, students who demonstrate mid to high levels of proficiency in both home and school languages will likely benefit from being assessed in both languages. On the other hand, language minority students with more novice levels of proficiency in a language may not benefit by being assessed in that language.

Language minority and language majority learners

Genesee et al. (2004) profile eight distinct dual language learners with varying backgrounds and schooling experiences. In their final chapter, they make recommendations about appropriate assessment and intervention practices for each of these fictional learners. They argue that educators need to consider the individual's language dominance when making decisions about the language(s) of assessment.

For example, the authors recommend using the first, or dominant, language when assessing second language learners like Samantha who was learning Spanish in an immersion program. In contrast, they suggest first determining language dominance for more balanced bilinguals like Pasquala, who use Spanish and English in both the home and the school, using standardized tests in both Spanish and

English. Similarly, their recommendations for Carlos, nearly monolingual in Spanish after a full year of schooling in U.S. schools in English, include assessment in Spanish in addition to English.

Research shows that certain dual language learners, in particular English language learners in U.S. schools, benefit by being assessed in their first/home language as well as the second/immersion language (Genesee et al., 2004; Gouin, 1998; Kahmi & Catts, 1999; Kohnert, 2008; Ortiz, 2002, 2003; Petzold, 2004; Wiss, 1987). By assessing a learner in both languages, practitioners can identify any discrepancies between performance in the language of instruction and the first/home language. Discrepancies may result from what should be seen as a typical delay in a dual language learner's language acquisition process, whereas similar deficit patterns that surface in both of the learner's languages and mirror those of monolinguals with language-impairment may indicate a language impairment or disability (Kohnert, 2008; Paradis, Crago, Genesee & Rice, 2003; Petzold, 2004).

It is also important to keep in mind that bilinguals typically develop proficiency in some domains and not others. Such distribution of proficiency across two languages or even within one language does not indicate language impairment. For example, English learners may have language for home activities in L1, but use their L2 (English) for school subject knowledge. Similarly, English-speaking immersion students may have academic language related to school subjects in L2, but lack the social language of everyday situations in L2.

Due to the lack of assessment tools in languages other than English, educators sometimes resort to translating tests from one language to another. However, both researchers and practitioners caution that test translations may lose their content and construct validity (Anderson with Lindholm-Leary, Wilhelm, Boudreaux, & Ziegler, 2005; Genesee et al., 2004; Kohnert, 2008).

As with many of the questions posed with struggling immersion learners, decisions about the language(s) of assessment are best addressed on a case-by-case basis (Genesee et al., 2004; Kohnert, 2008; Petzold, 2004; Woelber, 2003).

Language majority learners

Wiss (1987) recommends the Boder method (Boder & Jarrico, 1982) in order to accurately evaluate a language majority learner's difficulties. This method requires students to spell a list of ten known words as well as ten unknown words; any errors are then analyzed for patterns. This method can be used to assess students' reading-spelling patterns in both the L1 and L2 as a means to identify possible language-related learning disabilities.

Ochoa & Ortiz (2003) propose that when making decisions about the language(s) of assessment, the instructional program history of the learner needs to be taken into account as well as the language of initial literacy instruction. Most learners in foreign language immersion programs (as opposed to non-native English speakers in two-way models) fall into Ochoa and Ortiz' Language Profile 6: L1 fluent, L2 emergent. According to their Multidimensional Assessment Model for Bilinguals, these learners should be assessed in their L1 in grades K-7. Once learners enter grade 5, however, assessment in L2 is a secondary or optional mode of assessment that may provide additional valuable information, yet which will likely result in an underestimation of the learner's abilities.

GUIDING PRINCIPLES

Based on the research reviewed above, and on the collective experiences of veteran immersion educators, we offer the following principles to guide practice.

Focus on implementing interventions and monitoring growth before, during, and after the administration of a comprehensive assessment plan. To identify children who qualify for special education services, implementation and progress monitoring of the three-tier model of Response to Intervention (RTI) should be used, instead of the pre-IDEA 2004 discrepancy model of identification that emphasized IQ and achievement testing. Such practices necessitate ongoing collaboration among classroom teachers, special education teachers, and other educational specialists.

Use a wide range of assessment information from a variety of educational specialists. It is important to carry out a comprehensive assessment. For example, vary the sources and types of evaluative information used to inform a decision about a struggling learner. Best practice also suggests that information come from multiple contexts, time frames and professional perspectives, including school psychologists, speech language pathologists, special educators, social workers, health care providers, classroom teachers, art/music/physical education/technology specialists, and administrators. Possible sources for assessment information include:

Learner assessments

- *Informal* (observational checklist, interview, anecdotal records, questionnaires, etc.) and *formal* (standardized assessments, etc.)

- *Ability* (verbal and nonverbal reasoning, speed of processing, etc.) and *achievement* (criterion- and norm-based, etc.)

- *Innate* (L1 and L2; oral and written; receptive and expressive, physical health, emotional well-being) and *contextual* (family support and home environment)

Content area assessments

- *Subject matter* (math, science, social studies, music, etc.) and *language-related* (reading, writing, spelling, phonemic awareness, language arts, etc.)

Classroom assessments

- *Formative* (journals, learning logs, daily work samples, etc.) and *summative* (tests, end-of-unit performance tasks, presentations, projects, etc.)

Use assessments that provide rich comparative information over time including:

- Struggling learner vs. self

- Struggling learner vs. other struggling learners in the same context

- Struggling learner vs. other struggling learners in different contexts

- Struggling learner vs. siblings

- Struggling learner vs. whole class

- Struggling learner vs. same grade peers in the program/school (CBMs)

- Struggling learner vs. same grade peers in the district

- Struggling learner vs. same grade peers in the state

- Struggling learner vs. same grade peers in the nation

Develop program-specific measures based on the curriculum. Petzold (2004) recommended using Curriculum-Based Measurements (CBMs) (e.g., reading fluency tests, "mad minutes" [i.e., timed math computation tests], etc.) to establish program-specific norms for the immersion context. To learn more about developing CBMs and how such program-specific norms are used in **St. Paul Public Schools' immersion programs**, see Petzold (2006).

Montgomery County Public Schools in Maryland also administer a writing assessment in the immersion language to an entire class in order to create a program-specific comparison group (Gouin, 1998).

Hawaiian immersion programs recently engaged in a two-year project to translate the state's English-medium standardized assessments used for No Child Left Behind. After two consecutive efforts at English-to-Hawaiian test translation, Hawaiian educators decided to design an alternate assessment portfolio system that will be used with Hawaiian immersion students (Anderson with Lindholm-Leary, Wilhelm, Boudreaux, & Ziegler, 2005).

Use nonverbal cognitive ability tests and non-traditional and orally based language proficiency tests to assess struggling learners who are not yet literate (Joyce & Bushey, 2004; Woelber, 2003).

Interpret standardized test results after accounting for linguistic and cultural bias. Devise a system of evaluating the degree of cultural load (for ethnically diverse learners) and language demand (for all students learning through their L2) on each standardized assessment administered. Consider the cultural load and language demand implications of any type of assessment. When the assessments will be used to qualify a learner for special education services, it becomes even more important that some system of cultural-and-linguistic-bias determination be in place.

Take L1 background into consideration. Language majority and language minority students benefit from assessment in both L1 and L2. Language minority learners will also benefit by considering issues of language dominance in both of their languages; for language majority learners in K-1, results from language assessments given in English can be used to help identify the need for early intervention and additional instructional support.

Provide opportunities for learners to display knowledge in any and all languages. Ideally, assessment information would include some data gathered using truly bilingual tools, that is to say, tools in which both of their languages could be used to respond to the questions as needed. However, such assessments are few. Many practitioners recommend testing in each of a struggling learner's developing languages.

Consider program model and learner characteristics as well as the particular assessment tool.

Offer teachers and other support professionals high-quality professional development and in-program support for conducting multiple, appropriate assessments for the immersion context.

Identify, isolate, remediate. Often educational professionals insufficiently assess struggling immersion learners and prematurely initiate interventions for remediation. Imagine, for example, if we were to clearly determine through a series of measures a child's difficulty with walking. If medical experts then prescribed any number of general therapeutic activities to address the problem, results might or might not be successful. If, on the other hand, the doctor had pinpointed the exact nature of the child's walking disorder (e.g., hip dysplasia, bone fracture, inner ear disturbances, muscle deterioration, etc.), the potential effectiveness of the treatment would increase significantly. When it comes to struggling learners, educational specialists do well to first identify the existence of a language and/or learning disorder, and then persist to isolate the specific nature of the disability at hand. Once isolated, a plan for remediation can begin in a well-targeted manner.

USEFUL RESOURCES

Below are selected online and print resources that pertain to issues discussed in this chapter.

1. *AIMSWeb*
   Pearson Education, 2008

   www.aimsweb.com

   This Internet-based student academic progress-monitoring software and materials program, created by several of the researchers who originally developed CBM, includes downloadable directions for administration and scoring of oral reading, math computation and written expression. Materials can be adapted for use in the immersion language.

2. *DIBELS (Dynamic Indicators of Basic Early Literacy Skills) Home Page*
   University of Oregon Center on Teaching and Learning

   http://dibels.uoregon.edu

   A set of standardized, individually administered measures of early literacy based on student development of phonological awareness, alphabetic understanding and reading fluency are available on this website.

3. *Learning Disabilities Resource Kit: Specific Learning Disabilities Determination Procedures and Responsiveness to Intervention*
   National Research Center on Learning Disabilities, 2007

   http://www.nrcld.org/resource_kit/

   The National Research Center on Learning Disabilities developed this kit to help educators navigate the changes in the process of determining a specific learning disability and the implementation of Responsiveness to Intervention (RTI). It includes general information, tools for change, a getting started manual, an RTI manual, and PowerPoint presentations.

4. *Assessment of Struggling Elementary Immersion Learners: The St. Paul Public Schools Model*
   Petzold, 2006

   http://www.carla.umn.edu/immersion/ACIE/vol9/feb2006_bpractices_strugglinglearners.html

   This article describes the curriculum-based model used during the assessment and special education assessment process in the St. Paul Public School District.

5. *Improving Academic Performance Among American Indian, Alaska Native, and Native Hawaiian Students: Assessment of Learning and Identification of Learning Disabilities*
   National Institute of Child Health and Human Development, NIH, DHHS, 2005

   http://www.nichd.nih.gov/publications/pubs/upload/native_american_learning_2005.pdf

   On March 16-18, 2005, several federal agencies, professional organizations, and associations joined forces to hold a national colloquium to address the educational needs of Native American students. Researchers and educational practitioners discussed the key issues and challenges for improving educational performance among Native American students, and began creating a blueprint for research and practice. This document summarizes these discussions.

6. *Two-way Immersion (TWI) Toolkit*
E. R. Howard, J. Sugarman, M. Perdomo, and T. T. Adger, 2005

http://www.cal.org/twi/toolkit/index.htm

This Toolkit is designed to meet the growing demand from teachers, administrators, and parents for guidance related to the effective implementation of TWI programs. Although the Toolkit is primarily intended to support teachers, administrators, and parents who are new to two-way immersion, those with experience in TWI may also find the Toolkit useful. The Toolkit is composed of three segments: program design and planning, classroom instruction, and parent involvement. The pages that specifically address the assessment question are 43-47.

7. *The Oral Language Acquisition Inventory (OLAI), PreK-3*
L. M. Gentile

This informal, repeated measures assessment tool is recommended by speech language pathologists to provide additional information about an individual learner's control of commonly-used language structures. Such information helps to identify a child's stage of language development and appropriate instructional practices that are learner-specific.

PART TWO

Best Practice at the Classroom- and Program-Level

CHAPTER

KEY QUESTIONS

- As we work to support immersion teachers with struggling learners, what research-based adaptations to instruction are known to be effective with these students?

- Which strategies are most likely to be implemented by teachers?

Chloe is a six-year-old first grader in a total French immersion program, which is located in a large metropolitan school district. Since students receive all their academic instruction in French, initial literacy begins in French right away in Kindergarten. English is formally introduced as a subject in the second half of fourth grade, for two 45-minute sessions a week. Fifth graders receive 45 minutes a day of English instruction.

Chloe came to the immersion program from a family in which only English was spoken in the home. Her mother speaks enough French to help her daughter with homework, but not enough that she spoke it to Chloe as a home language. Both parents have advanced degrees, and work as professionals outside the home. When Chloe was in Kindergarten, a second child was born, a sister. Chloe also has siblings from her dad's first marriage.

When Chloe entered first grade, she was at a level considerably below that of her peers. In Kindergarten her teacher referred her to a special team, following the school's process for recognizing students for whom classroom best practices didn't seem to be working. At parent meetings, parents described argumentative, contrary, obstinate behavior, as well as off-topic comments and a reluctance and inability to do homework. In class, Chloe exhibited very immature behavior, often being inappropriately affectionate

REAL STORIES

In response to questions addressed in this chapter, we offer two stories from experienced immersion professionals: one from the one-way foreign language immersion perspective, the other from the perspective of the two-way bilingual immersion program.

Donna M. Gouin

French Immersion Program Coordinator

Sligo Creek Elementary School

Silver Spring, Maryland

Program Model: One-way foreign language immersion, total, K- Gr. 5

Program Environment: Strand program, Urban

Language(s): French

REAL STORIES

Donna M. Gouin

with classmates and teachers, whining, laughing, clinging to other students, and making loud, off-topic comments; she also had toileting accidents.

Academically, Chloe was not learning sound-letter relationships, class poems or number names, despite working one-on-one with a para-educator. She had vision problems, necessitating her wearing a patch on one eye part of the day. Parents considered retention, but the team felt that, given her eyesight issues, as well as the fact that a new baby had entered her family at the beginning of the Kindergarten year, that Chloe should go into grade one with the teacher implementing many best practices at the beginning of the year, and that all adults would monitor her progress (or lack there of) closely.

She was placed in grade one, knowing only 26 of the 54 upper and lower case letter names, and not knowing any of the 25 sight words Kindergarteners are expected to know. The grade one immersion teacher is a veteran of immersion, as well as having been a teacher in Head Start and a mainstream Kindergarten teacher in a school with a physically challenged population.

Chloe's current teacher in grade one implements several of the research-tested instructional adaptations presented in this chapter; differentiation is principal among them. Sometimes, differentiation takes place within the classroom, and sometimes outside the classroom, at a table in the hallway with an instructional assistant, a high school intern, a parent or another adult who speaks French.

Differentiation takes place in many ways. Chloe's workload is adjusted; when other students need to answer five questions, she needs to answer two. Also, since she expresses herself best orally, the teacher makes sure that she can answer the questions orally before she asks Chloe to dictate her answers.

The teacher also differentiates by modifying tasks to Chloe's cognitive level. She has a great deal of difficulty identifying a story's beginning, middle and end. The teacher started the year by giving Chloe every day real life events to sequence visually—her morning routines, a birthday party, and the school day. And since November, the teacher gives her three pictures of the story being read and asks her to sequence those.

During guided reading and center time, Chloe has begun working with the teacher and/or helper adult and a small group of beginning level students in first grade to learn letter names, sounds, blending and sight words. They do constant repetition of words, and sounds, identifying them visually and writing them. She now knows all letter names and sounds, can identify all 25 Kindergarten sight words and most of the 50 first grade sight words. She can read

REAL STORIES

level 1 and 2 guided reading books, but she cannot yet answer comprehension questions by herself or retell the story with a beginning, middle, and end. She is able to manipulate sight word flash cards to form simple sentences, and read the sentences, but still cannot compose a sentence by herself. In fact, her journal entries are mostly incomprehensible.

Another way Chloe's teacher differentiates is by specifically choosing the type of questions to ask her. Although she may ask more open-ended questions of other students, she often asks Chloe questions about content by giving her a choice of answers of which one is the right answer, and one is blatantly wrong. Chloe then can choose the right answer, giving her positive reinforcement in content, as well as helping her feel good about herself.

Chloe responds well to adult attention. The teacher always keeps her in close proximity, and often the teacher will give her a physical cue when she is inattentive, such as touching her shoulder, or tapping on her desk. Although Chloe still has socialization issues, they are less inappropriate than those exhibited in Kindergarten. She also works well with certain peers. However, because of her socialization issues, cooperative grouping is not the most beneficial grouping arrangement for her. The teacher thus pairs her with one other student from a group of students who like her, accept her immature behavior, and want to help her succeed.

Chloe's teacher uses a lot of multi-sensory materials in class; students routinely use paint, markers, art, and movement as part of their daily work. Chloe responds well to these stimuli.

Chloe was identified this year as having multiple learning disabilities, and has been put on medication very recently for Attention Deficit Hyperactivity Disorder. Once again, her parents would like her to be retained; the team is waiting until June to make that decision.

Whatever happens next year, the teacher will want to continue to use the best practice strategies that have helped Chloe make progress in her first grade class: differentiation of tasks by simplifying work and reducing workload, use of visualization techniques like using manipulatives to develop sequencing skills, providing either-or options in questioning, pairing with a buddy or another adult helper, and using multi-modal activities that tap into her non-language-based strengths.

Furthermore, as Chloe makes some progress in her academic skills through the implementation of the strategies described above, it might be time for the teacher to work on some of the strategies that Arnett (2003) identifies as part of the expression stage (see Figure 5.4 on page 74). She can give Chloe advance warning to let her

REAL STORIES

Mary T. Cazabon, Ed.D.

Former Director of Bilingual and English Language Acquisition Programs

Cambridge Public Schools

Cambridge, Massachusetts

Program Model: Two-way bilingual immersion, 50:50, K- Gr. 8

Program Environment: Whole school, Urban

Language(s): Spanish/English

know that she will be asking her a question; this might lead her to be more comfortable answering more open-ended questions. Her teacher can permit her to use alternate forms of expression, especially since she seems comfortable with manipulatives and visualization techniques. The teacher might also engage her in instructional conversations, which will bring the learning to another level, develop her metacognitive abilities, and develop more receptive and expressive vocabulary in the target language.

Anthony Johnson's mom is very enthusiastic about placing her four-and-a-half-year-old son Anthony in the 50:50 two-way Spanish-English immersion school in their district, which is located in the northeastern region of the U.S. She has heard wonderful comments from other parents and she knows about several children who have been very successful in the school. Anthony's dad lives in another city and does not speak any Spanish, but he is willing to go along somewhat reluctantly with the immersion placement. Anthony's mom spent a semester in Mexico in college and has good conversational Spanish and a solid literacy foundation. She has purchased some Spanish DVDs and books in Spanish to promote the Spanish language at home, and has been teaching Anthony some Spanish songs and incorporates some Spanish nursery rhymes into her play with him at home. Anthony exhibits difficult behaviors at home with mom and also with dad on his every other weekend parent-child time and the parents think that as he matures he will grow out of these behaviors.

In September of the new school year, when Anthony was placed in the pre-Kindergarten class in the two-way immersion school, he quickly exhibits some difficult behaviors in both English and Spanish lessons. He tends to speak loudly, does not interact well with his classmates, has a hard time sitting in circle time, and will get up and wander around the room. He looks away when speaking with adults and has difficulty making eye contact. He is happiest when he is left alone to build with Legos™ and he has made several intricate vehicles that astound his teacher and his classmates alike. Anthony's mother comes often to observe in the classroom and she notices that her son is not interacting well with the other students. The teacher and the mom have discussed Anthony's issues and both feel that they should give him a couple of more months to see how he adapts as he is only four-and-a-half years old. Ms. Johnson reveals that Anthony developed speech on the late side and he seems to have difficulty understanding directions and demonstrates a restricted range of interests, preferring to play by himself with his toy cars and trucks rather than romping in the playground with other children. His actual speech is quite formal and his mother states that he seems like a little professor. Unfortunately, his behavior does not improve much even after a few months in school.

Because there is little change in Anthony's behavior, the decision is made to have Anthony tested for special needs. Anthony receives testing and screening by a speech pathologist and other clinicians. This screening and testing determine that he has Pervasive Developmental Disorder Non Specific (PDD NOS) indicating impaired development in social interaction and communication and a severely restricted range of interests. Anthony's mom and dad have been told that children with PDD are on a spectrum or continuum and that Anthony falls into the higher functioning end of the spectrum. A plan is developed that gives Anthony weekly speech lessons with a specialist that includes speech pragmatics and group therapy with 3 or 4 other children, some physical therapy to improve gross motor development, and additional occupational therapy. Anthony responds well to the extra support and is learning how to read social cues from his teacher and other students. He is able to sit for longer periods during circle time and has begun to respond appropriately to questions. He still prefers to play by himself but he is able to label the parts of his created vehicles and share this information with his peers in both English and Spanish. When he is motivated to work, he is diligent and can concentrate for long periods of time. Transitioning to new tasks causes him to dig in his heels and he becomes very obstinate and stubborn. Any change in the daily classroom schedule is a problem for him.

Mom and dad are implementing strategies at their respective homes to assist Anthony in the daily basics of brushing teeth, bathing, eating, and other routine behaviors. They are in weekly communication with the teacher to make sure that the lines of communication are open regarding Anthony. Both parents look for ways to involve Anthony with other children but they do not force him into social situations unless he is willing to engage with others.

By the end of the school year, Anthony has made progress. He will be going on to Kindergarten where his new teachers will be mindful of his needs and the necessity to keep the lines of communication open with his family. There are certain adaptations that the teachers will be making for him. Social stories in both languages are very effective ways to engage students with PDD, like Anthony, in the realities of school life and can give them the knowledge capital

REAL STORIES

they need to understand social interactions by learning how to preview, predict, plan for and analyze social situations. Teachers need to be able to predict when students like Anthony might be feeling heightened stress in order to mitigate the situation before there is a crisis. Staff members need to take the opportunity to help foster empathy in Anthony so he begins to understand the feelings of others and so too must Anthony's classmates come to realize that we all have different ways of being that make us unique and yet we share similarities too.

Anthony will potentially benefit greatly from two-way schooling as it will help him navigate communication in two languages in very explicit ways and he will be building up a true repertoire of communication skills. His behaviors, while challenging, ought to be more under control as he gets older if the early support systems are in place and if he has sustained and continual support throughout his school years and into young adulthood.

An Addendum: Dr. Corinne Varon-Green is an elementary two-way language immersion teacher with many years of experience. She offers these suggestions for improving the classroom environment for students with PDP:

- *Student Conducted Interviews.* Use one-on-one interviews as tools to have students learn about each other, to find out about their families, and explore similarities and differences.

- *Portraits of Each Other.* Have students do portraits of each other—"You do my portrait and I will do yours." As they do so, allow them to engage in informal conversation.

- *Think-Alone Board.* Create a special bulletin board where students can draw and write about anything that they want.

- *Structured Chaos.* Give students time to explore free movement in dance and art activities. Role-play to explore emotions and memories. What made you sad? Angry? Happy?

- *Sharing Ideas.* Invite students to share their ideas. All must agree to respect everyone else's ideas. There is no need to convince others of their way of thinking; they are just sharing and listening.

- *Stuffed Animal Friends.* Provide stuffed animals in the classroom for comfort so as to have a calming influence in instances of heightened anxiety.

- *Leadership Opportunities.* Find ways to make students like Anthony a leader in the classroom.

- *Puppet Theater.* Use puppets to practice social conventions and to explore how to react to social cues.

BACKGROUND INFORMATION

Teachers tend to have positive attitudes about the effectiveness of instructional adaptations for struggling learners (Scott, Vitale & Masten, 1998), yet research has shown that teachers are most likely to implement adaptations that are relatively straightforward and all encompassing. Substantive adaptations requiring specialized adjustments to meet the specific needs of an individual student are less likely to be implemented (Munson, 1987; Scott et al., 1998). Teachers need to believe that what they are doing pedagogically serves all learners, not just a few. They are more likely to implement research-based strategies that positively impact instruction for all students including the struggling ones.

It is important for teachers to understand that instructional strategies that are implemented to meet the needs of a struggling learner will not take away from the learning of other students in the classroom; in fact, often times strategies aimed at helping one student or a small group of students result in gains for other students as well (Bender, 2002). All of the research-based instruction techniques and approaches discussed below hold great potential for making a difference for all learners, especially those who are struggling to learn and those that are learning through the medium of an L2.

The five adaptations and strategies we will draw attention to in this review of the literature are:

1. Differentiated Instruction

2. Multi-modal Teaching and Learning

3. Strategies-based Instruction

4. Five Standards of Effective Pedagogy

5. Cooperative Learning

We will briefly discuss each adaptation strategy and how it contributes to the goal of more effective instruction in the relevant research findings section.

In the practitioner recommendation section, we will present the Arnett (2003) Framework for Adapting Immersion Instruction, which considers three aspects of language learning difficulty: perception, information processing, and expression. These areas serve as a way of organizing and presenting specific strategies or adaptations. It is important to keep in mind, however, that changes to the instructional process are only one piece of curriculum implementation. Thus, before implementing any particular change, teachers need to account for the interdependence of all curricular elements including teaching strategies, content, instructional setting, and student behavior (Hoover & Collier, 2001).

In addition, research in the area of language teacher education indicates that teachers need high quality professional development that is sustained over time to make lasting changes in their teaching practice. Professional development that focuses on current research in second language acquisition, metalinguistic learning strategies, and language-specific reading strategies needs to be developed and made accessible to educators. This will provide them with the necessary tools and skills to most effectively implement immersion methodology (Boschung & Roy, 1996; Calderón & Minaya-Rowe, 2003; Cummins, 1984). Creating school-based professional learning communities and offering mentor coaching on site are some effective ways to facilitate ongoing commitment to integrating supportive techniques and strategies for struggling immersion learners.

RELEVANT DISCUSSIONS AND RESEARCH FINDINGS

DIFFERENTIATED INSTRUCTION

Differentiated instruction is a teaching practice based upon the notion that different learning needs require varied and adapted instruction; this is true not only for struggling learners but for those who are making "normal" progress and/or excelling as well. With differentiated instruction, students have more than one way of taking in information and making sense of their ideas; rather than students adapting to the curriculum, it requires that teachers be flexible and adjust the curriculum and presentation of content to meet the particular learning needs of students. Its goal is "to maximize each student's growth and individual success by meeting each student where he or she is, and assisting [them] in the learning process" (Hall, 2002, Definition section, ¶ 1). In order to effectively carry out this technique, teachers must know their learners well. Learning styles and preferences, background knowledge, readiness, current level of ability, motivation, and interests all need to be considered when differentiating instruction.

Content, process, and what learners are expected to produce can be modified to meet a learner's unique needs (Tomlinson, 2001). While the specific content to be covered is often out of the control of the teacher, the teacher can control how the content is presented. All students should learn the same concepts but the level of complexity or detail presented can be adjusted according to the needs of learners in the classroom. Teachers can differentiate the learning process by varying how students interact with the content. Flexible grouping strategies, learning centers, and a variety of learning activities promote differentiation in the learning process. The product, the means by which teachers assess student mastery of content, is also flexible in the differentiated instruction approach. Well-designed products will promote "varied means of expression, alternative procedures, and provide[s] varying degrees of difficulty, types of evaluation, and scoring" (Hall, 2002, Products section, ¶ 3).

Research has shown that small group instruction is more effective than large, whole group instruction (Elbaum, Vaughn, Hughes, & Moody, 2000). Small group instruction can take many forms, and students with learning disabilities often find success in classrooms that offer a variety of instructional grouping options (Bender, 2002).

MULTI-MODAL TEACHING AND LEARNING

That learners are diverse is well accepted in the educational community. Multiple intelligences (Gardner, 1983, 2000) and learning styles (Scarcella & Oxford, 1992) are just two of the many ways that they differ. Presenting content in a variety of ways affords learners the opportunity to interact with information in ways that match their particular style; by doing so, teachers are attending to the individual learning preferences and innate strengths of students.

The theory of multiple intelligences helps to explain how learners approach learning. Intelligence, according to Gardner (1999), "is a biopsychological potential to process information that can be activated in a cultural setting to solve problems or create products that are of value in a culture" (p. 34). Such potential can be realized in various ways and can be further developed and expanded. Intelligence then is not best expressed psychometrically as a single IQ score, rather it is more appropriately viewed in broader terms as a set of unique capacities.

To date, eight intelligences have been identified: intrapersonal/introspective, interpersonal/social, logical/mathematical, verbal/linguistic, bodily/kinesthetic, visual/spatial, musical/rhythmical, and naturalist. Multiple intelligences theory enables educators to understand how a learner might more easily grasp a concept and consciously plan to present information in unique and complementary ways. For example, when learning about Paul Revere's ride in a history lesson, musically intelligent learners might benefit from learning a song about his ride. In this way, they could associate the content information with the rhythm and music of the song and would be more able to learn the new information.

Similarly, sensory preference is one of the five dimensions of language learning styles identified by Scarcella and Oxford (1992). This particular dimension focuses on the physical, perceptual methods for learning such as through visual, auditory, kinesthetic, and tactile cues. Because learners differ in their approaches to learning, it is important that teachers know how students learn best and provide them with opportunities to interact with content in the manner that is most appropriate for them. For example, in a lesson about three-dimensional shapes (prisms, pyramids, spheres, cones, etc.), teachers might show pictures or models of these shapes to reach their visual learners, tell a story about how different cultural groups have used these shapes in their communities to reach auditory learners, ask students to trace the edges of the shapes and feel the models with their hands to reach tactile learners, and have pairs or triads make the shapes with their bodies to reach kinesthetic learners. While learning for all students can be deepened and enriched by presenting concepts in many and varied ways, multi-modal teaching helps to ensure more successful learning for struggling students who are likely to have difficulty with more traditional, language-based instruction on its own.

Recent research on the human brain also highlights the need for using a multi-sensory approach. Brain-based research suggests that motor skills are remembered much longer than cognitive skills because (1) motor skills learning takes place in a different place in the brain, and (2) the brain considers these skills more essential to survival. This finding suggests that teachers should pair factual information and academic skills with physical movements. Additionally, because the human brain is drawn to novelty and differences in stimuli, enhancements to the color, size, and shape of lesson materials have been shown to increase learning and are recommended techniques for classroom teaching.

While multi-modal instruction is beneficial for all learners, researchers identify it as essential for those who struggle. As an example, Sparks et al. (1998) review the literature on secondary students identified as likely to struggle to learn a foreign language. Based on this review, they report that learning Spanish through multi-sensory structured language techniques resulted in students making significant gains on measures of both native language skill and foreign language aptitude over one and two years. Moreover, the levels of oral and written proficiency these students attained in Spanish were similar to those of other students.

In the field of immersion education, practitioners and researchers have also consistently identified multi-sensory techniques as core strategies for making instruction comprehensible to students learning through a second language (Boutin, 1993; Lorenz & Met, 1988; Salamone, 1993; Snow, 1987, 1990). For example, Snow (1990) distills the essence of teaching in a language immersion classroom down to ten core strategies, among them, making extensive use of realia, visuals, hands-on experiences and manipulatives to create multi-sensory experiences. By doing this, she finds immersion teachers help students to "associate language with its concrete referent through pictures and real-life objects" (Snow, 1990, p. 161). Boudreaux (1994) and others point out the clear match between techniques found to be effective

with struggling learners and those cited as essential for students learning through a second language. In sum, multi-modal instruction is indispensable for struggling immersion learners.

STRATEGIES-BASED INSTRUCTION

A common area of struggle for underperforming learners is managing the learning process. This occurs both in a physical sense of keeping track of learning materials and in a cognitively strategic sense in that they do not know when and how to apply specific skills they have learned. In a recent chapter, Bergström (2006) reports on a Swedish immersion learner with diagnosed dyslexia whose ability to use a broad range of strategies to assist with L2 writing was dwarfed by a preoccupation with spelling challenges. The amount of attention paid to spelling details from the start inhibited the child's ability to construct meaningful text and create a story.

A number of researchers advocate teaching learning strategies to students for use with particular tasks (cf. Chamot & O'Malley, 1994; Day & Elksnin, 1994; Keeler & Swanson, 2001; Marks, Laeys, Bender & Scott, 1996; Sousa, 2001; Vaughn, Gersten & Chard, 2000). Learning strategies are defined as "procedures or techniques that learners can use to facilitate a task" (Chamot, Barnhardt, Beard El-Dinary, & Robbins, 1999, p. 2). They fall into two broad categories: metacognitive and task-based strategies. Task-based strategies are further grouped as: (1) Use what you know, (2) Use your imagination, (3) Use organizational skills, and (4) Use a variety of resources. Some strategies, like making use of graphic organizers in a pre-writing task, are observable; most, however, like using visual imagery to recall information, are not.

Strategies-based instruction has been found to have a positive impact on content learning (Christensen & Cooper, 1991; Dole, Brown & Trathen, 1996) and second language learning (Cohen, Weaver & Tao-Yuan-Li, 1995; Kern, 1989). Within the elementary immersion context specifically, "good" learners have been found to monitor and adapt their strategy use more than less effective learners (Chamot & El-Dinary, 1999). In addition, upper elementary immersion learners who reported greater strategy use were found to be more confident learners (National Capital Language Resource Center, n.d.). Furthermore, robust research findings from studies with English language learners has led to the inclusion of learning strategy development as a separate standard within each of the three main goal areas that comprise the *National English as a Second Language Standards for PreK-12 Students* (Teachers of English to Speakers of Other Languages, 1997).

Creating independent learners who can appropriately use learning strategies is the goal of strategies-based instruction (Chamot et al., n.d.). Through this technique, students acquire specific language to talk about the learning process, and adopt techniques used by effective learners to acquire new knowledge and skills. It is important that students learn not only what the strategies are, but how and when to apply them. Chamot and O'Malley (1994) proposed a five-step cycle for implementing effective strategies-based instruction for second language learners: (1) Preparation, (2) Presentation, (3) Practice, (4) Evaluation, and (5) Expansion. All five steps are essential to effectively implement this type of instruction. Providing second language learners with opportunities to work with a strategy and then reflect upon its effectiveness in accomplishing a specific task helps them to internalize the strategy and understand when and how to use it.

Rousseau (1998) carried out a two-year research study evaluating the effectiveness of a French Immersion Learning Disabilities Program (FILDP), a short-term (two-year) program carried out in a separate, self-contained immersion classroom for LD learners, in which parts of the program took place in French. FILDP was designed to provide these struggling learners with the skills needed to be able to return to the regular French immersion classroom. It embedded a specific learning strategies component as one of four program elements: (1) strategy instruction based upon each child's needs, (2) weekly learning disabilities awareness sessions, (3) English reading intervention, and (4) communication between school and home. Program goals included internalization of learned strategies and better self-perception. To qualify for program participation,

all students met eligibility criteria for a Specific Learning Disability as defined by the Edmonton Public School Board Guidelines (Edmonton Public Schools, 1996).

FILDP participants, parents and their teacher reported a more positive attitude toward school and learning as well as perceived improvement in school-related tasks. This is noteworthy in the case of parents because these same parents had expressed earlier dissatisfaction with the English language remedial help provided to their children prior to this program.

With respect to assessed French language abilities, Rousseau found that students increased their word identification and passage comprehension. French spelling abilities, on the other hand, deteriorated slightly. Rousseau hypothesized that this could be a result of more difficult exams over time. Students also improved their English decoding, spelling, and reading comprehension skills. When compared with French immersion students who participated in the English-only remediation program the previous year, FILDP students performed as well as or better. For example, 60% FILDP students increased their reading level by two grades whereas only 29% of English-only remediation program participants did the previous year. Additionally, 100% of FILDP students performed at grade level on the writing measure whereas only 40% of the English-only students did so.

FIVE STANDARDS OF EFFECTIVE PEDAGOGY

The Five Standards of Effective Pedagogy are the end result of a long-term research agenda into teaching and learning standards that have been shown to be effective for all learners, regardless of language background, educational experiences, and ability. These standards have found support in research studies that evidence a relationship between their use in the classroom and improvements in affective, behavioral, and cognitive areas of student performance (Doherty & Pinal, 2002; Doherty, Hilberg, Pinal, & Tharp, 2003; Estrada, 2000; Hilberg, Tharp & DeGeest, 2000; Padron & Waxman, 1999; Tharp, Estrada, Dalton & Yamauchi, 2000).

The goals of the Five Standards are to engage learners actively in co-constructing new understandings, to cultivate the ability to think and articulate critically about complex ideas, and to develop language and literacy skills in the language of instruction across the content areas. The standards as described and graphically summarized by Dalton (1998, p. 10) are outlined below.

Figure 5.1: Five Standards of Effective Pedagogy (Dalton, 1998)

Standard I: **Joint Productive Activity (JPA)**

Facilitate learning through joint productive activity between teacher and students.

Standard II: **Language and Literacy Development (LLD) Across the Curriculum**

Develop competence in the language and literacy of instruction across the curriculum.

Standard III: **Making Meaning (MM)**

Connect teaching and curriculum with experiences and skills of students' home and community.

Standard IV: **Teaching Complex Thinking (CT)**

Challenge students toward cognitive complexity.

Standard V: **Teaching Through Conversation (IC)**

Engage students through dialogue, especially Instructional Conversation (IC).

Figure 5.2: Graphic Summary of Five Standards of Effective Pedagogy (Dalton, 1998)

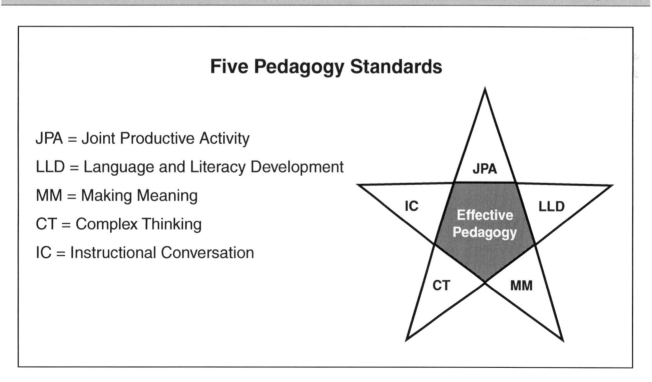

These standards are intended to serve as guiding principles for teachers as they promote learner-centered, effective learning environments. They are also intended to supplement other approaches, such as those discussed throughout this paper. Doherty, Hilberg, Pinal & Tharp (2003) describe what implementing these strategies might look like in an abstract way:

> "[It] consists of a teacher and a small group of students having an instructional conversation while collaborating on a cognitively challenging activity contextualized in students' personal, social, or cultural knowledge and experience. Other students engage in multiple, diverse activities occurring simultaneously." (p. 5)

The immersion research literature also emphasizes the effectiveness of joint collaborative activities for developing language and content knowledge (Standards I and V), in particular activities that necessitate language production such as joint writing activities, and partner and small group tasks (Fortune, with Fernandez del Rey, 2003; Punchard, 2002; Swain, 2001). Making explicit meaningful connections between children's home and school lives (Standard III), between language/literacy and content (Standard II), and between their first and second languages is especially important with strugglers learning through a non-native language. Finally, keeping in mind the need for developmentally appropriate learning challenges when working with struggling learners can help ensure that learning experiences are not reduced to repeated review of basic skills (Standard IV).

COOPERATIVE LEARNING

In cooperative learning, students interact with one another in pairs and small groups in order to accomplish a task together. As a result, cooperative learning activity structures are a means of promoting both positive interdependence between students and individual accountability. They provide an alternative to the more traditional, competitive structures focused on individual performance, such as whole class question-answer techniques (Kagan, 1990).

Figure 5.3: Key Tenets of Cooperative Learning (Johnson, Johnson & Holubec, 1993)

Positive interdependence. Each learner has a unique role in the activity and only together can learners reach their goal.

Face-to-face interaction. Students need to share resources, help, support, and encourage each other's efforts and success while doing real work together.

Individual and group accountability. Individuals must be accountable for contributing their part and learning while groups must be accountable for meeting their goals.

Interpersonal and small group skills must be taught. Leadership, decision-making, trust-building, communication, and conflict-management skills do not automatically appear; therefore, these skills need to be taught.

Group processing. Reflecting upon how well the group is meeting its goals and maintaining effective working relationships result in improvements in the process of working together and greater learning.

Kagan (1990) promotes the use of cooperative learning activity structures as a means to distribute the responsibility for learning among all students. Some examples of cooperative learning activity structures are: round robin, numbered heads together, think-pair-share, jigsaw, four corners, and match mine/information gap (to learn more about these techniques and others, see Kagan, 1990). These activity structures can be used in any content area, for any group of students, and at any grade-level. When deciding upon an appropriate activity structure, it is important to consider the kinds of cognitive and social development it promotes, how it fits into instructional planning, as well as the language students will need to successfully complete the activity.

Researchers have found that cooperative learning in contrast to competitive learning results in a) higher achievement and productivity, b) more supportive and committed relationships, and c) greater psychological health, social competence, and self-esteem. For these reasons, use of cooperative learning techniques are found to be especially important for two-way immersion settings that include both language majority and language minority learners.

Second language education researchers have also shown that cooperative learning promotes more sustained language use among immersion students (Fortune, 2001). Use of language during student interaction, in turn, results in language learning (Swain, 2001). Importantly, this added language acquisition opportunity is not at the expense of learning content since research finds similar amounts of content coverage during teacher-fronted and cooperative learning activities (Porter, 1986; Rulon & McCreary, 1986). These findings are further supported by those of Lee (2000) who found that second language learners who participate in group work recall twice as many ideas as those involved in teacher-fronted discussions both immediately after and one week later.

In the second language classroom, cooperative learning can also provide a safe context in which students can practice their new language among peers without excessive concern for accuracy and teacher monitoring (Calderón & Minaya-Rowe, 2003). McGroarty (1989) identifies additional benefits to students from cooperative learning arrangements in second language and bilingual classrooms: 1) greater frequency and variety in L2 practice, 2) possible L1 development as it is used to support cognitive development or L2 skills, and 3) more active role as information providers in the learning process. When implemented correctly, cooperative learning clearly provides for high levels of student interaction and engagement in the learning process.

GUIDING PRINCIPLES

Based on the research reviewed above, and on the collective experiences of veteran immersion educators, we offer the following principles to guide practice.

Balance use of strategies across all stages of Arnett (2003) Framework for Adapting Immersion Instruction. Arnett (2003) identifies three stages of the learning process in which struggling learners experience difficulty: perception, processing, and expression. Learners may struggle in only one area or they may struggle in any combination of the three. Perception is the act of decoding and assigning meaning to the stimuli in one's environment; it is a cognitive activity that allows recognition of what is touched, seen, tasted, heard, and smelled. Processing is much more closely connected to memory and metacognition/learning strategies; it is the "ability to decipher, organize, and store previous and current stimuli in a manner that will enable the individual to eventually express this understanding and knowledge in a clear, logical presentation" (p. 7). Finally, "expression is the act of externalizing the knowledge and understanding that has been achieved" (p. 10). Expression can take many forms—written, verbal, or physical, and because this stage is more easily observed, educators often use it to monitor how well students have perceived and processed the stimuli they have encountered.

Arnett argues that maintaining a balance between all three learning stages is important. Many teachers are prone to focusing mainly on students' ability to express what they know rather than considering the whole learning cycle. By maintaining an awareness of and honing skills in the areas of perception and processing, in addition to expression, teachers may enable both struggling and other students to become more efficient learners who are then better able to interact with both language and content. Another advantage to breaking the learning cycle into its component parts is that it will lend itself more readily to identifying particular strategies that can be used to support each phase.

Most adaptations and strategies presented in this section were identified by experienced immersion practitioners as ones they have found useful with struggling learners. All of these instructional strategies can be implemented within the various pedagogical practices presented in the previous section. They are organized according to the related phase of the learning process (perception, processing, or expression).

Figure 5.4: Arnett (2003) Framework for Adapting Immersion Instruction

Perception: Strategies to help students increase perception and decode language

- Give students extra time to "decode" language.
- Use visuals to focus attention and clarify content.
- Allow students to collaborate.
- Engage multiple modalities.
- Repeat key words and phrases.
- Incorporate gestures, facial expressions, and vocal intonation into "teacher talk."
- Provide concrete materials that students can manipulate.
- Draw learners' attention to key parts of text and key parts of words.
- Activate prior knowledge.
- Reduce the amount of background noise in the classroom.
- Use a microphone for teacher and student presentations.
- Present lessons in a predictable, consistent manner: State the topic and proceed in a structured manner. Move from the obvious to the concrete to the abstract.

Processing: Strategies to help students process and organize prior and new knowledge

- Use mnemonic devices to organize and recall certain information.
- Chunk tasks into smaller, more manageable steps.
- Have students envision the end product (both form and content) and describe the steps needed to get there.
- Invite students to predict what will happen next.
- Provide checklists to monitor progress on a task.
- Use graphic organizers to classify and organize information.

- Provide a context that makes the task and language more comprehensible.
- Make explicit comparisons between the two languages and/or two ideas.
- Require students to keep a learning journal in which they reflect upon what they are learning, what strategies they are using, what is clear to them, and what they still do not understand.
- Create an environment in which students feel safe and are encouraged to ask questions.

Expression: Strategies that promote student expression and classroom participation

- Ask open-ended questions.
- Provide students with possible answers to questions.
- Provide wait time.
- Give advance warning to students who are anxious about participating or may need more time to formulate their response.
- Post starter expressions around the room that can help "jump start" a student's response.
- Provide students with an outline of the presentation or demonstration.
- Permit alternative forms of expression.
- Always provide models of "right" answers.
- Scaffold and expand on verbal responses as necessary.
- Use techniques for instructional conversations with students such as clarification (e.g., What does this mean to you?), validation (e.g., How do you know this?), and confirmation (e.g., Does everyone agree?).

USEFUL RESOURCES

Below are selected online and print resources that pertain to issues discussed in this chapter. Resources related to the five instructional techniques discussed in the relevant research findings section are provided first.

DIFFERENTIATION

1. *Learning Centers: Meaningful Context for Language Use in the Primary Immersion Classroom*
   J. Click, 2004

   www.carla.umn.edu/immersion/acie/vol8/vol2_bridge3.pdf

2. *Differentiated Instruction*
   V. Eaton, 1996

   http://www.ualberta.ca/~jpdasddc/incl/difinst.htm

3. *Differentiated Instruction Resource, 2006*
   Staff Development for Educators

   http://www.sde.com/teacher-resources.asp

4. *What is Differentiated Instruction?*
   Sacramento City Unified School District

   http://www.scusd.edu/gate_ext_learning/differentiated.htm

5. *Enhance Learning with Technology*
   P. Theroux, 2004

   http://members.shaw.ca/priscillatheroux/differentiatinglinks.html

MULTI-MODAL TEACHING AND LEARNING

1. *Strategies for Helping Underperforming Immersion Learners Succeed*
   K. Arnett with T. Fortune, 2004

   http://www.carla.umn.edu/immersion/acie/vol7/bridge-7(3).pdf

2. *Curriculum and Project Planner, Revised Edition: For Integrating Learning Styles, Thinking Skills, and Authentic Instruction*
   I. Forte and S. Schurr, 2008 Available to order at http://www.nprinc.com/curr/cppi.htm

3. *V.A.K. Learning Styles*
   https://olt.qut.edu.au/it/ITB116/gen/static/VAK/Index.htm

LEARNING STRATEGIES INSTRUCTION

1. *Strategy Training for Second Language Learners*
   A. Cohen, 2003

   http://www.cal.org/resources/digest/0302cohen.html

2. *Teaching Learning Strategies in Immersion Classrooms*
   A. U. Chamot, 2001

   http://www.carla.umn.edu/immersion/acie/vol5/Nov2001.pdf

3. *The Elementary Immersion Learning Strategies Resource Guide (2nd Ed.)*
   A.U. Chamot, K. Anstrom, A. Bartoshesky, A. Belanger, J. Delett, V. Karwan, et al.

   http://www.nclrc.org/eils/index.html

4. *Styles- and Strategies-Based Instruction*
   A. Cohen, n. d.

   http://www.carla.umn.edu/strategies/SBIinfo.html

5. *Helping struggling Students Become Good Language Learners*
   J. Robbins, J. and A. U. Chamot, 2007

   http://www.nclrc.org/about_teaching/topics/learner_diversity.html#helping_struggling_students

FIVE STANDARDS FOR EFFECTIVE PEDAGOGY

1. *Instructional Scaffolding With Graphic Organizers*
   L. Cammarata, L. with M.C. Bartolini, 2005

   http://www.carla.umn.edu/immersion/ACIE/vol8/2005BRIDGE8.2.pdf

2. *The Five Standards for Effective Pedagogy*
   Center for Research on Education, Diversity & Excellence, 2002

   Available to order at: www.crede.ucsc.edu or
   Center for Applied Linguistics
   Phone: 202.362.0700
   crede@cal.org
   www.cal.org/store

3. *Strategies for Effective Two-Way Immersion (TWI) programs: A Chinese-American perspective*
   J. Chang, 2003

   http://www2.sjsu.edu/faculty/chang/research_practice/documents/Dual%20immersion%20article.pdf

4. *Maximizing Language Growth Through Collaborative-Creative Writing*
   T. Fortune with C. Fernandez del Rey, 2003

   http://www.carla.umn.edu/immersion/acie/vol6/bridge-6(2).pdf

COOPERATIVE LEARNING

1. *Cooperative Learning*
   http://edtech.kennesaw.edu/intech/cooperativelearning.htm

2. *The Cooperative Learning Network*
   D. Galambos, 2005

   http://www-acad.sheridanc.on.ca/scls/coop/cooplrn.htm

3. *Improving Immersion Student Oral Proficiency by Fostering the Use of Extended Discourse*
   I. Punchard, 2002

   http://www.carla.umn.edu/immersion/acie/vol6/bridge-6(1).pdf

GENERAL RESOURCES

1. *Foreign Languages and Students with Learning, Hearing or Vision Disabilities*
   National Clearinghouse on Disability and Exchange, 2007

   http://www.miusa.org/ncde/tipsheets/foreignlang/

   The National Clearinghouse on Disability and Exchange collaboratively developed this tip sheet to provide practical suggestions for foreign language teachers working with students with a variety of disabilities so that more students with disabilities can successfully acquire foreign language and cultural skills that are becoming increasingly important.

2. *Developing Deficit-Specific Intervention Plans for Individuals With Auditory Processing Disorders*
   T. J. Bellis, 2002

   See page 13 for more information on this resource.

3. *Reciprocal Teaching*
   Florida Online Reading Professional Development (FOR-PD), 2005

   See chapter 3 for more information on this resource.

4. *Two-way Immersion (TWI) Toolkit*
   E. R. Howard, J. Sugarman, M. Perdomo, and T. T. Adger, 2005

   http://www.cal.org/twi/toolkit/index.htm

   This Toolkit is designed to meet the growing demand from teachers, administrators, and parents for guidance related to the effective implementation of TWI programs. Although the Toolkit is primarily intended to support teachers, administrators, and parents who are new to two-way immersion, those with experience in TWI may also find the Toolkit useful. The Toolkit is composed of three segments: program design and planning, classroom instruction, and parental involvement. The pages that specifically address instructional strategies are 48-50.

CHAPTER

6

KEY QUESTIONS

- Should interventions be provided in immersion students' first language, second language, or in both?

- If a particular language is recommended, which language should one use, when and why?

Luisa is 11 years old. She was born in Mexico and came to the United States almost a year ago with her mother, who can read and write and has good Spanish language skills. Since they have lived in Mexico their whole lives, neither Luisa nor her mother speaks any English. Prior to their move, Luisa completed fourth grade at an elementary school in Mexico.

Luisa is currently enrolled in a 50:50 two-way Spanish-English immersion (TWI) school located in an urban center in the eastern part of the United States. There she receives instruction half of the day in English and half of the day in Spanish. At her school, math, science, and Spanish language arts are taught in Spanish, while social studies and English language arts are taught in English.

Luisa was diagnosed by physicians in Mexico with Cornelia de Lange Syndrome (CdLS) a few days after she was born. CdLS is a medical condition that can be identified at birth. Physical characteristics include low birth weight, small head size, and other unique facial features such as eyebrows that meet at midline and a short upturned nose (Kline et al., 2007). It is typical for individuals with CdLS to exhibit developmental delay, ranging from mild to profound, with the majority of children in the mild to moderate range.

Once in the U.S., Luisa was diagnosed with a moderate cognitive impairment and, as a result, was eligible for special education

REAL STORIES

Patricia Martínez, Ph.D.
Bilingual Special Education Teacher and Math Coach

Francis Scott Key Elementary School

Arlington, Virginia

Program Model: Two-way bilingual immersion 50:50, K- Gr. 5

Program Environment: Whole school, Urban

Language(s): Spanish, English

REAL STORIES

Patricia Martínez

services. Her oral Spanish skills are very well developed. She can write and decode at the first-grade level in Spanish, and she can count up to fifty and solve addition and subtraction problems up to twenty. During the Spanish time of the day, she struggles with literal and concrete ways of thinking, which seems to impact all of her learning experiences. For example, in math while she can solve simple addition and subtraction problems, she is unable to understand the relationship between these two operations or identify the appropriate operation she needs to solve a word problem. In reading, she can decode better than comprehend, and it is difficult for her to use context strategies to help her read with accuracy. During instruction in English, her lack of even basic vocabulary greatly limits these learning experiences.

Luisa's mother has high expectations for her daughter. She believes that Luisa did not make more progress in Mexico because she had almost no help from special education. However, she recognizes that Luisa was very happy in her old school and that she misses the friends she made there very much. Furthermore, Luisa is transitioning to middle school next year. Her teachers and her mother worry about her transitioning to an English-medium school so soon. Luisa's mother also worries about her own ability to communicate with Luisa's teachers in the new school.

Luisa receives special education services in both languages, a practice in line with the practitioner and researcher recommendations made below. This is especially important given that Luisa needs both languages: English for schooling and to be able to interact with others in her community, Spanish to remain connected to her family.

Despite the difference in academic level, Luisa enjoys being part of her fifth-grade classroom; her general and special education teachers try to involve her in class activities whenever possible. Because of her high level of oral Spanish, she is integrated in a fifth-grade class during the Spanish part of the day, and she has been selected the "Spanish secretary" for her table. She participates in most science experiments, watches the science videos, and is exposed to the same science content as her fifth-grade peers. She enjoys looking at the pictures of the same books the other students are using and engages in conversations about them. The other children in her class appreciate Luisa. They try to help her follow the class routine and recognize and admire her command of the Spanish language. In this sense, Luisa is a model for them.

In English, Luisa is in a self-contained classroom with small groups of other fifth graders, who receive additional services for special needs. Luisa's special education English teacher who teaches

REAL STORIES

Luisa in this self-contained setting does not speak Spanish. At the beginning of the school year, her teacher was having a difficult time figuring out how to help Luisa. She reported that Luisa could not even name the letters or repeat the simplest sentences in English. After working with Luisa for a month, this teacher concluded that, in addition to her cognitive impairment, Luisa clearly had a speech problem. In the teacher's own words, "Luisa could not do anything in her class and should be moved to a life skills program." The English-speaking special education teacher also asked the other children to talk to Luisa in English so that she would have more opportunities to practice using English. She felt the other students pity Luisa and treated her as if she were a baby. She wanted to see Luisa become more independent. In the self-contained English class, Luisa was usually quiet, and she visited the bathroom a lot.

The English-speaking special education teacher eventually requested help from a bilingual assistant based on her difficulty meeting Luisa's Individual Education Plan (IEP) goals in this small group, where the rest of the students were two or three grade levels ahead of her in English. A bilingual assistant has since started to work with Luisa in the self-contained classroom to help her improve her English.

The bilingual assistant, supervised by the English-speaking special education teacher, has focused on developing Luisa's oral skills in English (one of Luisa's IEP goals). She has been impressed by what Luisa is able to do; according to her, "she had received a mistaken image of Luisa." She feels her own knowledge of Spanish has helped facilitate communication with Luisa; she mostly speaks English to Luisa, but Luisa is allowed to use her Spanish to show she understands what the teacher is saying. The bilingual assistant began working with Luisa five months ago and reports progress in Luisa's communicative English skills. Luisa can now engage in simple conversations in English about the weather, the parts of her body, the calendar, or the clothes she is wearing. The bilingual assistant states that Luisa is currently using a combination of English and Spanish to communicate with her.

Luisa has made much progress and her mother would like to see Luisa continue on this track. Her progress suggests that intervention for Spanish-speaking learners with special needs may be more effective in two languages than in one, especially in cases where the language of instruction is also a second language for the student. This is consistent with recent findings from a study of TWI learners, which shows that TWI learners with special needs do indeed continue to make progress towards closing the achievement gap over time (Howard, 2003).

BACKGROUND INFORMATION

In the following section, we draw upon the literature to present arguments for two commonly encountered approaches to offering intervention services to struggling immersion learners: (1) use one of the child's two languages, and (2) use both of the child's languages. For each of these options, we further distinguish between practices that are appropriate for language minority learners, those that best suit language majority learners, and those that are fitting for both groups of learners.

RELEVANT DISCUSSIONS AND RESEARCH FINDINGS

Research that directly investigates the effects of the language of intervention is made nearly impossible by the methodological requirements of a well-designed study (see Kohnert & Derr, 2004, for a complete analysis). For example, the number of individual variables with a possible influence on the outcome is vast, which makes finding students to form two matched comparison groups for so many factors difficult. Additionally, a longitudinal study of minimally ten years is necessary to investigate the long-term effects of the language of intervention; such longitudinal studies result in participant and researcher attrition challenges over time. Given the methodological rigors needed to carry out a well-designed study, research that addresses this topic is limited. The limited research base, particularly with regard to immersion learners from language minority and language majority backgrounds, has meant that researchers and practitioners must make inferences based on research carried out with language minority learners in English-medium (majority language) U.S. schools. Such inferences have led to one of two approaches for bilingually schooled immersion children: (1) exclusive use of one language, or (2) use of both languages (Genesee et al., 2004; Kohnert & Derr, 2004).

RESEARCH SUPPORT FOR USE OF ONE LANGUAGE

The "use-of-one-language" position grounds itself in three basic arguments that are outlined below.

Whether L1 or L2 is recommended for intervention varies for children whose first language is English (language majority learners), and those whose first language is other than English (language minority learners). Because of this, we will discuss each argument separately according to L1 background.

ARGUMENT #1: Educate the whole child

For language minority learners, use the L1 (minority language)

The social and emotional well-being of an individual is key to healthy development overall, including language, cognitive, and academic development (Thomas & Collier, 1997; 2002). The "at-risk language" for language minority learners in the U.S. is the minority language (in this case students' L1); therefore, intervention that supports this language and culture is a critical aspect of educating the whole child.

Language minority children who lack school-based support for their L1 are more likely to lose their home language and the ability to interact with members of their family. Such a loss has been shown to result in an individual's isolation within the community and the loss of intergenerational family connections and cultural links. The combined effect of all these losses is evidenced in impeded cognitive and social-emotional development (Wong-Fillmore, 1991). If the child's day-to-day reality both inside and outside of school involves regular contact with the L1 and the L1 is a minority language, then supporting development through that language is worthwhile (Kohnert, 2008).

For language majority learners, use the L1 (majority language)

There is very little in the research literature about this topic. One interesting study was carried out by a former French immersion teacher who was teaching at an international school in Paraguay. This teacher had long been frustrated by not knowing whether to use struggling students' L1 or L2 for instructional support. Holden (2000) found that language majority learner use of reading comprehension strategies (taught in the learners' L1) increased L2 reading comprehension. This held true for struggling and non-struggling learners alike. Moreover, the five struggling learners he studied increased the number of ideas and words retold after reading a passage and using self-corrections in L2; they also decreased the number of errors made when reading a passage aloud in L2. In his conclusion, Holden suggested that L1 remediation can transfer to the L2 making it an effective language for struggling learner support of instruction.

Foreign language immersion programs for language majority learners often encourage support for struggling learners in the immersion language (L2) only (see argument #3). In essence, this argument denies educators access to one of students' two languages during intervention and may in some cases unnecessarily delimit intervention. In the absence of research-based evidence, using only one of a child's two languages for intervention may not sufficiently consider the "whole child."

> **ARGUMENT #2:** Trust the achievement evidence based on typically developing children

For language minority learners, use the L1 (minority language)

Maintaining the L1 is not only good practice for language minority students as a means of promoting adequate social-emotional development, but also because L1 development has been shown to pave the way for higher achievement in L2 for minority language speakers. Evidence points to faster and greater L2 gains when a strong foundation is present in the L1 (see Gutiérrez-Clellan (1999) and Lindholm-Leary & Borsato (2006) for reviews). Studies suggest that children are able to transfer certain language and literacy skills from one language to another. Research also finds that language minority learners benefit from learning in an environment that allows for uninterrupted cognitive and linguistic development in the L1 (Collier, 1995).

If L1 literacy development and formal schooling in the L1 increase academic achievement in the L2 (English) for typically developing language minority

learners by the middle school years, then it can be inferred that intervention in the L1 will likewise further support academic achievement in the L2 for struggling language minority learners.

For language majority learners, use the L2 (minority language)

Conversely, decades of research carried out on immersion programs with typically developing language majority children clearly and consistently show that initial literacy development and full (100%) immersion in an L2 do not jeopardize English language or literacy development or subject matter achievement (Genesee, 1987; Swain & Lapkin, 1982; Turnbull, Lapkin & Hart, 2001). These studies clearly show that instructional use of the minority language in no way disadvantages language majority children; thus, intervention through this language should pose no problem. Furthermore, it is argued that if a learner is already struggling to keep pace with the content and language, reducing the amount of instructional time learning through the immersion language by offering intervention in English, may result in the learner falling further and further behind. This point leads to the third argument which follows.

> **ARGUMENT #3:** Time and intensity translate into proficiency

For language minority learners, use the L2 (majority language)

In U.S. schools, the "time and intensity" argument is also used to support instruction in all-English programs for language minority students. The research debate on bilingual education versus English-medium instruction has a long and highly contested history (for a recent review, see Krashen & McField, 2005) and takes us far beyond the scope of this project.

For language majority learners, use L2 (language minority)

If students are and will continue to be mostly schooled in language "X" for the near future, then intervention in language "X" is most appropriate because research with language majority learners in immersion contexts shows a relationship between more time and intensity of exposure in a language and greater proficiency gains in that language (Morrison, Bonyun, & Pawley, 1981; Morrison & Walsh, 1980; Swain & Lapkin, 1982).

Genesee (1987) found that "there is no evidence that increased use of English during the primary elementary grades as a result of either partial or delayed use of French as a medium of instruction yields greater proficiency in English than that achieved in early total immersion programs. At the same time, the reduced use of French in these alternative models usually results in reduced French language proficiency" (p. 40). Recently, Turnbull, Lapkin and Hart (2001) confirmed the English proficiency findings that Genesee (1987) identified once again with a large database comprised of French immersion students from an entire Canadian province.

RESEARCH SUPPORT FOR USE OF BOTH LANGUAGES

Kohnert & Derr (2004) argue that inferences made *without empirical evidence based on atypically developing learners* are insufficient to guide practices in educational intervention. They challenge the one-language-only intervention model and present a rationale for an alternative approach, bilingual intervention.

ARGUMENT #1: Language "dominance" is unpredictable

For language minority and language majority learners, use the L1 and the L2

Using research carried out predominantly on language minority learners in the U.S., language dominance has been found to be:

- *Topic-dependent* (Bialystock, 2001). For example, a bilingual child may likely have a well-developed linguistic repertoire for cooking because he cooks at home often, but not know many similar words in the school language since cooking rarely occurs in that environment.

- *Cognitive demand-dependent* (Kohnert & Bates, 2002). Learners are likely to shift to a more familiar language when the degree of cognitive challenge increases.

- *Time-dependent* (Silva-Corvalán, 1991). One's stronger language at a particular age and in a particular environment will likely evolve and change over time and in new contexts.

- *Skill-dependent* (Kohnert, Hernandez, & Bates, 1998). Research shows that bilingual individuals may have access to certain words only in one of their two languages depending on where and how the words were used.

In a nutshell, these authors reference research that supports the complex, changing nature of language development in an individual. Given that language proficiency is likely to be distributed across the dual language learner's two languages and to change over time, the effects of intervening in one language may be limited and limiting.

ARGUMENT #2: Bilingual life? Bilingual intervention!

For language minority and language majority learners, use the L1 and the L2

This argument essentially mirrors the "educate-the-whole-child" argument presented above and pertains mainly to language minority learners whose daily lives are regularly impacted by their ability to function in more than one language. Fostering monolingualism in a bilingually developing child by intervening in only one language does the child and the family a disservice.

ARGUMENT #3: Emerging achievement evidence lends positive support

For language minority and language majority learners, use the L1 and the L2

The vast majority of research referenced to promote intervention in one language only has been carried out with typically developing dual language learners. Recent findings from research on two-way immersion learners with special needs show that learners with special needs continue to make progress in closing the achievement gap over time. Both English home language and Spanish home language students who were learning disabled were advancing towards the achievement levels of same-language peers while remaining in the two-way immersion program (Howard, 2003). The argument here is essentially that continued support of both languages is not detrimental to educational performance.

> **ARGUMENT #4:** L1-L2 transfer evidence for certain reading skills

For language minority and language majority learners, use the L1 and the L2

Recent research supports the idea that specific skills can and do transfer across some alphabetic languages, in particular, those languages that are closely related such as Spanish-English and French-English. For example, phonemic awareness support for French immersion students provided in French only has been found to positively effect phonemic awareness skills in both French and English (MacCoubrey, Wade-Woolley, & Kirby, 2007); vocabulary support in Spanish and English for bilingual English language learners with low oral language proficiency resulted in faster learning than vocabulary support in English only (Perozzi & Sanchez, 1992); and language-disabled bilingual children were more efficient vocabulary learners if they were introduced to the words in their first language before being asked to learn them in their second (Thordardottir, Weismer, & Smith, 1997). Further support for this argument is also discussed in chapter 3, pages 33-36.

GUIDING PRINCIPLES

Based on the research reviewed above, and on the collective experiences of veteran immersion educators, we offer the following principles to guide practice.

Place child's social-emotional well-being above all. When deciding upon the language of intervention for bilingual learners, several notions must be kept in mind. First, social, emotional, identity, and self-esteem development are more important than language. So, if the L2 is key to the learner's social and emotional development, maintaining support for both languages during intervention is important. It follows that what is appropriate for a sequential bilingual or a second language learner may differ from the most appropriate intervention path for simultaneous bilinguals. Among the needs that should be considered are: the need of the individual to communicate and function in his/her family and the larger community, and the need to maintain any professional and/or economic advantages that may result from being bilingual.

Second, it is important to remember when considering the intervention plan that choosing one language or another for intervention will not automatically solve the problem. Demers (1994) suggests that learners not only need language remediation but also need to be instructed in "how to learn" skills and concepts. Any attempt at remediation must include instruction in metacognitive processes and memory organization as well.

Use a bilingual approach to intervention whenever possible. While there is limited empirical evidence that strongly supports the use of one language or the other, many practitioners recommend that intervention be bilingual if at all possible. (Genesee et al., 2004; Gutiérrez-Clellan, 1999; Kohnert, 2008; Kohnert & Derr, 2004).

There is disagreement, however, about how dual language input affects the language development of children with language impairments. Some argue that two languages must be exponentially more difficult to learn than one for children with language impairment (e.g., Toppelberg, Snow, & Tager-Flusberg, 1999); others argue that under the right circumstances all children, even those with language impairment, are able to learn two languages (Genesee et al., 2004; Kohnert, 2008). Genesee (2004) further argues that dual language educators need not worry about overloading children by providing them with input in more than one language as children come into the world with brains that are "wired to learn languages."

Kohnert and Derr (2004) propose two different approaches to dual language intervention: a bilingual approach and a cross-linguistic approach. Both approaches develop first and second language systems and develop metacognitive and memory organization skills as recommended by Demers (1994). The bilingual approach focuses on cognitive-linguistic skills common to both languages, improving communicative competence in both languages simultaneously. The cross-linguistic approach in contrast focuses on the linguistic features that are unique to each language; attention is focused upon each language at different times during the intervention session and/or process. This requires that schools have professionals that are qualified and trained in bilingual intervention methodologies.

In a review of the immersion literature, Cummins (2000) concurs with the notion that strict separation of languages may not be necessary once a solid foundation in the L2 is established. He also notes the importance of the linguistic interdependence principle when it comes to intervention, explicitly stating its implication for struggling learners:

"An implication of the interdependence principle is that children who are experiencing difficulties in the early stages of a French immersion program might be helped by encouraging the two-way transfer of skills across languages. In other words, if students are slow in learning to read through French (L2) it makes sense to promote literacy development in their stronger language (English) and work for transfer to their weaker language after they have made the initial breakthrough into literacy" (Cummins, 2000, p. 5).

Much as the two language systems (home language and immersion language) are interdependent, language and literacy are interdependent, not independent, systems. For this reason, support should not be exclusively in the home language or to the exclusion of the home language. Phonological awareness and learning strategies transfer across languages,

yet students may need assistance in making explicit connections between the two languages. Because a student struggles with learning to read in the immersion language does not mean that he/she is incapable of reading in that language; students must be given support and patience to develop literacy skills in a positive environment that recognizes that reading takes time and learning to read in a second language can be a lengthy process.

While bilingual intervention may ultimately be best practice . . .

- **For language minority learners whose stronger language is the minority language, use the child's first language (minority language) for support services initially.** If there is limited to no change after a period of time and continual monitoring for improvement, add intervention in the second language as well as the first (Gutiérrez-Clellan, 1999; Kohnert & Derr, 2004).

- **For language majority learners in early total immersion programs whose stronger language is the majority language, use the immersion language first to offer additional support for struggling learners.** If there is limited to no change after a period of time and continual monitoring for improvement, add support and intervention in the first language as well as the second (immersion) language (Genesee, 2008).

Match the language used to the skill being developed, and to the learning context. Some one-way immersion schools fortunate enough to have bilingual special education teachers and/or speech language pathologists have implemented intervention in the immersion language for language majority students. One such program is the Montgomery County, MD French Immersion Program. Gouin (1998) reports that immersion teachers in this particular program provide support in the immersion language to develop skills in memory, sequencing, organization, etc. for learners with information processing challenges. Moreover, for learners who are first developing basic literacy skills in alphabetic languages that include access to the sound-symbol relationships of the language system, intervention is provided in the language of literacy instruction, which for this program is the L2. Only once French literacy has been established are teachers permitted to use English for support and intervention.

USEFUL RESOURCES

Below are selected online and print resources that pertain to issues discussed in this chapter.

1. *Language Intervention from a Bilingual Mindset*
   E. Thordardottir, 2006

   http://www.asha.org/publications/leader/archives/2006/060815/f060815a.htm

   This short article, written for clinicians, reviews research on bilingualism and argues that specialists need to have a "bilingual mindset" when making decisions regarding intervention for children with communication impairments. Thordardottir reminds specialists that bilingualism is indeed a feasible goal for all and that it is their responsibility to provide a learning context in which children are able to attain this goal.

CHAPTER

KEY QUESTIONS

- In your program, are there any services available for struggling students in the early primary grades?

- If so, what are they and how do students qualify for these services?

- If no, does this impact your program's pre-referral process in any way?

Jeremy is a hard working second grader attending an early total Spanish immersion school in a suburban/rural area in the Midwest where he spends the majority of his school day in Spanish. Jeremy has been experiencing trouble developing his reading and writing skills in Spanish. His mother, whose native language is English, tries to help him at home, but she does not know the sounds all the letters are supposed to make in Spanish and does not understand the sight words he brings home. If Jeremy's reading assignments were in English, his mother could be of more help, but he will not begin reading instruction in English for another year. For now, his parents do their best to help him with the work that the reading specialist sends home, and they continue to read aloud to him in English.

Jeremy knows the sounds each letter makes and is able to blend short words while sitting with a teacher. He can also make predictions about new books and retell stories he has read with support. His Spanish language development is not noticeably behind his peers, yet he struggles to coordinate his language and literacy skills to independently and successfully pull meaning out of text. Jeremy often needs reminders to read carefully and notice each sound and word. His teachers also note that, even when prompted to take time with reading, he often does not understand the point of what he has just read and he does not seem to recognize this lack of meaning

REAL STORIES

Kaari Berg Rodriguez

Basic Skills Support Teacher

Lakes International Language Academy

Forest Lake, Minnesota

Program Model: One-way foreign language immersion, total, K- Gr. 5

Program Environment: Whole school, Suburban/Rural

Language(s): Spanish

REAL STORIES

Kaari Berg Rodriguez

as a cue to reread or employ another strategy so that the text can become meaningful. His peers will read in Spanish, for instance, '*comí*' [I ate], and make a meaning connection to a related word they are familiar with, for example, '*come*' [eats]. "*That* makes sense," explains the reading specialist, "*[but] he's not catching that.*"

The immersion program Jeremy attends uses Rigby's PM Benchmark kits, made up of leveled texts and teacher recording sheets to assess students' reading levels each trimester. The levels range from 1 to 30. The first grade goal is for students to reach levels 14-16 by year's end. The grade-level average for all four first grade classrooms in November was 3.5, March average was 8.7 and the June average was right on target at level 15. Jeremy began below average at level one, moved up to level 2 by March, and had only reached level 3 by June.

In describing Jeremy, his kindergarten teacher said, "He always said he couldn't do it. He said, 'I can't read. I can't write.'" Similarly, his first grade teacher commented he still seems to have the attitude that he cannot do it. In addition to these teacher reports, the basic skills teacher observed some behavior that indicated a lack of confidence during both small group instruction and a whole-class writing lesson. For example, while in a guided reading group with the first grade reading specialist, Jeremy often looked up at the teacher, seeming to want approval and assistance. During writing time, whenever the teacher or a peer would walk by and get too close to him, he often hugged his writing board to himself, as if to hide his work from others.

Jeremy spent less time than other students engaged in reading and writing activities. The reading specialist indicated that she struggled with finding ways to keep him focused and with encouraging him to use their time together productively. She also noticed that during independent reading time Jeremy rarely concentrated on reading when she wasn't sitting right next to him. While she listened to the others in the group, he took a long time sorting through his books, or when he finally did sit down to read, he seemed to page through the book quickly, skipping over many words rather than taking the time to try out one of the many strategies she had modeled for the class.

At first, the reading specialist felt that Jeremy struggled with attention, but in talking to the classroom teacher, it became apparent that his lack of focus was most pronounced during reading time. The off-task behaviors observed during reading groups and other reading activities were not as apparent during math or morning meeting. In conversations, the reading specialist, the classroom teacher and the basic skills teacher at the school hypothesized that while some students have a hard time focusing on any task, others, like Jeremy, are most task-avoidant when they lack confidence in their ability to perform the task well. One approach that seemed to counter Jeremy's apparent avoidance of reading was the incorporation of reading into familiar routines. After implementing this intervention, the reading specialist and the classroom teacher reported that he was generally engaged and focused during the routine warm-up activity for guided reading in which students read sight words. He also attended and was able to participate successfully in reading activities connected to the morning message.

During the course of first grade, Jeremy's low scores identified him as needing additional support. He worked with a reading teacher two days a week for twenty to thirty minutes in a small pull-out group of two to four students. These groups followed a guided reading format. The classroom teacher also met with small reading groups regularly and listened to students read individually each morning. In addition, the reading teacher and classroom teacher sent home letter, sound, syllable, and other reading activities with Jeremy. Within the guided reading format, the reading teacher paid special attention to Jeremy's need to experience success and build confidence. For example, during the portion of the lesson when each student read the day's book on his or her own, the reading teacher tried to sit with Jeremy first. If she was there to help him pick up the pattern of a new book, he was less likely to be off task while she listened to each of the other students in the group.

Now, as a second grader, he continues to be one of 20 students to receive additional small group support from a basic skills teacher. This support alternates between pull-out and push-in, depending on the day of the week. Unlike many of his classmates, Jeremy did not lose any ground in his Spanish reading over the summer. By the end of the first trimester of second grade he was reading at Rigby's PM Benchmark level 7. He now seems excited about reading and is proud of the many books he has been able to read. He can read many words fluently and is much more willing and able to sound out longer words. He remains one of the lowest performing readers in his grade, but his recent progress has been at a faster rate than his second-grade peers, including those identified as struggling readers.

All of the support Jeremy has received is being documented and his progress is closely monitored by the basic skills teacher. He will likely be referred to the school's pre-referral team, known as Estrella (Star, in Spanish), before the end of second grade. If the current early support interventions in Spanish and English reading do not

REAL STORIES

result in significant progress by the end of second grade, the Estrella team will refer Jeremy to the Student Study Team. This team may then choose to create an evaluation plan that would provide further insight into the underlying reasons for Jeremy's struggles and determine whether or not he is eligible for special education services. Jeremy is fortunate to attend an immersion program that offers additional professional support for struggling learners from a reading/basic skills specialist in the critically important primary years.

While it is still not clear why Jeremy is behind his peers in his reading development, he seems to have benefited from the additional school-based support he has received during his K-2 years. The classroom teachers and reading specialist have provided Jeremy with large amounts of small group and individualized instruction. They have worked hard to give him opportunities to be successful, build his confidence, and focus his efforts on reading. They have also worked hard to provide him with a variety of strategies to coordinate his discrete skills such as letter-sound knowledge, Spanish vocabulary, and listening comprehension so that Jeremy can enjoy more successful and meaningful reading experiences. His recent growth spurt in reading is promising. If he continues to progress at this quick pace through second grade, he will be less than a year behind by the end of the year and will be much better prepared to succeed with the third grade curriculum.

BACKGROUND INFORMATION

The needs of many struggling immersion learners are not being met, particularly in the early primary years—programs that make special services available to struggling students in these grades are uncommon. In the case narrative above, Jeremy is fortunate to have access to additional reading support from the school's bilingual reading/basic skills specialist. But such schools are not the norm. More common is the situation where program-based support specialists are lacking, or if reading specialists are available in the school, they likely lack proficiency in the immersion language and thus may not be able to provide appropriate support. A few schools, however, have reported on successful early support programs that

have been developed with the struggling K-2 immersion student population in mind. A description of these programs follows.

In this next section, a distinction has been made between programs that have research support and are commercially available to immersion programs, and those that have been developed locally by immersion educators in a particular program setting. Full citations for programs that have been studied are available in the reference section. Each support program description includes the following information: (1) intended audience, (2) qualifying criteria, and (3) program overview. Local program support initiatives are also presented to encourage replication as appropriate.

RELEVANT DISCUSSIONS AND RESEARCH FINDINGS

TRADEMARKED AND RESEARCH-BASED INSTRUCTIONAL SUPPORT PROGRAMS

The Peer Tutoring Literacy Program™

(Chipman, Roy, & Naylor, 2001)

Intended audience: Grade 2 or 3 students with minor reading difficulties, also described as "nearly independent readers" (Chipman, Roy, & Naylor, 2001, p. 5); not appropriate for those whose difficulties are moderate to severe.

Qualifying criteria: Selection of teacher and learning assistance (LA) teacher is based on various assessments, including classroom teacher's informal reading inventories and anecdotal records, and LA teacher's phonics or curriculum-based assessments. Other learner characteristics are also considered for program selection, such as eagerness for learning, good work habits, comfort being taught by older students, etc. (Chipman, Roy, & Naylor, 2001).

Program Overview

While primary students who are experiencing moderate to severe reading difficulties are given extra support by resource teachers, those with minor reading difficulties may not have any specific support outside the classroom. The Peer Tutoring Literacy Program™ was developed with these students in mind. The objective of the program is to raise their reading abilities to grade-level fluency through guided reading sessions with specially trained intermediate students as tutors. The following logistical features describe the day-to-day learning experience:

- 30-minute tutoring time twice a week

- Typically occurs during language arts time, silent reading time preferred

- Library offers an ideal location

- Tutor (grades 5-7)—reader (grades 2-3) partnerships

- Trained parent volunteer supervisors

Essential components of The Peer Tutoring Literacy Program™ that lead to its efficacy in improving literacy and fostering collaborative relationships among parents, students, and educators include:

- Forging partnerships

- Promoting reading

- Including peer tutors

- Including parent volunteers

- Emphasizing social responsibility/leadership

- Supporting volunteerism

Program developers, Mary Chipman and Nicole Roy (2006), report that after seven years of implementing the program at Lord Tennyson French Immersion Elementary, program advantages can easily be seen. Near-fluent primary grade readers receive specially focused academic support and achieve grade level fluency after two to three terms of eight- to ten-week peer tutoring sessions. Anecdotally reported outcomes of program participation are increased self-esteem and confidence, and a more positive attitude toward and interest in reading and learning at the individual level (Bournot-Trites & Lee, 2001) and at the school level; in addition, a heightened sense of community that promotes leadership, caring, and volunteerism has been observed (Chipman & Roy, 2006).

Reading Recovery (Clay, 1993)

Descubriendo la lectura (Spanish translation, Escamilla, 1992)

Intended audience: Grade 1 students experiencing difficulty learning to read and write.

Qualifying criteria: Teacher recommendation based upon an "alternate-ranking" procedure (Escamilla, 1994, p. 62); that is to say, teacher ranks all students based upon his/her experiences and perceptions of student reading abilities, alternating between the strongest and weakest readers until all have been ranked.

Program Overview

Reading Recovery/Descubriendo La Lectura (DLL) is a reading support program intended to accelerate the progress of struggling, beginning readers in grade 1 as a means of enabling them to catch up with their independently reading peers (Escamilla, 1992). This pull-out program involves one-on-one interaction with a Reading Recovery certified teacher for 30 minutes daily over a period of twelve to sixteen weeks. Supportive conversations between teacher and child are the principal method of instruction.

Each lesson has six distinct parts:

1. *Familiar reading:* This is an opportunity for the student to work on fluency and strategy use in addition to developing a self-concept as a reader.

2. *Running record:* The teacher observes the student reading a book first introduced in the previous lesson, cues and strategies are the focus of observation.

3. *Letter identification and word analysis (optional):* This is especially useful for students who know few letters.

4. *Writing:* The student dictates and writes a self-generated sentence or short story. As a result, he/she is able to hear sounds in words and further develop conventions of print. The teacher can then cut up and rearrange the sentence/story for the student to put back into order.

5. *New book:* The teacher introduces a new book as well as the main idea and any necessary words or phrases to the student, and then the student attempts to read it with some teacher support. The story is then re-read together.

6. *Conclusion:* The student practices writing high frequency words.

(Escamilla, 1992)

Research carried out on Spanish dominant children in U.S. bilingual schools found the DLL program to be as successful when implemented in Spanish as in English. Specifically, this program was able to provide effective reading support for children during the allotted twelve- to sixteen-week time frame, and after participating in the program, struggling readers successfully returned to their regular literacy classroom (Escamilla, 1994). Moreover, in a later study, Escamilla, Loera, Rodriguez, and Ruiz (1998) investigated long term effects of the reading intervention program and reported that DLL students performed as well as or better than grade-level peers who were not in the DLL program. These authors argue that Spanish dominant learners will benefit from and may need sustained Spanish literacy support beyond that provided by current bilingual programs. They also emphasize the need for teachers to attend to the challenging social and societal issues that greatly impact the educational success of low-income Latino learners in urban schools.

Signing Strategies for Reading (Tucker, 2001)

Park Spanish Immersion School, St. Louis Park, Minnesota (Reyes-Wrede & Sala-Healey, 2008)

Intended audience: All beginning readers in kindergarten, struggling readers in grades 1-3.

Qualifying criteria: Teacher observations and informal assessments in grades 1-3 based on Developmental Reading Assessment (DRA) results.

Program Overview

This strategy for enabling beginning readers to connect the written representations of sounds with the corresponding sound is based upon the work of Bethanie Tucker (2001). Tucker developed a series of kinesthetic movements made with the left hand to help students remember the sound of each written grapheme. Students in English-medium schools who were instructed in this particular reading strategy have been found to make greater progress in decoding sight words than peers who did not receive such instruction (Cole & Majd, 2005); researchers suggest that it is an appropriate means of improving decoding skills in all learners, including those who have diagnosed language and/or learning disabilities (Cole & Majd, 2003, 2005).

Teachers at Park Spanish Immersion adapted the symbols developed for English grapheme-sound correspondences to Spanish. When first teaching the signs, immersion teachers focus on forming the sign appropriately and establishing the connection between the sign, symbol, and sound. After the physical movement becomes automatic, the sign-sound-symbol association is of primary importance. This technique is a strategy for beginning readers. Students begin by signing regularly, gradually moving to using the signs only when they need help decoding a specific word. Students drop the signs when this support is no longer needed. Teachers have found that this reading strategy aids students in isolating sounds and decoding words as well as encoding (writing) sounds. While this reading strategy is of particular use to struggling immersion readers, it benefits all students; by the end of kindergarten, approximately 80% of their students have learned to read (Reyes-Wrede & Sala-Healey, 2008).

LOCAL INSTRUCTIONAL SUPPORT PROGRAMS

Academic Support Programs Maryvale Elementary School French Immersion Program, Montgomery County

Public Schools, Rockville, Maryland (Essama, 2006)

This French immersion school developed a few academic support programs as a means of increasing standardized test scores and improving student learning. Two of the programs, Intensive Basic Math Facts and Reading Program for Grades 1 and 2, are carried out during the academic school day; others take place either before or after school.

Program #1: Intensive Basic Math Facts Program

Intended audience: All students

Qualifying criteria: Does not apply

Program Overview

This is a school-wide program implemented once a week during the school day. All teachers and students participate in the Basic Math Facts program simultaneously, starting and ending with direction given over the school intercom system. Students and teachers find the fact that it is on the intercom and happening school-wide particularly motivating.

Each grade level establishes grade-level goals. For example, grade 2 teachers might decide to give 100 addition problems in 5 minutes and aim for 80% success. Teachers begin with a focus on addition, and then move students on to subtraction and multiplication. Individual students are recognized when they meet goals, earning a certificate and having their name published in the school bulletin, as are whole classrooms, receiving recognition on bulletin boards in the school entrance.

Program #2: Reading for Grades 1 and 2

Intended audience: K-2 immersion students who are performing lower on French literacy assessments

Qualifying criteria: Teacher recommendation based on lower reading performance

Program Overview

This program is designed to foster the transfer of French literacy skills to English by ensuring that students have a strong foundation in French literacy prior to beginning English literacy in the second semester of grade 4. In line with county-wide initiatives, the French immersion program has implemented 90-minute literacy blocks for K-2 groups of no more than 15 learners. During this time, the French immersion teacher team teaches with the reading initiative teacher.

As part of the county's program, all K-2 students' reading and comprehension skills are assessed three times a year. To participate fully in the reading initiative program immersion teachers adapted the entire program in French so that the immersion students take the same assessments as their non-immersion peers, but in French. The French immersion assessment material has been reviewed repeatedly over time and is an important tool for within-program discussions about students' academic and literacy development progress. As such, it has become a useful tool in identifying students who are struggling with reading. Recently, the French immersion reading initiative teacher in grade one was allocated more time (from .50 to .75 position). This additional time allows for focused pull-out support for the lowest performing K-2 students to make sure that they will reach the county's literacy goal of all students being proficient readers by grade 2.

Program #3: Additional Math and Language Arts Support

Intended audience: All grade 2-5 students

Qualifying criteria: Does not apply

Program Overview

Since greater emphasis has been placed on state-mandated tests in grades 3 and 5, teachers send math and reading packets home with the hope that parents will take the time to work on them with their children. Additional videos and booklets, developed by Maryvale French immersion teachers, offer support in math for grades 2-5, as well as in language arts for grade 2, and have proved to be very useful. When funding allows, they are offered in conjunction with additional test preparation and homework support programs for students and parents.

Foundations of Learning

Normandale French Immersion, Edina Public Schools, Edina, Minnesota

Intended audience: Kindergarten through grade 5 students who are struggling with math and language arts; students in grades 3-5 who have scored at or below 40% on standardized tests for the district

Qualifying criteria: Teacher referral

Program Overview

The Foundations of Learning (FOL) class provides extra academic support in a small group format, focusing on math and language arts remediation. It is a pull-out option during the school day. Student achievement while participating in these two services can be used as additional evidence either for or against a learning disabilities diagnosis during the special education evaluation process (see chapter 2, page 24).

Some key program elements are:

- Certified teachers in the FOL classroom

- Small group format

- Progress reports for parents as part of the regular grade-level report card

- Regular communication between FOL and classroom teachers regarding student progress

- FOL teacher participation in parent-teacher conferences

Special education teachers view this early support program as a kind of intervention that provides a "safety net" for students who are unlikely to qualify for services, but are likely to benefit from the support. The district funds this program on its own, i.e., special education dollars are not used.

Program Impact

Woelber (2003) states that in-school academic support programs, such as her school's Foundations of Learning or Success Center, are a critical part of responding to the needs of struggling immersion learners. She describes services provided in these programs as "an intervention to be tried before a child is referred for a special education evaluation" and acting as "a 'safety net' for many individuals that need the extra academic support but who wouldn't necessarily qualify for special education services" (p. 38).

Having a functional professional process in place within the school, such as a Child Study Team or a Teacher Assistance Team, serves as a relief for classroom teachers. In the words of one immersion teacher, "the feeling of urgency to solve the problem quickly is calmed when suggested interventions can be used immediately in the classroom while the rest of the process is taking place" (Woelber, 2003, p. 62). According to the school psychologist in Woelber's study, team-based processes also facilitate a proactive response that serves to prevent premature assessment and identification.

Conocimiento Fonológico (Phonological Awareness Curriculum for Spanish Immersion Teachers)

Adams Spanish Immersion Magnet School, St. Paul Public Schools, St. Paul, Minnesota (Joyce, 2004)

Intended audience: Spanish immersion/bilingual teachers of struggling readers, immersion/bilingual teachers grades K and 1, remedial reading teachers, parents at home, parent volunteers at school, teaching assistants, speech-language pathologists, learning disability teachers

Qualifying criteria: Spanish immersion children who have not mastered phonological awareness (PA) skills.

Program Overview

This curriculum is a hierarchically arranged collection of multi-sensory Spanish PA lessons that begin with the most basic PA skills (sound awareness) and proceed through the most advanced PA skills (phoneme substitution). An alphabet song with hand symbols for each letter is part of the daily lesson plan. Lessons include oral activities, games, songs, reproducible worksheets, and reproducible games.

Some key program elements are:

- Flexible group size (small group or whole class)

- Easily implemented by target language proficient individuals (even a sixth grade peer)

- Integrates traditional Latin American rhymes and songs as well as Spanish-medium adaptations of American songs

- Hierarchical

- Includes many examples of ways that parents can assist their child's PA development at home

- Multi-sensory

Learners need phonological awareness (PA) in preparation for accessing the alphabetic code (phonics/reading). The goal of this curriculum program is that all K/1 teachers are doing some PA activities *each day* in their Spanish immersion classrooms. This curricular program makes lesson planning simple. Additional PA time for those learners who really need it could be given in a guided reading group at Readers or Writers Workshop times by the teacher, a parent volunteer, or a special education teacher, for instance.

GUIDING PRINCIPLES

Based on the research reviewed above, and on the collective experiences of veteran immersion educators, we offer the following principles to guide practice.

Use research-supported instructional adaptations known to be effective for LLD students (see chapter 5 for further discussion).

Track student progress with effective record-keeping (e.g., anecdotal, logs, etc.).

Pursue grant support for after-school homework clubs and additional academic support programs that include L2 support.

Provide ongoing professional development for all educators involved.

Make time for collaborative teaching and planning among teachers and specialists.

Communicate clearly and consistently with parents during this time so that parents are not caught off guard, should their child be referred for special education evaluation.

Focus on what teachers can change, not on how learners and their families need to be different. One excellent model that appears to be grounded in this principle is found in Ortiz (2002).

Ortiz (2002) proposes a phase-based framework to proactively address the needs of all English language learners. A synopsis of her recommended process follows.

Figure 7.1: Ortiz (2002) Framework of Learning Support

Phase I: Prevention of School Failure
- A. Characteristics of Positive School Climates for English Language Learners
- B. Characteristics of Effective Instruction for English Language Learners

Phase II: Early Intervention for Struggling Learners
- A. A Clinical Teaching Cycle
- B. Teacher Assistance Team (TAT) Process
- C. Alternative Programs and Services

Phase III: Referral to Special Education
- A. Referral Committee Process

Phase I begins with prevention through developing an "educational environment [that] reflects the belief that all students can learn and that educators are responsible for seeing to it that they do" (Ortiz, 2002, p. 34). In the second phase, three approaches to *early* intervention for struggling English language learners are identified. Importantly, the first approach begins with the teacher and his/her practice, emphasizing the need to differentiate and monitor student progress closely. Next, teachers are encouraged to call on the assistance and input of other teachers as well as other professionals in the school (e.g., school nurse, special education teacher, etc.). The focus of this part of the process is still very much oriented to changes that educators can make to improve learner success, instead of placing the onus of the difficulties on the learner and/or the learner's family. The third part of phase II involves use of alternative general education programs, such as those described above in the "relevant research findings" section of this chapter.

Finally, Phase III, implemented only when all other efforts have not met with success, ultimately calls for the initiation of the referral process. The majority of the actions during this third phase are once again efforts to ensure that classroom teachers and others in the school have employed as many strategies and adaptations as possible to assist the struggling learner. After careful review and collective agreement that necessary intervention techniques have been tried for a sufficient amount of time, this committee can recommend a comprehensive student evaluation (see chapter 4). Throughout this process, Ortiz emphasizes that intervention efforts occur as soon as the learner begins experiencing difficulties, not once a teacher feels a need to refer the child for outside screening.

USEFUL RESOURCES

Below are selected online and print resources that pertain to issues discussed in this chapter.

1. *Descubriendo La Lectura: An Application of Reading Recovery in Spanish.*
K. Escamilla, 1992

This English to Spanish translation (with Spanish to English back translation) of Reading Recovery Materials includes:

- Descubriendo la Lectura lesson format
- List of Spanish literature books for Descubriendo la Lectura Program
- Observation tasks
- Data collection forms

2. *Preventing Reading Problems: Factors Common to Successful Early Intervention Programs*
John J. Pikulski, 1997

http://www.eduplace.com/rdg/res/prevent.html#1

Based on research findings carried out with students acquiring literacy in L1, Pikulski reviews several successful early intervention programs and synthesizes the characteristics these programs share.

3. *Peer Tutoring Literacy Program*™
Canadian Parents for French

http://www.cpf.ca/eng/resources-programs-tutoring.html

The Canadians Parent for French (CPF) website includes information about the Peer Tutoring Literacy Program™ for French Immersion Schools: A Parent-Teacher Collaborative Approach™ on their website. They address the following questions:

- What is the Peer Tutoring Literacy Program™ (PTLP)?
- How does the PTLP work?
- Who runs the Peer Tutoring Literacy Program?
- What are the benefits of the Peer Tutoring Literacy Program?
- How do I know the Peer Tutoring Literacy Program will help my child?
- How do I get a copy of the Peer Tutoring Literacy Program?

4. *The Peer Tutoring Literacy Program*™: *Achieving reading fluency and developing self- esteem in elementary school students*
Mary Chipman and Nicole Roy, 2006

http://www.carla.umn.edu/immersion/acie/vol10/Bridge_Nov06.pdf

This *ACIE Newsletter* BRIDGE Insert provides readers with some issues to consider when implementing a *Peer Tutoring Literacy Program*™. It also reviews the benefits for participants in this program in one Canadian elementary school.

5. *Supporting Literacy Learning for Children with Autism*
Stanley L. Swartz

http://www.stanswartz.com/SwedenPresentation/supportingliteracy.html

This study investigates two methods that support literacy learning: Reading Recovery (Clay, 1979; 1985) used as an individual intervention, and Guided Reading (Swartz, Shook, & Klein, 2003) used both in individual and small group applications. Findings suggest that both methods were helpful for six children with autism and may be worth implementing.

6. *Signing Strategies: A Reading Tool in the Spanish Immersion Classroom*
St. Louis Park Public Schools

http://www.rschooltoday.com/se3bin/
clientschool.cgi?schoolname=school461

Kindergarten teachers at Park Spanish Immersion School use video to present the signs they use when creating sound-symbol associations during literacy instruction in their classrooms, adapted from Tucker (2001). There is also a video of students using the reading signs to decode words.

To get to this link, first go to the school's homepage: http://www.rschooltoday.com/se3bin/clientschool.cgi?schoolname=school461. Next, click on the "Students" tab, and then the "K" link, and the "actividades para leer" link. Once on the "actividades para leer" page, you will find a final link to the Tucker Signing Links on the left-hand menu list. Click on this link and you can view videos of Park Spanish immersion teachers using the signing strategies adapted for Spanish immersion students.

7. *Tucker Signing Strategies for Reading (English)*
B. Tucker, 2006

http://www.tuckersigns.com/index.html

This on-line resource provides links to Tucker's (2001) instructional manual, *Tucker Signing Strategies for Reading*, as well as research on the effectiveness of this approach to reading instruction.

8. *Raconte—Moi Les Sons (Tell Me the Sounds)*
Josée Laplante, October 2001

In this innovative approach to teaching the correspondence of sounds to letters in French, Laplante associates sounds to gestures to facilitate decoding abilities for early readers. This color-illustrated book contains all the little stories on the spellings and the corresponding sounds and visual cues associated with them. This publication has earned the author Josée Laplante the Germaine Huot 2002 awarded by the College of Pathologists and Audiologists of Quebec.

To order:
Title: Raconte—moi les sons (Tell me the sounds)
Author: Josée Laplante
Publisher: SEPTEMBER
Subject: READ-WRITE-LANGUAGE
ISBN: 9782894711361 (28947113611)
Reference Renaud-Bray: 290041397

9. *Brille, La Chenille (Brille, the Caterpillar)*
Nathalie Paquin, Nathalie Lagroix-Othmer, 2002
Published by Ottawa, ON: Centre franco-ontarien de ressources pédagogiques (CFORP)

https://www.librairieducentre.com/pdf/frs-156-se.pdf

This educational resource book serves as a phonological awareness teaching guide for the French language.

CHAPTER

KEY QUESTIONS

When it comes to communicating with immersion parents . . .

- How and when does the teacher raise the issue of transferring out with a parent?

- How and when does the teacher encourage a parent to keep their child in the immersion program?

- What tools can immersion educators give or recommend to parents to help their struggling, learning disabled, and/or language and learning disabled immersion student at home?

A PARENT'S PERSPECTIVE

REAL STORIES

BACKGROUND INFORMATION

Jay Risner is 8 years old. He loves bowling, fishing, and ice-skating. At age 2 years 8 months, Jay was removed from his birth home due to severe neglect. At the time he was removed from his birth family, he could say only four words. In the birth home, Jay experienced many untreated ear infections and most likely suffered a ruptured eardrum on one side resulting in borderline high frequency hearing loss in one ear. This may have impacted his speech issues. Jay also has Sensory Integration Disorder (SID), attachment issues, an Anxiety Disorder, ADHD, some signs of Post Traumatic Stress Disorder (PTSD), and most significantly Alcohol Related Neurological Disorder (ARND).

In foster care, Jay was identified as "language delayed" and began receiving speech and language services three days a week through Early Childhood Special Education for a period of three months. Jay spent eleven months in the foster care system where we came to know him as foster parents. We finalized Jay's adoption when he was four years and one month. After the adoption, he began receiving clinical services for Speech Articulation and Occupational Therapy

We have opted to respect this immersion parent's request to remain anonymous. The immersion program in question uses the early total one-way Spanish immersion model. It exists in a whole school setting and is part of a large urban district.

REAL STORIES

(OT) for SID. He continues to receive clinical OT services to this day.

Jay's schooling began in an English language four-year-old program in a public school where his language skills improved greatly. He was exited from clinical speech and language services just after his fifth birthday. For kindergarten, we enrolled Jay in a one-way total Spanish immersion program.

All members of Jay's family speak Spanish and have attended the same Spanish immersion program. I am an immersion educator and have taught Spanish Language Arts in the district's secondary continuation program for many years. Due to Jay's complex issues, we were not planning to send him to the Spanish immersion program until we heard him complain to the speech clinician, "I am the only one in this family who does not speak Spanish." We knew we had to give the immersion program a try so Jay could feel part of our family.

KINDERGARTEN

Before the start of kindergarten we wrote a description of Jay's strengths and challenges. To facilitate communication, I also met with his teacher during opening week. Testing in November of his kindergarten year indicated that Jay demonstrated an overall IQ of 126 (scores from 120-129 are considered "superior," i.e., reflective of the top 6.7% of the population), and a visual processing speed of 137 (meaning he is really good at puzzles and tanagrams, and he benefits from a fast-paced, visual learning environment). Even though kindergarten was a difficult year for both Jay (in terms of his behaviors) and his teacher (in trying to deal with him), we maintained an open line of communication and worked to problem solve his more challenging behaviors.

After the first few months of schooling, we requested an Individualized Education Program (IEP) evaluation and in January of his kindergarten year, Jay qualified for speech articulation services. The school added OT as a secondary service and social work services at our request. Jay did not qualify, however, under the Other Health Disabilities (OHD) or Emotional or Behavioral Disorders (EBD) categories at that time, as he was doing grade level work and was academically "on target" even though he had many behavioral challenges.

Half way through kindergarten, Jay was diagnosed with ADHD and an Anxiety Disorder. At one parent-teacher meeting, his teacher said, "You know, immersion is not for every student." I responded that I felt it was too early to make that determination for our son,

REAL STORIES

and that we were well aware of his special challenges. She agreed. Jay then began taking medication for ADHD and the teacher noted remarkable improvement. By the end his first year in the program, he was performing in Spanish on par with his peers.

After reflecting back on the kindergarten experience, here is what we learned: Jay needs more space than most people. Due to his sensory issues, he has a hard time joining the group or standing with the group (especially to sing). If he can be given a job (like cleaning the tables) while the singing is taking place, he will participate and sing along as much as he can. Lining up is hard for him as there is a lot of physical touching and bumping. Practicing with the entire class and giving Jay a big "bubble" made a huge difference. He also has trouble with transitions or change. He needs forewarning if there are going to be changes to the routine, for example, the introduction of a substitute teacher or a fire drill or an assembly. He needs extra supervision in less structured times such as lunchtime, recess, and on the bus. Routine and structure and clear rules that are consistently followed work best. Jay has trouble reading social cues and as a result social interactions with peers are his biggest challenge.

FIRST GRADE

Jay had a great year in first grade. His teacher really took the time to build a positive relationship with him (and us) and Jay responded by working very hard. He had some issues with one particular student that were ongoing throughout the year. He also struggled with handwriting as his fine motor skill deficits became more noticeable. For his sensory issues, the school tried a sisal seat, a slant board, chewing gum during writing time, etc. When Jay needed re-direction for his challenging behaviors, the teacher would take him into the hallway and talk to him in English. This technique of using English outside the classroom provided clarity for Jay regarding his behaviors and was very effective. When he did something that was impulsive (which was often) the teacher would re-direct him by having him practice the appropriate behavior. By the end of first grade, Jay was performing academically right "in the middle" in all areas. He had one significant behavioral issue in first grade that resulted in a three-day suspension. We requested a Functional Behavior Assessment (FBA) in an effort to better understand Jay's social, affective behaviors and he was found "not discrepant" from his peers so no special interventions were implemented.

REAL STORIES

SECOND GRADE

In second grade, Jay began to have some real difficulties. His off-task behaviors escalated. He was negative about school and his ability to be successful. He would often refuse to do the work. He was dismissed and suspended frequently. We tried to raise the point that his behavior struggles are part of his disability and that we need to move away from the punishment model of responding to his behaviors, as it was clearly not working. One morning before leaving for school he said, "Just shoot me now, I can never follow the rules well enough. I hate school. I wish I were dead." We met several times with the teacher and support staff. We initiated a new IEP evaluation for him and requested a second FBA be completed and the new behavioral interventions be implemented.

It became clear to us that the teacher-student relationship was not working. We asked for a teacher change. While the transition to the new classroom was a difficult one, the new teacher took time to prepare the other students in his class, get to know Jay, and build on his strengths. Jay was very good at math computation and became the "helper" in class. The teacher differentiated the instruction for writing time so Jay could complete the work and feel successful. In this new classroom, Jay also had a half-time aide who the principal assigned to him using regular education funds. His role was to work with him especially during writing time. The aide made different things out of origami for Jay. As long as Jay continued to write, the aide would fold. Jay got to keep or give away any origami that was made during this time. This worked to help him stay on task.

Grade 2 achievement tests showed that Jay was reading at a first grade 9-month level (approximately 8 months behind) in Spanish. He was reading at grade level in English. In computation skills in math, he was performing at a fourth grade 6-month level (almost two years ahead). He qualified for gifted and talented services. The special education staff said we should not worry about the reading lag, as this was not atypical in immersion settings. Since the teacher change, Jay was doing very well, so again he did not qualify for special services under OHD or EBD.

Our experiences with parenting Jay through his second grade year gave us additional important information about Jay's developmental needs. We learned that avoiding power struggles with Jay is key. We also learned that Jay benefits from immediate feedback for both positive and negative behaviors and still needs help to negotiate social situations. To assist with his writing issues, he will need keyboarding skills and access to other assistive technology. Finally, we learned again that the teacher-student relationship is critical for Jay.

REAL STORIES

To ensure appropriate support for his third grade year, we requested an aide for sensory and calming breaks. This was written into his IEP. Even though he was doing very well after the transition to the new teacher, we were still very concerned about what would happen the following year; so we requested that this same teacher be allowed to loop to third grade, so he could continue to work with our son. This request was denied.

THIRD GRADE

After these experiences, I began to look at other schooling options for Jay. I was particularly looking for a school that employed a full-time social worker, offered a take-a-break room with a full-time staff member, and implemented a philosophy that helped behaviorally challenged children problem solve and do fix-it plans instead of using punishment via exclusion from learning and suspensions. We found a school that met my criteria and signed him up. Over the summer, we made the decision to try the immersion program for one more year since change is hard for Jay and we were still committed to the importance of learning Spanish.

During the summer at the immersion school, a new principal came on board and removed the aide support for Jay. The new third grade teacher did not have time to meet with us before the school year began. We met her briefly at an early fall Open House and she shared that she was not aware Jay had an IEP. We started the school year with many concerns about our relationship with this new teacher and Jay's ability to be successful in her classroom.

Jay never developed any kind of positive relationship with his third grade teacher. The supports that had helped him be successful in second grade had been removed. The aide for calming and sensory breaks was only implemented at the end of September after we pointed out that the school was out of compliance with regards to his IEP. The sensory breaks were often not helpful as he had difficulty transitioning in and out of the classroom. Sometimes he would refuse to leave and other times he would refuse to return. The last email communication we received from his third grade teacher regarding his behaviors (which had become more and more concerning) was during the second week of the school year. We began receiving behavior reports from the assistant principal in the mail two to four days after the behavioral issues had taken place. We felt powerless to intervene and work through problem behaviors with our son, as we were not informed about the issues in a timely manner. It felt as though the school had given up on our son.

REAL STORIES

We participated in several IEP meetings that were extremely frustrating as the school seemed intent on continuing to use the punishment model for Jay. We believe the teacher gave up on him and did not want him in her classroom. She sent him out of class on a regular basis and did not communicate with us regarding his behaviors after the second week of the school year. Jay became increasingly anxious, easily frustrated, and oppositional. Some of his behaviors were dangerous to himself and others. Jay began to declare he "hated Spanish" both at home and at school. He was continually punished and often removed from class for his behaviors. He was a child in crisis.

Jay has had behavior challenges since kindergarten. In response, he was sent out of class for more than 30 minutes on a regular basis.[3] Jay was sent out regularly starting in kindergarten (for more than 30 minutes, he was sent to a "buddy classroom" of fifth and sixth graders); he was sent out about twice a week in the first part of second grade and almost daily in third grade. In spite of all these occurrences, we never once received the required documentation, a Conditional Procedure Form, until mid-October of his third grade year. By the time, he was sent out a second time and we scheduled a meeting at the school, a total of four Conditional Procedures Forms had been completed. We did not receive the paperwork for the other three Conditional Procedures until mid-November.

At the mandatory IEP meeting to discuss the Conditional Procedures with school staff and district special education staff, a district expert described the level of disruptive behavior Jay was exhibiting based on a new preliminary FBA report. After her report, we were told that the immersion setting could no longer meet his escalating social-emotional needs. At this point, our son's IEP only addressed his need for speech articulation. As parents, we realized we had no other choice but to remove him from what had come to be an unhealthy situation for Jay. During this meeting, Jay had another behavior incident in the classroom and was going to be suspended again. Instead, he was allowed to come back the next day to have some closure and say good-bye. Sadly, he spent most of his last day in the principal's office as a punishment for his behavior the day before and the speech clinician's office (over the years she had become a great support person for Jay). I am not sure if he was given any opportunity to say good-bye.

---

3. IDEA mandates that removal of a student with an IEP from planned instruction for more than 30 minutes, whether planned or in an emergency situation, is a "Conditional Procedure," a response that requires documentation and immediate notification of parents. If a Conditional Procedure happens twice in the same month an IEP meeting must occur to make appropriate modifications to the IEP.

REAL STORIES

Jay was a student in the Spanish immersion program up and through the first two months of third grade. My husband and I believe that the issue of transferring out of this immersion school was handled very poorly. We thought we were meeting to discuss the Conditional Procedures reports when all of a sudden, we were being told the school could no longer meet his needs. The very next day was Jay's last day at the immersion school. In the process, we feel Jay's self-esteem was damaged. The message he came away with was, 'These people don't want me here any more. They don't care about me. I am not good enough to be able to stay here.'

While we all ultimately recognized that a change was necessary, we believe that had appropriate support services been offered from kindergarten onward Jay might have been able to be successful in the immersion setting and have access to the Spanish language support that could help him feel like a full-fledged member of his Spanish-proficient family. After all, his oral Spanish language skills were quite strong even though he performed slightly below grade level in Spanish reading. Beginning midway through kindergarten and during the rest of his time at the immersion school, his primary IEP was for speech articulation services with limited OT and social work services. For a child with FASD, ADHD and an anxiety disorder that impaired his ability to function successfully at school, these services were clearly insufficient. Approximately one month after leaving the immersion program Jay qualified for a new IEP label, Other Health Disabled, one that takes into account his multifaceted educational needs.

Jay is now in a school where English is the language of instruction. It is a Federal Level III setting self-contained program for EBD students. There are 10 other students in his class with a teacher and two aides. He still has behavior struggles, but they have diminished a great deal. At his new school, there is sufficient aide support and programming to meet his needs. Academically, he is doing extremely well. He is now reading a full year above grade level (in English) and recently tested out at the fifth grade level in math (two years above grade level). When we asked Jay, what it is about the new school that is working for him, he responded without any hesitation, "My new teachers like me and they care about me. I can tell by the way they treat me. They want me to stay in class and learn new things."

BACKGROUND INFORMATION

Research identifies a number of reasons that families leave an immersion program. These reasons cited at the elementary level tend to differ from those at the secondary. Elementary students reference the following motivators for transferring out:

- Poor attitudes, lack of motivation, comfort level using the immersion language, and behavioral challenges (Bruck, 1985)

- Difficulties in language arts, either in the immersion language or in the student's first language, and low test results (Dubé, 1993; Halsall, 1991; Hayden, 1988)

- Limited access to or ineffective special education resources in the immersion program (Dubé, 1993; Hayden, 1988)

- High student frustration levels (Dubé, 1993; Hayden, 1988; Stern, 1991)

- Low teacher expectations for student's success potential (Boschung & Roy, 1996; Trites, 1976)

Secondary students allude to a different set of concerns:

- Lack of course variety and scheduling limitations (Boschung & Roy, 1996; Cadez, 2006; Halsall, 1991; Johnson, 2003; Lewis & Shapson, 1989)

- Concern about level of difficulty and the potential for earning higher grades in English-medium coursework (Cadez, 2006; Lewis & Shapson, 1989)

- Forced choice between immersion and other advanced or challenge options (Boschung & Roy, 1996; Johnson, 2003)

- Transportation and logistical challenges due to the limited number of high schools that offer an immersion continuation program (Boschung & Roy, 1996)

- Poor quality teaching (Cadez, 2006; Husum & Bryce, 1991; Lewis & Shapson, 1989)

In sum, students and families enrolled in elementary-level immersion programs are likely to consider transferring out if learners are not making appropriate academic and literacy progress and if special education resources are lacking. Attitudinal and behavioral issues are also seen as important indicators of dissatisfaction. While the majority of elementary-level concerns focus on individual learner characteristics, secondary-level concerns have more to do with programmatic and academic performance issues.

RELEVANT DISCUSSIONS AND RESEARCH FINDINGS

Both parents and teachers comment on the influence of the other in the decision-making process. According to one study, parents follow teacher recommendations approximately 90% of the time (Stern, 1991); similarly, teachers note that on occasion the recommendation for transfer comes from parents, not them (Hayden, 1988).

A power differential between educators and parents frequently surfaces in transfer meetings. When more than just the teacher and parent(s) are present, the educational terminology and complicated material presented by educational professionals such as school psychologists and principals who have prepared for the meeting can be difficult for parents to interpret. Many parents are unfamiliar with educational jargon. As a result, parents rarely ask questions and may tacitly accept the decisions made by the principal decision-makers: principals, school psychologists, and teachers (Stern, 1991).

Demers (1994) outlines three guidelines for determining whether a student should transfer out of an immersion classroom to a non-immersion classroom.

1. Review Demers's list of characteristics of successful and unsuccessful immersion learners in addition to establishing the learner's level of success in their native language. (This list can be found on page 11.)

2. Consider the personal dedication and/or motivation of the learner; those who are unmotivated and/or frustrated may be good candidates for transfer.

3. Consider using psychometric measures to gather additional information for possible transfer. Demers (1994) suggests that immersion students who display weaknesses in their L1 language scores and/or exhibit auditory deficits may be good candidates for transfer.

Importantly, he concludes by reminding educators, "Any decision to change the placement of a child must be in the interest of the child, not of the program, the parents or the teachers" (p. 4).

Woelber (2003) reports use of the Vancouver School Board's document titled *Possible Factors Influencing Student Performance in French Immersion* (Roy, 1997b) during discussions with parents whose children are struggling (see page 110 for resource information). She finds that this document facilitates clear and open communication about a child's performance and assists educators in addressing difficult questions concerning the appropriateness of the immersion program for the child.

Alberta Education (1997) suggests that parents consider transfer

- when leaving an immersion program gives a student access to critical language and learning support services,

- when the child is not motivated or has a negative attitude,

- or when parent concerns affect the child's motivation.

Alberta Education (1997) identifies some grade-level-specific behaviors that should encourage teachers and parents to come together and discuss learner progress. Figure 8.1 specifies these early signs worthy of parental attention.

Figure 8.1: Early Signals That Merit Discussion With Immersion Teacher

Grade Level(s)	Observable Behaviors that Merit Discussion
Kindergarten	Difficulty expressing oneself clearly in L1 Difficulty articulating certain sounds in L1
Grade 1	Attention difficulties even for brief periods of time Unable to echo words/phrases in L2 Limited letter/sound recognition
Grade 2	Limited word identification Attention difficulties for more extended periods of time
Grade 3	Difficulty understanding or recalling information either heard or read Difficulty giving information about something just seen or heard Difficulty with phonetic analysis of words
Grades 4/5	Persistent letter reversal Phonetic analysis difficulties inhibit comprehension
All grades	Ongoing unhappiness at school Persistent behavioral or social problems Sudden changes in behavior Notable lack of confidence Notable lack of interest in immersion language

Source: Alberta Education. (1997). Yes, you can help!: Information and inspiration for French immersion parents. Edmonton, Alberta, Canada: Author.

Hughes, Vaughn, and Schumm (1999) examined the perceptions and practices of 80 Hispanic parents regarding literacy-related activities in the home. Educators can sometimes presume that a learner's literacy struggles are due to lack of parent interest and support for literacy in the home. Forty study participants were parents of learning-disabled children and the remaining 40 were parents of high-achieving Latino learners. All children were in grades 3-5. Hispanic parents of both learning-disabled and high-achieving learners reported reading books at home and making frequent trips to the library with their children; writing activities occurred less frequently. Researchers concluded that most parents understood the importance of supporting literacy in the home and were interested in doing so.

Several researchers also identify specific ways that parents can help their struggling child. For example, parents can assist by

- promoting language development and literacy in the L1 at home with activities such as interactive reading between parent and child (August & Shanahan, 2006; Fortune & Tedick, 2003) as well as natural oral correction in the L1 (Demers, 1994);

- establishing good study habits at home;

- being open and honest with the child about his/her struggles and/or learning disabilities, discussing the child's strengths and weaknesses together, and then developing ways to cope with the disability and together overcome the weakness. This is the idea behind the French Immersion Learning Disabilities Awareness Program described in Rousseau (1998, 1999).

Several researchers point out that transferring a child out of immersion can result in a loss of self-esteem and feelings of frustration and unhappiness (e.g., Bruck, 1979; Cummins, 1984). Along a similar vein, findings suggest that while some learners may experience better academic performance and greater school satisfaction upon transfer, many will face similar educational challenges regardless of the language of instruction (Demers, 1994).

GUIDING PRINCIPLES

Based on the research reviewed above, and on the collective experiences of veteran immersion educators, we offer the following principles to guide practice.

Provide accurate, research-based information to parents on an ongoing basis. Parents need to know what to expect from the beginning, prior to enrolling their child. In enrollment meetings "the good" and "the bad" of immersion needs to be shared; this includes disclosing that not all learners find success in the immersion classroom as well as information about the common struggles of immersion learners and the types of remediation/assistance available to those who struggle.

Set realistic and developmentally sensitive expectations for each learner. What constitutes success for one child may look very different from that of another child. Anton (2004) argued that individual student goals can help to motivate a learner and later monitor his/her success. Goals should include content objectives as well as objectives in both language systems; in order for a struggling learner to be successful in an immersion program, both language systems need to be developed (Arnett & Fortune, 2004).

Educate parents about possible benefits and costs of transfer out of immersion. It is important that parents understand that switching to a non-immersion program may not eliminate their child's struggles in school.

Maintain open lines of communication between educators and parents. Parents appreciate a teacher who will share concerns and work with them to discuss possible causes and solutions. "When educators and parents dialogue together in constructive ways, there is a greater opportunity for possible 'at-risk' children to feel positively about themselves and to develop as successful learners" (Dubé, 1993, p. 65).

See parents as partners in the educational process. Parents are experts on their child and may have valuable insights to share. It is important to spend time eliciting parents' knowledge and understanding of their child's development. Encouraging them to observe their child at home and providing them with certain behaviors to observe will also allow them to be an active participant rather than passive recipients of what others say. Moreover, using common, non-technical language allows parents to better understand the situation and provides them with greater entry into the discussion.

Expect all parents to be invested in the literacy development of their children. Educators need to guard against a tendency to assume that parents of underperforming students and parents from diverse linguistic and cultural backgrounds are not interested in or able to support their child's literacy development at home.

Remain open-minded and patient with the process. It is likely that there will be differences in teachers' and parents' experiences of a child. No one individual holds all of the information that may be needed to better meet the needs of a given learner. Nor does any one individual have the "one and only" solution. A positive, child-centered outcome results when all stakeholders act as contributors and co-participants who work collaboratively and stay committed over time.

Stay positive. Children are susceptible to the attitudes of adults. Therefore maintaining positive attitudes or not dwelling on negative concerns enables learners to remain more positive about their learning experience (Alberta, 1997).

USEFUL RESOURCES

Below are selected online and print resources that pertain to issues discussed in this chapter.

1. *"Yes You Can Help! Inspiration for French immersion parents"*
Canadian Parents for French (CPF)

Yes, You Can Help! was written by unilingual parents who relied on their joint 30 years of experience with French immersion in three provinces, as well as their active involvement with CPF. They were assisted by an advisory committee of teachers, administrators, researchers, and education department staff. The book is published by Alberta Education, Canadian Parents for French and is available to order online at: http://www.cpfalta.ab.ca/yesuhelp.htm

2. *The Special Needs French Immersion Student*
Government of Alberta, 2008

http://www.education.gov.ab.ca/french/adt_scol/frImm/default.asp

Click on the English button to view the website in English. This online resource addresses the question, "Can French Immersion offer an appropriate quality education for a student with special needs?" You will find a set of references for suggested readings on topics for gifted students and students with learning disabilities, specifically children who display the following disabilities:

- Hearing problems;
- Blind and visually impaired;
- Behavioral or emotional disorders; and
- Attention difficulties and/or hyperactivity.

3. *Tools to Work With the School*
LD OnLine

http://www.ldonline.org/features/idea2004
Information about IDEA

http://www.ldonline.org/article/107
How parents can be advocates for their children by Coordinated Campaign for Learning Disabilities

http://www.ldonline.org/article/14615
Sample letters parents can use to write the school by National Dissemination Center for Children with Disabilities

http://www.ldonline.org/parents (General information for parents of LD and ADHD children)
LD OnLine recommends that parents work cooperatively with the school system to get the best education for their children and avoid court. These websites provide information on special education laws and advocacy for parents.

4. *Learning Difficulties in French Immersion*
Canadian Parents for French, Alberta Branch

http://www.cpfalta.ab.ca/Parents/LDinFI.htm

This resource page, developed by Canadian Parents for French, provides parents with information and resources to support their child(ren) in French immersion programs. Some of the highlights include:

- Parental coaching strategies

- Literacy development in French immersion

- Ways for creating language-rich environments

- Parental handbooks developed by Alberta Education

5. *Parenting Perspectives . . . Ideas to Help Your Child Succeed: New Directions in Identifying Learning Disabilities*
Canter, 2002

http://www.teachersandfamilies.com/open/parent/idea1.cfm

This website explains what a learning disability is, how it is identified, and some of the changes that have been made recently in the legislation around the identification of learning disabilities.

6. *Two-way Immersion (TWI) Toolkit*
E. R. Howard, J. Sugarman, M. Perdomo, and T. T. Adger, 2005

http://www.cal.org/twi/toolkit/index.htm

This Toolkit is designed to meet the growing demand from teachers, administrators, and parents for guidance related to the effective implementation of TWI programs. Although the Toolkit is primarily intended to support teachers, administrators, and parents who are new to two-way immersion, those with experience in TWI may also find the Toolkit useful. The Toolkit is composed of three segments: program design and planning, classroom instruction, and parental involvement. The pages that specifically address parent involvement are 167-214.

7. *Possible Factors Influencing Student Performance in French Immersion*
Vancouver School Board, reprinted with permission in The ACIE Newsletter, May 2004

http://www.carla.umn.edu/immersion/acie/vol7/May2004_Student_Performance_Factors.html

This document arose out of district-wide concerns for students who experienced difficulties in French immersion. This profile was therefore developed to facilitate discussion among the classroom teacher(s), learning assistance teacher(s), and other school-based team members. The profile could also be used when working with parents during educational planning for their children.

CHAPTER

KEY QUESTIONS

- Is it appropriate to pre-assess potential students' readiness to enter an immersion program?

- If so, how might this be carried out and by whom?

BACKGROUND INFORMATION

According to Fortune and Tedick (2003), the vast majority of language immersion programs are accessible to all learners. There are cases, however, a kind of prescreening is warranted. TWI programs, for example, which need participation rates of at least one-third of each of two language groups for quality implementation, may use a prescreening process to ensure the appropriate linguistic balance in their student population. In such cases, the goal is not to determine students' readiness for an immersion learning experience, but to determine the relative L1/L2 proficiencies of incoming students and adhere to best practices for program implementation. Pre-assessment may also occur when newcomers wish to begin the immersion program after the initial K-1 grades. As before, the purpose of such pre-assessment of skills in the languages of instruction is to support the learner's academic success and maintain program integrity. Immersion programs that do not consider the program-level impact of admitting new students in grade 2 and beyond who lack the requisite

proficiency in the instructional languages may run the risk of compromising the student's, teacher's and program's ability to be successful.

Beyond the situations outlined above, best practice suggests that pre-assessment of potential participants to identify the appropriateness of immersion for a particular learner is unwarranted. This is because research findings on issues related to program suitability remain inconclusive. Nonetheless, the question of determining prior to admission whether or not a student is well suited for the immersion learning environment continues to surface for parents and educators alike. Parents are committed to finding the best educational program match for their children. Immersion educators are likewise committed to facilitating each child's linguistic and academic development and social well-being. Both parents and educators are interested in preventing individual instances of academic failure that may result in transfer out of immersion, so as not to incur the associated personal and programmatic cost of such failures on all concerned.

111

It is understandable that families and schools would seek to adopt practices that avert the hardship of an educational mismatch, especially given the fact that immersion programs are optional. That said, promoting learner pre-assessment as an educationally endorsed response requires a thoughtful analysis of the underlying assumptions that motivate prescreening practices.

Some assumptions driving the quest for prescreening are:

- Immersion is not the only educational option for a given child. If more appropriate schooling options exist, there should be a way to determine this.

- All educational programs, in particular specialty programs such as immersion, need to be a good match for every learner.

- Learning through a language one is still acquiring demands a particular, within-learner skill set.

- *Within-learner* factors exist that will result in a child's inability to succeed.

- Immersion programs and practitioners cannot effectively adapt to certain within-learner factors that are known to prevent learning through a second language.

- *Within-learner* factors that forecast an individual's success and failure potential in immersion are reliably identifiable.

- Educators should be able to provide prospective immersion learners and their families with a "scientifically based prognosis" concerning the learner's future success potential.

- A prescreening test is an effective way to assess a learner's success potential.

RELEVANT DISCUSSIONS AND RESEARCH FINDINGS

The "to screen or not to screen" debate among immersion researchers and practitioners has brought to light both positive and negative consequences that prescreening practices might bring. Figure 9.1 below summarizes the principal arguments on this topic.

Figure 9.1: Possible Pros and Cons of Prescreening

Possible Prescreening Pros	Possible Prescreening Cons
• Avert discomfort and trauma of school failure due to participation in an immersion program (Cummins, 1984; Trites, 1976; Wiss, 1989)	• Fuel perception of immersion education as an "elitist" program suitable only for some, not all (Genesee, 1987; Keep, 1993; Wiss, 1989)
• Reduce high rate of attrition and immersion program drop out rates (Mannavarayan, 2002)	• Lead to eventual demise of the immersion program within a district in the long run (Genesee, 1987; Keep, 1993)
• Conserve educational resources that would be used to support the learner's success when the program is not in fact suitable for that learner	• Deny a given learner what may be their best opportunity to acquire some level of proficiency in a second language and the benefits associated with this (Bruck, 1985; Genesee, 1987; 1992; Genesee et al., 2004)
• Ensure appropriate linguistic balance between groups of linguistically diverse students in a two-way immersion program	• Misidentify an individual learner's potential for success due to lack of valid and reliable prescreening assessment tools (Bruck, 1985; Genesee, 1992, 2007; Halsall, 1998; Mannavarayan, 2002; Wiss, 1989)
• Determine appropriate levels of proficiency in all languages of instruction to make certain that Gr. 2+ newcomers, teachers, and programs can be successful	

Some researchers have discussed the specific question(s) that a prescreening tool would need to answer, as well as the characteristics it would need to exhibit. Before educationally sound adoption and implementation of any immersion prescreening tool can take place, research suggests that certain characteristics and functions be present (see Figure 9.2 below).

Figure 9.2: Necessary Characteristics and Functions of an Immersion Prescreening Tool

Necessary Characteristics	Necessary Functions
• Manageable in terms of cost and time • Learner-friendly • Reliable (results are replicable) • Valid (measures what it says it measures) • Able to be administered by school personnel	• To validly and reliably determine a within-learner deficit predictive of academic failure • To distinguish between a learner's academic success potential in a L2-medium versus a L1-medium program (Cummins, 1984; Wiss, 1989)

Select Quotes From the Literature

Many researchers have voiced their perspective about the question of prescreening. Below we present a few of the more compelling quotes.

". . . to say that French immersion may not be appropriate for all children is not to say that it is inappropriate and should be abandoned. Almost any educational program will have a few drop-outs, a few individuals who do not succeed" (Carroll's response to Trites, 1976, p. 208).

". . . we do not yet have ways of identifying students who will not benefit from immersion. Researchers should be encouraged to continue to find the characteristics of students which enable them to succeed in immersion" (Halsall, 1998, p. 12).

"At present, there exists no single or simple criterion that can validly determine the suitability of immersion for individual children. Decisions regarding suitability can probably only be made with accuracy once the child's actual performance in immersion can be judged; that is, once they have been in immersion for some time" (Genesee, 1992, p. 211).

"We know that in appropriate circumstances, children, even those with language impairment, have the capacity to learn two languages.

Professionals and parents need to assess whether the circumstances that a given child is in are conducive to dual language learning. They should never automatically assume that having two languages is the exclusive domain of children with typical development" (Genesee et al., 2004, p. 212).

"At present, we lack sufficient evidence to exclude students on the basis of specific risk or impairment profiles" (Genesee, 2007a, p. 680).

GUIDING PRINCIPLES

Based on the research reviewed above, and on the collective experiences of veteran immersion educators, we offer the following principles to guide practice.

Focus on learner needs and strengths when assessing. Assessments should not be conducted for the purpose of screening, but rather to provide information for parents, teachers, support service professionals, and administrators about the individual needs and strengths of the child so that the individual child's needs can best be met.

Educate parents. Inform prospective parents of the factors that influence second language development, the stages of language acquisition, and how these can vary among individuals.

Challenge yourself to think beyond all or nothing parameters. Early total immersion is not the only immersion program model available. If a district has concerns about suitability and believes it advisable to introduce literacy in English for all students, then a middle (beginning in grades 4 or 5) or late (beginning in grades 7-9) immersion program may be an option.

Develop useful tools for late entry immersion students. While immersion programs do not prescreen for initial admission in K-1, most programs do screen for late entry of newcomers to ensure that these students bring the requisite language proficiencies for learning content in two languages.

FINAL THOUGHTS

In the face of emerging findings from research carried out in language immersion programs and the significant challenges of investigating such highly complex issues, it seems premature to focus efforts on the development of a prescreening tool. Instead of attending to questions of learner-program suitability, pursuing ways to more specifically pinpoint the highly particular struggle an individual learner is experiencing will likely allow educators to make more appropriate use of limited resources. This shift in focus away from the need to identify within-in-learner deficits that preclude academic success towards a need to identify teachable compensatory strategies that complement within-learner strengths is critical. Such a change in perspective complements recent legislative initiatives such as *Response to Intervention* and holds potential for reorienting immersion educators. Most importantly, it engages them in exhausting all possible efforts to change what they themselves can change for the ultimate good of the individual struggling immersion learner. In so doing, educators mentor through modeling a productive, proactive stance for struggling immersion learners and their families.

USEFUL RESOURCES

Below are selected online and print resources that pertain to issues discussed in this chapter.

1. *Two-way Immersion (TWI) Toolkit*
   E. R. Howard, J. Sugarman, M. Perdomo, and T. T. Adger, 2005

   http://www.cal.org/twi/toolkit/index.htm

   This Toolkit is designed to meet the growing demand from teachers, administrators, and parents for guidance related to the effective implementation of TWI programs. Although the Toolkit is primarily intended to support teachers, administrators, and parents who are new to two-way immersion, those with experience in TWI may also find the Toolkit useful. The Toolkit is composed of three segments: program design and planning, classroom instruction, and parental involvement. The pages that specifically address late entry into TWI programs are 50-52.

SURVEY OF EXCEPTIONALITIES AND THE IMMERSION CLASSROOM
CARLA SUMMER CHALLENGES INSTITUTE
AUGUST 2003 AND 2004

Professional Title: _____

Years of Experience in Immersion Education: _____

As an educational practitioner experienced in immersion education, think back on your experiences with struggling students. Which of the categories or sub-categories below best describe the underachieving students with whom you have worked?

Exceptionality Categories Recognized by Individuals with Disabilities Education Act (IDEA)	Never	Rarely	Sometimes	Often	Always
Mental Retardation (Mild Intellectual Disability): Significantly sub-average general intellectual functioning existing concurrently with deficits in adaptive behavior and manifested during the development period.					
Auditory Impairment: Hearing impairment, permanent or fluctuating, includes any degree of hearing loss ranging from mild to profound resulting in a diagnosis of hard of hearing or deaf.					
Speech or Language Impairment: Communication disorder, such as stuttering, impaired articulation, and language or voice impairments that adversely affects educational performance.					
Visual Impairment and Blindness: Visual impairment includes any type of sight problem which, even with correction, adversely affects educational performance.					

Exceptionality Categories Recognized by Individuals with Disabilities Education Act (IDEA)	Never	Rarely	Sometimes	Often	Always
Emotional Disturbance: A diagnosis of emotional disturbance means that the student exhibits one or more of specified characteristics that are not the result of a temporary reaction to home, school, or community situations.					
Orthopedic Impairment: A severe orthopedic impairment that adversely affects educational performance, including those caused by congenital anomaly, disease, or other causes.					
Autism: A developmental delay that significantly affects verbal and nonverbal communication and social interaction.					
Asperger's Syndrome					
Traumatic Brain Injury: A sudden injury to the brain caused by an external event, resulting in total or partial functional disability or psychosocial impairment or both that adversely affects the student's educational performance.					
Other Health Impaired: Limited strength, vitality, or alertness, including a heightened alertness to environmental stimuli, that results in limited alertness with respect to the educational environment.					
Attention Deficit/Hyperactive Disorder (ADHD/ADD)—Inattentive only					
Attention Deficit/Hyperactive Disorder (ADHD) — Impulsive/ Distractible only					
Attention Deficit/Hyperactive Disorder (ADHD)—Inattentive and Impulsive/Distractible Combined					

Exceptionality Categories Recognized by Individuals with Disabilities Education Act (IDEA)	Never	Rarely	Sometimes	Often	Always
Specific Learning Disability: A disorder in one or more of the processes needed to receive, understand, or express information. The student can have difficulty with basic reading skills, reading comprehension, written expression, mathematics calculation, listening comprehension, and/or oral expression.					
Oral Expression					
Listening Comprehension					
Written Expression					
Basic Reading Skills (typically letter/word recognition and decoding)					
Reading Comprehension					
Mathematics Calculation					
Mathematical Reasoning					
Deaf-Blind: Combination of hearing and visual impairments that causes severe communication and other developmental and educational problems.					
Multiple Impairment: Multiple disabilities that occur in combination with each other and cause severe educational problems.					

APPENDIX B

SURVEY RESULTS OF
EXCEPTIONALITIES AND THE IMMERSION CLASSROOM
CARLA SUMMER CHALLENGES INSTITUTE
AUGUST 2003 AND 2004

As an educational practitioner experienced in immersion education, think back on your experiences with struggling students. Which of the categories or sub-categories below best describe the underachieving students with whom you have worked?

Exceptionality Categories Recognized by Individuals with Disabilities Education Act (IDEA)	Never	Rarely	Sometimes	Often	Always
Mental Retardation (Mild Intellectual Disability): Significantly sub-average general intellectual functioning existing concurrently with deficits in adaptive behavior and manifested during the development period.	32	14	10	2	0
Auditory Impairment: Hearing impairment, permanent or fluctuating, includes any degree of hearing loss ranging from mild to profound resulting in a diagnosis of hard of hearing or deaf.	15	22	15	2	2
Speech or Language Impairment: Communication disorder, such as stuttering, impaired articulation, and language or voice impairments that adversely affects educational performance.	6	13	21	11	6
Visual Impairment and Blindness: Visual impairment includes any type of sight problem which, even with correction, adversely affects educational performance.	33	19	4	1	0

Exceptionality Categories Recognized by Individuals with Disabilities Education Act (IDEA)	Never	Rarely	Sometimes	Often	Always
Emotional Disturbance: A diagnosis of emotional disturbance means that the student exhibits one or more of specified characteristics that are not the result of a temporary reaction to home, school, or community situations.	12	16	20	5	3
Orthopedic Impairment: A severe orthopedic impairment that adversely affects educational performance, including those caused by congenital anomaly, disease, or other causes.	30	18	6	1	2
Autism: A developmental delay that significantly affects verbal and nonverbal communication and social interaction.	29	19	8	0	0
Asperger's Syndrome	24	19	6	1	1
Traumatic Brain Injury: A sudden injury to the brain caused by an external event, resulting in total or partial functional disability or psychosocial impairment or both that adversely affects the student's educational performance.	42	15	0	0	0
Other Health Impaired: Limited strength, vitality, or alertness, including a heightened alertness to environmental stimuli, that results in98 limited alertness with respect to the educational environment.	5	12	11	2	3
Attention Deficit/Hyperactive Disorder (ADHD/ADD)—Inattentive only	6	4	23	17	5
Attention Deficit/Hyperactive Disorder (ADHD) — Impulsive/ Distractible only	5	5	19	21	4
Attention Deficit/Hyperactive Disorder (ADHD)—Inattentive and Impulsive/Distractible Combined	4	6	18	19	5

Exceptionality Categories Recognized by Individuals with Disabilities Education Act (IDEA)	Never	Rarely	Sometimes	Often	Always
Specific Learning Disability: A disorder in one or more of the processes needed to receive, understand, or express information. The student can have difficulty with basic reading skills, reading comprehension, written expression, mathematics calculation, listening comprehension, and/or oral expression.	3	7	25	8	3
Oral Expression	3	20	21	11	3
Listening Comprehension	2	8	30	13	2
Written Expression	2	5	27	16	4
Basic Reading Skills (typically letter/word recognition and decoding)	1	7	29	11	7
Reading Comprehension	0	6	26	16	7
Mathematics Calculation	3	11	29	5	4
Mathematical Reasoning	3	10	25	10	3
Deaf-Blind: Combination of hearing and visual impairments that causes severe communication and other developmental and educational problems.	51	2	1	0	0
Multiple Impairment: Multiple disabilities that occur in combination with each other and cause severe educational problems.	37	7	7	2	2

REFERENCES

Alberta Education. (1990). *Information document: Immersion and Francophone programs.* Alberta: Author.

Alberta Education. (1997). *Yes, you can help! Information and inspiration for French immersion parents* (National ed.) [Handbook]. Edmonton, Alberta: Alberta Education Cataloguing in Publication Data.

Alberta Learning. (2002). *Yes you can help! Information and inspiration for French immersion parents.* (Revised ed.) [Handbook]. Edmonton, Alberta: Alberta Learning, French Language Services Branch.

American Speech-Language-Hearing Association. (2008). *Impairment, disorder, disability.* Retrieved April 1, 2009, from http://www.asha.org/public/hearing/disorders/impair_dis_disab.htm

American Speech-Language-Hearing Association. (2009). *Child speech and language.* Retrieved April 1, 2009, from http://www.asha.org/public/speech/disorders/ChildSandL.htm

Anderson, M. (with Lindholm-Leary, K., Wilhelm, P., Boudreaux, N., & Zeigler, M.) (2005, May). Meeting the challenges of No Child Left Behind in U.S. immersion education [Bridge insert]. *The ACIE Newsletter, 8*(3), 1-8. Retrieved April 1, 2009, from http://www.carla.umn.edu/immersion/acie/vol8/bridge_vol8_no3.pdf

Anton, M. (2004). Dyslexia in the immersion classroom [Electronic version]. *The ACIE Newsletter, 7*(3). Retrieved April 1, 2009, from http://www.carla.umn.edu/immersion/ACIE/vol7/May2004_Dyslexia_in_the_Immersion_Classroom.html

Arnett, K. (2003, August). *Effective teaching in immersion: Helping underperforming learners succeed.* Presented at CARLA Meeting the Challenges of Immersion Education Institute, Minneapolis, MN.

Arnett, K. (with Fortune, T.) (2004). Strategies for helping underperforming immersion learners succeed [Bridge Insert]. *The ACIE Newsletter 7*(3), 1-8. Retrieved April 1, 2009, from http://www.carla.umn.edu/immersion/acie/vol7/bridge-7(3).pdf

Arthur, G. (2004, February). Partial Spanish immersion program expands by offering academic excellence for all [Electronic version]. *The ACIE Newsletter, 7(2).* Retrieved April 1, 2009, from http://www.carla.umn.edu/immersion/acie/vol7/Feb2004_Partial_Spanish.html

August, D., & Hakuta, K. (1997). *Improving schooling for language minority children: A research agenda.* Washington, D.C.: National Academy Press.

August, D., & Shanahan, T. (2006). *Developing literacy in second language learners: Report of the National Literacy Panel on Minority-Language Children and Youth.* Mahwah, NJ: Lawrence Erlbaum.

Barik, H.C., & Swain, M. (1975). Three-year evaluation of a large scale early grade French immersion program: The Ottawa study. *Language Learning, 25,* 1-30.

121

Beckman, P. (2002). *Strategy instruction.* Retrieved April 1, 2009, from http://www.ericdigests.org/2003-5/strategy.htm

Bellis, T. J. (2002). Developing deficit-specific intervention plans for individuals with auditory processing disorders. *Seminars in Hearing, 23*(4), 287-295.

Bellis, T. (2004). Understanding auditory processing disorders in children [Electronic version]. *Audiology Information Series, ASHA's Consumer Newsletter.* Retrieved April 1, 2009, from http://www.asha.org/public/hearing/disorders/understand-apd-child.htm

Bender, W. N. (2002). *Differentiating instruction for students with learning disabilities: Best teaching practices for general and special educators.* Thousand Oaks, CA: Corwin Press.

Bentz, J., & Pavri, S. (2000). Curriculum-based measurement in assessing bilingual students: A promising new direction. *Diagnostique, 25*(3), 229-248.

Bernhardt, E. B. (1991). *Reading development in a second language: Theoretical, empirical, and classroom perspectives.* Norwood, NJ: Abelex.

Bergström, M. (2006). Writing in a second language: Case studies dealing with the challenges faced and the strategies used by immersion students at secondary school. In S. Björklund, R. Mård-Miettinen, M. Bergström, & M. Södergård (Eds.), *Exploring dual-focused education: Integrating language and content for individual and societal needs* (pp. 7-21). Vaasa, Finland: University of Vaasa.

Bialystock, E. (2001). *Bilingualism in development: Language, literacy and cognition.* New York: Cambridge University Press.

Bishop, D. V. M. (2004). Specific language impairment: Diagnostic dilemmas. In L. Verhoeven & H. Balkom (Eds.), *Classification on developmental language disorders* (pp. 309-326). Mahwah NJ: Lawrence Erlbaum.

Boder, E., & Jarrico, S. (1982). *The Boder test of reading-spelling patterns* [Manual]. New York: Grune and Stratton.

Boschung, S., & Roy, N. (1996). *Appendix A: Issues surrounding transfer out of French immersion: A literature review.* Nanaimo, Vancouver Island, Canada: University of British Columbia, Modern Language Department.

Boudreaux, E. (1994, June). *Shared teaching strategies immersion language and special education.* Paper presented at the Advocates for Language Learning conference, Anaheim, CA.

Bournot-Trites, M. (2004). The French-second-language peer tutoring programme. In Canadian Parents for French (Ed.), *The state of French second language education in Canada* (pp. 56-57). Ottawa, Ontario: Canadian Parents for French.

Bournot-Trites, M., & Lee, E. (2001). *Implementing and evaluating a school-based peer tutoring program, Report #2: Evaluating the program.* Vancouver, British Columbia, Canada: British Columbia Teachers' Federation.

Bournot-Trites, M., Lee, E., & Séror, J. (2003). Tutorat par les pairs en lecture: une collaboration parents-école en milieu d'immersion française. *La Revue des Sciences de l'Education, 29*(1), 195-210.

Boutin, F. (1993). A study of early French immersion teachers as generators of knowledge. *Foreign Language Annals, 26*(4), 511-524.

Boyd-Batstone, P. (2006). Supporting reading instruction. In P. Boyd-Batstone (Ed.), *Differentiated early literacy for English language learners: Practical strategies* (pp. 70-92). Boston, MA: Pearson Education.

Brownell, R. (2000). *Expressive one-word picture vocabulary test (3rd ed.)* Novato, CA: Academic Therapy Publications.

Brownell, R. (2001). *Expressive one-word picture vocabulary test (Spanish-English ed.)* Novato, CA: Academic Therapy Publications.

Brown, G., & Yule, G. (1983). *Discourse analysis.* Cambridge: Cambridge University Press.

Bruck, M. (1979). Switching out of French immersion. *Interchange, 9,* 86-94.

Bruck, M. (1982). Language impaired children's performance in an additive bilingual education program. *Applied Psycholinguistics, 3,* 45-60.

Bruck, M. (1985). Predictors of transfer out of early French Immersion programs. *Applied Psycholinguistics, 6,* 39-61.

Burns, G. E. (1983). Charges of elitism in immersion education: The case for improving program implementation. *Contact, 2*(2), 2-7.

Cadez, R. (2006). *Student attrition in specialized high school programs: An examination of three French immersion centres.* Unpublished master's thesis, University of Lethbridge, Alberta, Canada.

Caldas, S., & Boudreaux, N. (1999). Poverty, race, and foreign language immersion: Predictors of math and English language arts performance. *Learning Languages*, 5(1), pp. 4-15.

Calderón, M., & Minaya-Rowe, L. (2003). *Designing and implementing two-way bilingual programs: A step-by-step guide for administrators, teachers, and parents.* Thousand Oaks, CA: Corwin Press.

Calderón, M., & Slavin, R. (2001). Success for all in a two-way immersion school. In D. Christian & F. Genesee (Eds.), *Bilingual education* (pp. 27-40). Alexandria, VA: Teachers of English to Speakers of Other Languages.

Cammarata, L. (with Bartolini, M.C.) (2005). Instructional scaffolding with graphic organizers [Bridge insert]. *The ACIE Newsletter 8*(2), 1-12. Retrieved April 1, 2009, from http://www.carla.umn.edu/immersion/ACIE/vol8/2005BRIDGE8.2.pdf

Canadian Parents for French. (n.d.). *Learning difficulties in French immersion.* Retrieved April 1, 2009, from http://www.cpfalta.ab.ca/Parents/LDinFI.htm

Canadian Parents for French. (n.d.) Resources: *Programs & skill building: Peer tutoring.* Retrieved April 1, 2009, from http://www.cpf.ca/eng/resources-programs-tutoring.html

Canter, A. (2002). *Parenting perspectives…Ideas to help your child succeed: New directions in identifying learning disabilities.* Network for Instructional TV, Inc. Retrieved April 1, 2009, from http://www.teachersandfamilies.com/open/parent/idea1.cfm

Carroll, J. B. (1976). Response to R. L. Trites: Children with learning difficulties in primary French immersion. *Canadian Modern Language Review, 33*, 208-211.

Carroll, J. B. (1993). *Human cognitive abilities: A survey of factor analytic studies.* New York: Cambridge University Press.

Catts, H. W., Fey, M. E., Zhang, X., & Tomblin, J. B. (1999). Language basis of reading and reading disabilities: Evidence from a longitudinal study. *Scientific Studies of Reading, 3*(4), 331-361.

Center for Advanced Language Proficiency Education and Research. (2008). *Dynamic assessment.* CALPER and The Pennsylvania State University. Retrieved October 15, 2008, from http://calper.la.psu.edu/dyna_assess.php

Center for Applied Linguistics. (2008). *Directory of two-way bilingual immersion programs in the U.S.* Retrieved April 1, 2009 from http://www.cal.org/twi/directory

Center for Applied Linguistics. (2006). *Directory of foreign language immersion programs in U.S. schools.* Retrieved April 1, 2009 from http://www.cal.org/resources/immersion/

Center for Research on Education, Diversity & Excellence. (2002). *The five standards for effective pedagogy.* Retrieved April 1, 2009, from http://www-gse.berkeley.edu/research/crede/standards/standards.html

Centre franco-ontarien de ressources pédagogiques (n.d.). Retrieved November 15, 2009, from https://www.librairieducentre.com/pdf/frs-156-se.pdf

Chamot, A. U. (2001). Teaching learning strategies in immersion classrooms [Bridge insert]. *The ACIE Newsletter, 5*(1), 1-8. Retrieved April 1, 2009, from http://www.carla.umn.edu/immersion/acie/vol5/Nov2001.pdf

Chamot, A. U., Anstrom, K., Bartoshesky, A., Belanger, A., Delett, J., Karwan, V., et al. (n.d.). *The elementary immersion learning strategies resource guide* (2nd ed.). Retrieved April 1, 2009, from National Capital Language Resource Center Web site: http://www.nclrc.org/eils/.

Chamot, A. U., Barnhardt, S., Beard El-Dinary, P., & Robbins, J. (1999). *The learning strategies handbook.* White Plains, NY: Addison-Wesley Longman.

Chamot, A. U., & El-Dinary, P. B. (1999). Children's learning strategies in language immersion classrooms. *Modern Language Journal, 83*(3), 319-338.

Chamot, A. U., & O'Malley, J. M. (1994). *The CALLA handbook: Implementing the cognitive academic learning approach.* Reading, MA: Addison-Wesley Publishing.

Chang, J. (2003). Strategies for effective two-way immersion (TWI) programs : A Chinese American perspective. [Electronic version]. *NABE News*, 28-31. Retrieved April 1, 2009, from http://www2.sjsu.edu/faculty/chang/research_practice/documents/Dual%20immersion%20article.pdf

Chipman, M., & Roy, N. (2005). *The Peer Tutoring Literacy Program™ for French immersion schools: A parent-teacher collaborative approach.* Vancouver, British Columbia, Canada: Canadian Parents for French.

Chipman, M., & Roy, N. (2006). The Peer Tutoring Literacy Program™: Achieving reading fluency and developing self-esteem in elementary school students [Bridge insert]. *The ACIE Newsletter, 10* (1), 1-8. Retrieved April 1, 2009, from http://www.carla.umn.edu/immersion/acie/vol10/Bridge_Nov06.pdf

Chipman, M., Roy, N., & Naylor, C. (2001). *Implementing and evaluating a school-based peer tutoring program, Report #1: Implementing the program.* Vancouver, British Columbia, Canada: British Columbia Teachers' Federation.

Christensen, C., & Cooper, T. (1991). The effectiveness of instruction in cognitive strategies in developing proficiency in single-digit addition. *Cognition and Instruction, 8*(4), 363-371.

Clay, M. M. (1979). *Reading: The patterning of complex behavior.* Portsmouth, NH: Heinemann.

Clay, M. M. (1985). *The early detection of reading difficulties* (3rd ed.). Portsmouth, NH: Heinemann.

Clay, M.M. (1993). *Reading Recovery: A guidebook for teachers in training.* Portsmouth, NH: Heinemann.

Click, J. (2004). Learning centers: Meaningful context for language use in the primary immersion classroom [Bridge insert]. *The ACIE Newsletter, 8*(1), 1-8. Retrieved April 1, 2009, from http://www.carla.umn.edu/immersion/acie/vol8/vol2_bridge3.pdf

Cohen, A. (n.d.). *Styles- and strategies- based instruction.* Retrieved April 1, 2009, from http://www.carla.umn.edu/strategies/SBIinfo.html

Cohen, A. (2003). *Strategy training for second language learners.* ERIC Digest, EDO-FL-03-02. Washington, DC: ERIC Clearinghouse on Languages and Linguistics. Retrieved April 1, 2009, from http://www.cal.org/resources/Digest/digest_pdfs/0302cohen.pdf

Cohen, A., Weaver, S., & Li, T-Y. (1995). *The impact of strategies-based instruction on speaking a foreign language.* Minneapolis, MN: Center for Advanced Research on Language Acquisition.

Cole, C., & Majd, M. (2003). *Tucker signing strategies for reading: A national study.* Highlands, TX: Aha! Process. Retrieved April 1, 2009, from http://www.tuckersigns.com/files/Tuckernationalstudy_2003.pdf

Cole, C., & Majd, M. (2005). *The effect of Tucker signing strategies for reading on the decoding skills of students in four elementary schools.* Highlands, TX: Aha! Process. Retrieved April 1, 2009, from http://www.tuckersigns.com/files/Tuckernationalstudy_2005.pdf

Collier, V. P. (1987). Age and rate of acquisition of second language for academic purposes. *TESOL Quarterly, 21,* 617-641.

Collier, V. P. (1992). A synthesis of studies examining long-term language minority student data on academic achievement. *Bilingual Research Journal, 16*(1, 2), 187-212.

Collier, V. P. (1995). Acquiring a second language for school. *Directions in Language and Education, 1*(4). Washington, DC: The National Clearinghouse for English Language Acquisition. Retrieved April 1, 2009, from http://www.ncela.gwu.edu/pubs/directions/04.htm

Collier, V. P., & Thomas, W. P. (2004). The astounding effectiveness of dual language education for all. *NABE Journal of Research and Practice, 2*(1), 1-20.

Colorín Colorado. (2007). *Recognizing reading problems.* Retrieved April 1, 2009, from http://colorincolorado.org/article/14541

Cooperative Learning. (n.d.) *Cooperative learning.* Retrieved April 1, 2009, from http://edtech.kennesaw.edu/intech/cooperativelearning.htm

Coordinated Campaign for Learning Disabilities. (2000). *How parents can be advocates for their children.* WETA. Retrieved April 1, 2009, from http://www.ldonline.org/article/107

Cortiella, C. (2009). *The state of learning disabilities.* New York, NY: National Center for Learning Disabilities. Retrieved July 11, 2009, from http://www.LD.org/stateofld

Cummins, J. (1979). Should the child who is experiencing difficulties in early immersion be switched to the regular English program? A reinterpretation of Trites' data. *The Canadian Modern Language Review, 36,* 139-143.

Cummins, J. (1981). Age on arrival and immigrant second language learning in Canada: A reassessment. *Applied Linguistics, 2,* 132-149.

Cummins, J. (1984). *Bilingualism and special education: Issues in assessment and pedagogy.* Avon, England: Multilingual Matters.

Cummins, J. (1991). Interdependence of first- and second language proficiency in bilingual children. In E. Bialystok (Ed.), *Language processing in bilingual children* (pp. 70–89). Cambridge, U.K.: Cambridge University Press.

Cummins, J. (2000). *Immersion education for the millennium: What we have learned from 30 years of research on second language immersion.* Retrieved April 1, 2009, from http://www.iteachilearn.com/cummins/immersion2000.html

Cummins, J. (2001). Assessment and intervention with culturally and linguistically diverse learners. In J.V. Tinajero & S. Hurley (Eds.), *Literacy assessment of second language learners* (pp. 115-129). Boston: Allyn & Bacon.

Dalton, S. S. (1998). Pedagogy matters: Standards for effective teaching practice. *Center for Research on Education, Diversity & Excellence. Research Reports.* Paper rr04. Retrieved April 1, 2009, from http://repositories.cdlib.org/crede/rsrchrpts/rr04

Damico, J. S. (1991). Descriptive assessment of communicative ability in limited English proficient students. In E. V. Hamayan & J. S. Damico (Eds.), *Limiting bias in the assessment of bilingual students* (pp. 157-218). Austin: PRO-ED.

Day, V. P., & Elksnin, L. K. (1994). Promoting strategic learning. *Intervention in School & Clinic, 29*(5), 262-270.

Demers, D. (1994). *Learning disabilities and cross-linguistic interference in French immersion: When to transfer, when not to transfer?* Manitoba, Canada: Learning Disabilities Association of Manitoba (LDAM) and Canadian Parents for French.

Demers, D. (2000). *A changing perspective: Meeting the needs of all students.* Paper presented at Alberta's French Immersion Conference, Building the Future: Learning the Way, Alberta, Canada.

Demers, D. (2001). Why do we reinvent the wheel all the time? Special education and second language immersion programs. *The ACIE Newsletter, 5(1),* 6-7. Retrieved on April 1, 2009, from http://www.carla.umn.edu/immersion/acie/vol5/Nov2001_Wheel.html

Deshler, D., Warner, M., Schumaker, J., & Alley, G. (1984). Learning strategies intervention model: Key components and current status. In J. D. McKinney & L. Feagan (Eds.), *Current topics in learning disabilities* (Vol. 1). Norwood, NJ: Ablex.

Doherty, R. W., & Pinal, A. (2002, November). *Joint productive activity, cognitive reading strategies, and achievement.* Paper presented at the Annual Conference of National Council of Teachers of English, Atlanta, GA.

Doherty, R. W., Hilberg, R. S., Pinal, A., & Tharp, R. G. (2003). Five standards and student achievement. *National Journal of Research and Practice, 1*(1), 1-24.

Dole, J., Brown, K., & Trathen, W. (1996). The effects of strategy instruction on the comprehension performance of at-risk students. *Reading Research Quarterly, 31* (1), 62-88.

Donley, P. H. (2002). Teaching languages to the blind and visually impaired: Some suggestions. *Canadian Modern Language Review, 59*(2), 302-305.

Dubé, S. L. (1993). *French immersion withdrawal: Parental perspectives.* Unpublished master's thesis, University of Alberta, Edmonton, Alberta, Canada.

Durgunoglu, A. Y., & Öney, B. (2000) Literacy development in two languages: Cognitive and sociocultural dimensions of cross-language transfer [Electronic version]. In U.S. Department of Education, Office of Bilingual Education and Minority Language Affairs (OBEMLA) (Ed.), *Proceedings of a research symposium on high standards in reading for students from diverse language groups: research, practice & policy* (pp. 78-99). Washington, D.C.: U.S. Department of Education. Retrieved April 1, 2009, from http://www.ncela.gwu.edu/pubs/symposia/reading/literacy4.html

Durgunoglu, A. Y., & Verhoeven, L. (Eds.). (1998). *Literacy development in a multilingual context: Cross-cultural perspectives.* Mahwah, NJ: Erlbaum.

Dynamic Assessment. (n.d.). *Dynamic assessment.* Retrieved April 1, 2009, from http://dynamicassessment.com/_wsn/page2.html

Eaton, V. (1996). *Differentiated instruction.* Retrieved April 1, 2009, from http://www.ualberta.ca/~jpdasddc/incl/difinst.htm

Edmonton Public Schools. (1996). *Learning disabilities program review.* Unpublished document. November 1996, Edmonton, Alberta, Canada.

Elbaum, B., Vaughn, S., Hughes, M. T., & Moody, S. W. (2000). How effective are one- to-one tutoring programs in reading for elementary students at risk for reading failure? A meta-analysis of the intervention research. *Journal of Educational Psychology, 92*(4), 605-619.

Escamilla, K. (1992). *Descubriendo La Lectura: An application of reading recovery in Spanish* [Final Report]. Office of Educational Research and Improvement, Washington, D.C. ERIC Document (ED 356 622).

Escamilla, K. (1994). Descubriendo La Lectura: An early intervention literacy program in Spanish. *Literacy, Teaching and Learning, 1*(1), 57-70. (*Descubriendo La Lectura: Un programa en Español para las primeras etapas*, and translated by the author, 71-86).

Escamilla, K. (2000). Teaching literacy in Spanish. In J. V. Tinajero & R. A. DeVillar (Eds.), *The power of two languages 2000* (pp. 126-141). New York: McGraw-Hill.

Escamilla, K. (2003). An examination of sustaining effects in Descubriendo La Lectura Programs. In C. Briggs & S. Forbes (Eds.), *Research in reading recovery*, (Volume II, pp. 193-214). Portsmouth, NH: Heinemann.

Escamilla, K., Loera, M., Rodriguez, Y. & Ruiz, O. (1998). An examination of sustaining effects in Descubriendo La Lectura programs. *Literacy Teaching and Learning: An International Journal of Early Reading and Writing, 3*(2), 59-81.

Espin, C., & Wallace, T. (2004). *Descriptive analysis of curriculum-based measurement literature* [Working document]. University of Minnesota Institute for Research on Progress Monitoring.

Essama, L. (2006, November). *Total immersion programs: What makes them remarkable?* Presentation given at the annual meeting of the American Council on the Teaching of Foreign Languages, Nashville, TN.

Essama, L. (2007). Total immersion programs: Assessment data demonstrate achievement in reading and math [Bridge insert]. *The ACIE Newsletter, 11*(1),1-8. Retrieved April 1, 2009, from http://www.carla.umn.edu/immersion/acie/vol11/BridgeNov07.pdf

Estrada, P. (2000, October). *Pedagogy, professional development and reading performance in six linguistically diverse classrooms*. Paper presented at the UC ACCORD First Annual Conference on Education and Equity: Research, Policy, & Practice, San Jose, CA.

Fisher, T. (2004). Reading support for primary immersion students [Electronic version]. *The ACIE Newsletter, 7*(3), 1-2, 8, 15. Retrieved April 1, 2009, from http://www.carla.umn.edu/immersion/acie/vol7/May2004_Reading_Support.html

Fitzgerald, J. (1995). English-as-second-language learners' cognitive reading processes: A review of research in the United States. *Review of Educational Research, 65*, 145-190.

Flanagan, D. P. & Ortiz, S. O. (2002). Best practices in intellectual assessment. In A. Thomas & J. Grimes (Eds.), *Best practices in school psychology IV* (pp. 337-352). Washington, DC: National Association of School Psychologists.

Florida Online Reading Professional Development. (2005). *Reciprocal teaching, May, 2005*. Florida Department of Education and University of Central Florida. Retrieved April 1, 2009, from http://forpd.ucf.edu/strategies/stratreciprocalteaching1.html

Florida Online Reading Professional Development. (2005). *Reciprocal teaching, clarifying & summarizing, June, 2005*. Florida Department of Education and University of Central Florida. Retrieved April 1, 2009, from http://forpd.ucf.edu/strategies/stratreciprocalteaching2.html

Florida Online Reading Professional Development. (2005). *Reciprocal teaching, July, 2005*. Florida Department of Education and University of Central Florida. Retrieved April 1, 2009, from http://forpd.ucf.edu/strategies/stratreciprocalteaching3.html

Forte, I., & Schurr, S. (2003). *Curriculum and project planner for integrating learning styles, thinking skills, and authentic instruction*. Nashville, TN: Incentive Publications, Inc.

Fortune, T. W. (2001). *Understanding immersion students' oral language use as a mediator of social interaction in the classroom*. Unpublished doctoral dissertation, University of Minnesota, Minneapolis, Minnesota.

Fortune, T (Facilitator). (2003, August). *Struggling learners' discussion panel with educational specialists in immersion*. Focus group conducted at Meeting the Challenges of Immersion Institute, Minneapolis, MN.

Fortune, T. W., & Arabbo, M. A. (2006). *Attending to immersion language proficiency at the program level*. Paper presented at the Dual Language Immersion Pre-Conference Institute of the National Association of Bilingual Education (NABE), Phoenix, AZ.

Fortune, T. (with Fernandez del Rey, C.) (2003). Maximizing language growth through collaborative-creative writing [Bridge insert]. *The ACIE Newsletter, 6*(2), 1-8. Retrieved April 1, 2009, from http://www.carla.umn.edu/immersion/acie/vol6/bridge-6(2).pdf

Fortune, T.W., & Tedick, D.J. (2003). *What parents want to know about foreign language immersion programs*. ERIC Digest, EDO-FL-03-04. Washington, DC: ERIC Clearinghouse on Languages and Linguistics. Available: http://www.cal.org/resources/digest/0304fortune.html

Fortune, T.W. and Tedick, D.J. (2008). One-way, two-way and indigenous immersion: A call for cross-fertilization. In T.W. Fortune & D. J. Tedick (eds.) *Pathways to multilingualism: Evolving perspectives on immersion education (pp. 3-21)*. Clevedon: Multilingual Matters.

Fradd, S., & McGee, P. (1994). *Instructional assessment*. Reading, MA: Addison-Wesley.

Freeman, Y., Freeman, D., & Mercuri, S. (2005). *Dual language essentials for teachers and administrators*. Portsmouth, NH: Heinemann.

Fuchs, D., & Fuchs, L. S. (2005). Responsiveness to intervention: A blueprint for practitioners, policymakers, and parents [Electronic version]. *Teaching Exceptional Children, 38*(1), 57-61. Retrieved April 1, 2009, from http://www.advocacyinstitute.org/resources/TEC_RtIblueprint.pdf

Galambos, D. (2005). *The cooperative learning network*. Retrieved April 1, 2009, from http://www-acad.sheridanc.on.ca/scls/coop/cooplrn.htm

Ganschow, L. & Sparks, R. (2000). Reflections on foreign language study for students with language learning problems: Research, issues and challenges. *Dyslexia, 6*, 87-100.

Garb, E. (1997). *Dynamic assessment as a teaching tool: Assessment for learning from assessment*. English Teachers Network Israel. Retrieved April 1, 2009, from http://www.etni.org.il/etnirag/issue2/erica_garb.htm

Gardner, H. (1983). *Frames of mind: The theory of multiple intelligences*. New York: Basic Books.

Gardner, H. (1999). *Intelligence reframed: Multiple intelligences for the 21st century*. New York: Basic Books.

Genesee, F. (1983). Bilingual education of majority-language children: The immersion experiments in review. *Applied Psycholinguistics, 4*, 1-46.

Genesee, F. (1987). *Learning through two languages*. Cambridge, MA: Newbury House.

Genesee, F. (1992). Second/Foreign language immersion and at-risk English-speaking children. *Foreign Language Annals, 25*(3), 199-213.

Genesee, F. (October, 2004). *Dual language learning in the global village*. Keynote address given at the Pathways to Bilingualism: Evolving Perspectives on Immersion Education Conference, Minneapolis, MN.

Genesee, F. (2007a). French immersion and at-risk students: A review of research evidence. *The Canadian Modern Language Review, 63*(5), 655-688.

Genesee, F. (2007b). Literacy outcomes in French immersion [Electronic version]. In D. Jamieson, S. Rvachew, L. Siegel, H. Deacon, E. Geva, & N. Cohen (Eds.), *Encyclopedia of language and literacy development* (pp. 1-8). London, ON: Canadian Language and Literacy Research Network. Retrieved April 1, 2009, from http://www.literacyencyclopedia.ca/index.php?fa=items.show&topicId=27

Genesee, F. (October, 2008). *Learning to read in a second language*. Plenary address given at the Immersion Education: Pathways to Bilingualism and Beyond Conference, St. Paul, MN.

Genesee, F., Paradis, J., & Crago, M. (2004). *Dual language development and disorders: A handbook on bilingualism and second language learning*. Baltimore, MD: Brookes.

Gentile, L.M. (2003). *Oral Language Acquisition Inventory: Linking research and theory to assessment and instruction*. Parsippany, NJ: Dominie Press, Inc.

Goldstein, B. (2000). *Cultural and linguistic diversity resource guide for speech-language pathologists*. San Diego, CA: Delmar Learning.

Gouin, D. (1998). Report on current practice: Immersion program in Montgomery County, Maryland. In M. Met (Ed.), *Critical issues in early second language learning: Building for our children's future* (pp. 62-64). Glenview, IL: Addison-Wesley Educational.

Government of Alberta. (2008). *Can French immersion offer an appropriate quality education for a student with special needs?* Retrieved April 1, 2009, from http://education.alberta.ca/francais/admin/speced/parents/immersion.aspx

Government of Alberta. (2008). *The special needs French immersion student*. Retrieved April 1, 2009 from http://www.education.gov.ab.ca/french/adt_scol/frImm/default.asp

Goyette, C. H., Conners, K. C., & Ulrich, R. (1978). Normative data on Revised Conners Parent and Teacher Rating Scales. *Journal of Abnormal Child Psychology, 6*, 221-36.

Gutiérrez-Clellen, V. (1999). Language choice in intervention with bilingual children. *American Journal of Speech-Language Pathology, 8*, 291-302.

Gutiérrez-Clellen, V. F. & Peña, E. (2001). Dynamic assessment of diverse children: A tutorial. *Language, Speech and Hearing Services in Schools, 32*, 212-224.

Gutiérrez-Clellen, V., Simon-Cereijido, G., & Wagner, C. (2008). Bilingual children with language impairment: A comparison with monolinguals and second language learners. *Applied Psycholinguistics, 29*, 3-19.

Hakansson, G., & Nettelbladt, U. (1996). Similarities between SLI and L2 children: Evidence from the acquisition of Swedish word order. In I. Gilbert & C. Johnson (Eds.), *Children's language* (pp. 135-151). Mahwah, NJ: Erlbaum.

Håkansson, G., Salameh, E., & Nettelbladt, U. (2003). Measuring language development in bilingual children: Swedish-Arabic children with and without language impairment. *Linguistics, 41*, 255-288.

Hall, T. (2002). *Differentiated instruction.* Wakefield, MA: National Center on Accessing the General Curriculum. Retrieved April 1, 2009, from http://www.cast.org/publications/ncac/ncac_diffinstruc.html

Halsall, N. (1991). *Attrition/retention of students in French immersion with particular emphasis on secondary school.* Ottawa, ON: Canadian Parents for French.

Halstead, W. C. (1947). *Brain and intelligence: A quantitative study of the frontal lobes.* Chicago, IL: University of Chicago Press.

Harrison, B., & Papa, R. (2005). The development of an indigenous knowledge program in a New Zealand Maori-language immersion school. *Anthropology and Education Quarterly, 36*(1), 57-72.

Hart, B., & Risley, T. R. (1995). *Meaningful differences in the everyday experience of young American children.* Baltimore: Paul H. Brookes.

Hayden, R. H. M. (1988). French immersion drop-outs: Perspectives of parents, students and teachers. *Reading Canada Lecture, 6*(4), 222-229.

Henderson, A., Abbot, C., & Strang, W. (1993). *Summary of the Bilingual Education State Educational Agency program survey of states' limited English proficient persons and available educational services 1991-1992.* (Contract No. T292001001, U.S. Dept of Education, Office of Bilingual Education and Minority Languages Affairs). Arlington, VA: Development Associates.

Hilberg, R. S., Tharp, R. G., & DeGeest, L. (2000). The efficacy of CREDE's standards-based instruction in American Indian mathematics classes. *Equity and Excellence in Education, 33*(2), 32-29.

Holden, C. (2000). *Reading strategies instruction in Spanish and its influence on reading comprehension in English.* Unpublished master's paper, University of Minnesota, Minneapolis, MN.

Holtzman, W. H., & Wilkinson, C. Y. (1991). Assessment of cognitive ability. In E. V. Hamayan & J. S. Damico (Eds.), *Limiting bias in the assessment of bilingual students* (pp. 248-279). Austin, TX: ProEd.

Hoover, J. J., & Collier, C. (2001). Methods and materials for bilingual special education. In L. M. Baca and H. T. Cervantes (Eds.), *The bilingual special education interface* (pp. 264 – 289). Upper Saddle River, NJ: Merrill.

Howard, E. R. (2003) *Biliteracy development in two-way immersion education programs: A multilevel analysis of the effects of native language and home language use on the development of narrative writing ability in English and Spanish.* Unpublished doctoral dissertation, Harvard University, Cambridge, MA.

Howard, E. R., Olague, N., & Rogers, D. (2003). *The dual language program planner: A guide for designing and implementing dual language programs.* Santa Cruz, CA and Washington, DC: Center for Research on Education, Diversity & Excellence.

Howard, E. R., & Sugarman, J. (2001). *Two-way immersion programs: Features and statistics.* ERIC Digest, EDO-FL-01-01. Washington, DC: ERIC Clearinghouse on Languages and Linguistics. Retrieved April 1, 2009, from http://www.cal.org/resources/digest/0101twi.html

Howard, E. R., Sugarman, J., Perdomo, M., & Adger, C. T. (Eds.). (2005). *The two-way immersion toolkit.* Providence, RI: The Education Alliance at Brown University. Retrieved April 1, 2009, from http://www.cal.org/twi/toolkit/index.htm

Howard, E. R., & Sugarman, J. (2007). *Realizing the vision of two-way immersion: Fostering effective programs and classrooms*. Washington, D.C.: Center for Applied Linguistics and Delta.

Hudson, R. F., High, L., & Al Otaiba, S. (2007). *Dyslexia and the brain: What does current research tell us?* Retrieved April 1, 2009, from http://www.ldonline.org/article/14907

Hughes, M. T., Vaughn, S., & Schumm, J. S. (1999). Home literacy activities: Perceptions and practices of Hispanic parents of children with learning disabilities. *Learning Disability Quarterly, 22*(3), 224-235.

Husum, R. & Bryce, R. (1991). A survey of graduates from a Saskatchewan French immersion high school. *Canadian Modern Language Review, 48*(1), 135-143.

Individuals with Disabilities Act. (1999). Public—Law 105-17, Office of Special Education Programs (OSEP), U.S. Department of Education.

Individuals with Disabilities Education Improvement Act. (2004). Public–Law 108-446, Office of Special Education Programs (OSEP), U.S. Department of Education.

Institute of Education Sciences / U.S. Department of Education. (n.d.). *Glossary*. Retrieved April 1, 2009, from http://nces.ed.gov/programs/coe/glossary/s.asp

Johnson, D. W., & Johnson, R. T. (1989). *Cooperation and competition: Theory and research*. Edina, MN: Interaction Book.

Johnson, D. W., Johnson, R. T., & Holubec, E. J. (1993). *Cooperation in the classroom* (6th ed.) Edina, MN: Interaction Book.

Johnson, M. (2003). Parent activism: A critical component for secondary immersion [Electronic version]. *The ACIE Newsletter, 6*(3), pp. 1, 3-5, 19. Retrieved April 1, 2009, from http://www.carla.umn.edu/immersion/acie/theme_issues/2003.pdf

Jones, C. (2005). Spanish immersion and the academic success of Alamo Heights students [Electronic version]. *The ACIE Newsletter, 9*(1). Retrieved April 1, 2009, from http://www.carla.umn.edu/immersion/acie/vol9/nov2005_researchreport_spanishimmersion.html

Joyce, D. (2004, August). *Conocimiento fonológico*. Presentation at Meeting the Challenges in Immersion Education Summer Institute for the Center for Advanced Research on Language Acquisition, University of Minnesota, Minneapolis, MN.

Joyce, D., & Bushey, S. (2004, August). *Differentiating instruction and structuring consistent classroom environmental accommodations for special needs immersion learners*. Presentation at Meeting the Challenges of Immersion Education Summer Institute for the Center for Advanced Research on Language Acquisition, University of Minnesota, Minneapolis, MN.

Kagan, S. (1990). The structural approach to cooperative learning. *Educational Leadership, 47*(4), 12-15.

Kahmi, A., & Catts, H. (1999). The language basis of reading: Implications for classification and treatment of children with reading disabilities. In K. G. Butler & E. R. Silliman (Eds.), *Speaking, reading and writing in children with language learning disabilities: New paradigms in research and practice* (pp. 45-72). Mahwah, NJ: Erlbaum.

Keeler, M. L., & Swanson, H. L. (2001). Does strategy knowledge influence working memory in children with mathematical disabilities? *Journal of Learning Disabilities, 34*(5), 418-434.

Keep, L. J. (1993). *French immersion attrition: Implications for model building*. Unpublished doctoral dissertation, University of Alberta, Edmonton, Alberta, Canada.

Kehl, R., & Ballweg, J. (2007). *Launching into literacy and math*. Paula Srite (Ed.). Retrieved April 1, 2009, from www.madison.k12.wi.us/tnl/lilm/early_literacy/infants&toddlers/milestones0-3.html

Kern, R. (1989). Second language reading strategy instruction: Its effects on comprehension and word inference ability. *The Modern Language Journal, 73*, 135-149.

Klimpl, J. I., Amin, I. A., Gouin, D. M., & Sacks, R. I. (2007, November). *Elementary immersion programs and assessments in Montgomery County Public Schools*. Presentation at annual meeting of the American Council on the Teaching of Foreign Languages (ACTFL), San Antonio, TX.

Kline, A. D., Krantz, I. D., Sommer, A., Sliewer, M., Jackson, L. G., FitzPatrick, et al. (2007). Cornilia de Lange Syndrome: Clinical review, diagnostic and scoring systems, and anticipatory guidance. *American Journal of Medical Genetics, Part A, 143A*, 1287-1296.

Kohnert, K. (2004a). Children learning a second language: Processing skills in early sequential bilinguals. In B. Goldstein (Ed.), *Bilingual language development and disorders in Spanish-English speakers* (pp. 53 – 76). Baltimore: Brookes.

Kohnert, K. (2004b, August). *Language and learning disorders in the immersion classroom.* Presentation at Meeting the Challenges of Immersion Education Summer Institute for Center for Advanced Research on Language Acquisition, University of Minnesota, Minneapolis, MN.

Kohnert, K. (2008). *Language disorders in bilingual children and adults.* San Diego: Plural.

Kohnert, K., & Bates, E. (2002). Balancing bilinguals, II: Lexical comprehension and cognitive processing in children learning Spanish and English. *Journal of Speech, Language, and Hearing Research, 45,* 347-359.

Kohnert, K., & Derr, A. (2004). Language intervention with bilingual children. In B. Goldstein (Ed.), *Bilingual language development: A focus on Spanish-English speakers* (pp. 311-342). Baltimore: Brookes.

Kohnert, K., Hernandez, A., & Bates, E. (1998). Bilingual performance on the Boston naming test: Preliminary norms in Spanish and English. *Brain and Language, 65,* 422-440.

Krashen, S., & McField, G. (2005). What works? Reviewing the latest evidence on bilingual education [Electronic version]. *Language Learner, 7*(10), 34. Retrieved April 1, 2009, from http://users.rcn.com/crawj/langpol/Krashen-McField.pdf

Krueger, D. R. (2001). *Foreign language immersion in an urban setting: Effects of immersion on students of yesterday and today.* Unpublished doctoral dissertation, University of Wisconsin, Milwaukee, WI.

Krueger, D. (2008). Immersion education, ethnicity and income: How well do immersion students fare in immersion districts. *The ACIE Newsletter, 12(1),* 1, 6, 10-13.

Lambert, W. E., & Tucker, G. (1972). *The bilingual education of children: The St. Lambert experiment.* Rowely, MA: Newbury House.

Lantolf, J. P., & Poehner, M. E. (2004). Dynamic assessment: Bringing the past into the future. *Journal of Applied Linguistics, 1,* 49-74.

Laplante, J. (2001). *Raconte – moi les sons (Tell me the sounds).* Quebec, Canada: Septembre éditeur Inc.

Lazear, D. (2008). *"Multi-modal" learning.* Retrieved April 1, 2009, from http://www.davidlazeargroup.com/free_articles/multi-modal.html

Lee, J. F. (2000). *Tasks and communicating in language classrooms.* New York: McGraw-Hill.

Lemire, H. (1989). *Perceptions of principals of French immersion schools in Alberta.* Unpublished master's thesis, University of Alberta, Edmonton, Canada.

Lewis, C., & Shapson, S. (1989). Secondary French immersion: A study of students who leave the program. *Canadian Modern Language Review, 45*(3), 539-548.

Lindholm-Leary, K. J. (2001). *Dual language education.* Clevedon, England: Multilingual Matters.

Lindholm-Leary, K., & Borsato, G. (2006) Academic achievement. In F. Genesee, K. Lindholm-Leary, W. Saunders, & D. Christian, (Eds.) *Educating English language learners: A synthesis of empirical evidence.* New York: Cambridge University Press.

Lindholm-Leary, K., & Howard, E. (2008). Language development and academic achievement in two-way immersion programs. In T. W. Fortune & D. J. Tedick (Eds.) *Pathways to multilingualism: Evolving perspectives on immersion education* (pp. 177-200). Clevedon, England: Multilingual Matters.

Lorenz, E. B., & Met, M. (1988). *What it means to be an immersion teacher.* Unpublished manuscript, Office of Instruction and Program Development, Montgomery County Public Schools, Rockville, MD.

MacCoubrey, S. J., Wade-Woolley, L., & Kirby, J. R. (2007). *A phonemic awareness intervention for at-risk second language readers in French immersion.* Unpublished manuscript, Queen's University, Kingston, Ontario, Canada.

Mannavarayan, J. (2002). *The French immersion debate: French for all or all for French.* Calgary, Alberta, Canada: Detselig Enterprises.

Marks, J. W., Van Laeys, J., Bender, N. W., & Scott, S. K. (1996). Teachers create learning strategies: Guidelines for classroom creation. *Teaching Exceptional Children, 28*(4), 34-38.

Massachusetts Department of Elementary and Secondary Education. (2008). *Specific learning disability.* Retrieved April 1, 2009, from http://www.doe.mass.edu/sped/links/learndisability.html

McCloskey, D., & Athanasiou, M. S. (2000). Assessment and intervention practices with second-language learners among school psychologists. *Psychology in the Schools, 37*(3), 209-225.

McGroarty, M. (1989). The benefits of cooperative learning arrangements in second language instruction. *NABE: The Journal of the National Association for Bilingual Education, 13*(2), 127-143.

Milian, M., & Pearson, V. (2005). Students with visual impairments in a dual-language program: A case study. *Journal of Visual Impairment & Blindness, 99*(11), 715-720.

Minnesota Department of Children, Families & Learning. (1998). *SLD companion manual* (Catalog #E1040). [Electronic version]. Little Canada, MN: Author. Retrieved on April 1, 2009, from http://education.state.mn.us/mde-prod/groups/SpecialEd/documents/Manual/001529.pdf

Minnesota Department of Education. (2003). *The ELL companion to reducing bias in special education evaluation* [Electronic version]. Retrieved on April 1, 2009, from http://education.state.mn.us/MDE/Learning_Support/Special_Education/Evaluation_Program_Planning_Supports/Cultural_Linguistic_Diversity/ELL_Companion_Manual/index.html

Minnesota Department of Education (2007). *School report card for 2006-2007 school year.* Retrieved on April 1, 2009, from http://education.state.mn.us/ReportCard2005/index.do

Morrison, F., Bonyun, R., & Pawley, C. (1981). *Longitudinal and cross-sectional studies of French proficiency in Ottawa and Carleton schools (8th annual report submitted to the Ontario Ministry of Education).* Ottawa, Canada: Ottawa Board of Education Research Centre.

Morrison, F., & Walsh, M. (1980). *French proficiency and general progress: Students in the elementary core French programs, 1978-1980, and in immersion and bilingual programs, grades 8, 10, and 12, 1980 (7th annual report submitted to the Ontario Ministry of Education).* Ottawa, Canada: Ottawa Board of Education Research Centre.

Muñoz-Sandoval, A., Cummins, J., Alvarado, G., & Ruef, M. L. (2001). *Bilingual verbal abilities test. (BVAT).* Rolling Meadows, IL: Riverside Publishing.

Muñoz-Sandoval, A., Cummins, J., Alvarado, G., & Ruef, M. L. (2005). *Bilingual verbal abilities test—Normative update edition. (BVAT-NU).* Rolling Meadows, IL: Riverside Publishing.

Munson, S. M. (1987). Regular education teacher modifications for mainstreamed mildly handicapped students. *Journal of Special Education, 20*(4), 489-502.

National Association of Special Education Teachers. (2006/2007). *Legal information in special education.* Retrieved April 1, 2009, from http://www.naset.org/specialedlaw01.0.html

National Capital Language Resource Center. (n.d.). *Elementary immersion students' perceptions of language learning strategies use and self-efficacy.* Retrieved April 1, 2009, from http://www.nclrc.org/about_teaching/reports_pub/elementary_imm_students.pdf

National Center for Education Statistics. (2007). *Status and trends in the education of racial and ethnic minorities* (NCES 2007-039). Retrieved on April 1, 2009, from: http://nces.ed.gov/pubs2007/minoritytrends/ind_2_8.asp

National Center for Learning Disabilities. (2006). *Highlights of key provisions and important changes in the final regulations for IDEA 2004.* Retrieved April 1, 2009, from http://www.ldonline.org/article/11201

National Center to Improve the Tools of Educators. (n.d.) *Learning to read/Reading to learn information kit.* Retrieved on March 25, 2010 from http://www.disabilitycompass.org/searches/resources/national-center-to-improve-the-tools-of-educators/learning-to-read-reading-to-learn-information-kit

National Center to Improve the Tools of Educators. (n.d.). *Learning to read/reading to learn campaign: Helping children with learning disabilities to succeed.* Retrieved July 2, 2009, from http://idea.uoregon.edu/~ncite/programs/read.html

National Clearinghouse on Disability and Exchange. (2007). *Foreign languages and students with learning, hearing or vision disabilities.* Retrieved April 1, 2009, from http://www.miusa.org/ncde/tipsheets/foreignlang/

National Dissemination Center for Children with Disabilities. (2002). *Communicating with your child's school through letter writing.* WETA. Retrieved April 1, 2009, from http://www.ldonline.org/article/14615

National Institute of Child Health and Human Development, NIH, DHHS. (2005). *Improving academic performance among American Indian, Alaska Native, and Native Hawaiian students: Assessment of learning and identification of learning disabilities* (NA). Washington, DC: U.S. Government Printing Office.

National Institute on Deafness and Other Communication Disorders. (2004). *Auditory processing disorder in children.* Retrieved on April 1, 2009 from http://www.ldonline.org/article/8056

National Joint Committee on Learning Disabilities. (2005). *Responsiveness to intervention and learning disabilities.* Paper for NJCLD. Retrieved April 1, 2009, from http://www.ncld.org/index.php?option=content&task=view&id=497

National Research Center on Learning Disabilities. (2007). *Learning disabilities resource kit: Specific learning disabilities determination procedures and responsiveness to intervention.* Retrieved April 1, 2009, from http://www.nrcld.org/resource_kit/

Obadia, A. A., & Thériault, C. M. L. (1995). *Attrition in French immersion programs: Possible solutions.* Vancouver, British Columbia, Canada: Faculty of Education, Simon Fraser University.

Olsen, C. P. (1983). Inequality remade: The theory of correspondence and the context of French immersion in northern Ontario. *Journal of Education, 65*(1), 75-82.

Ortiz, A. (2002). Prevention of school failure and early intervention for English language learners. In A. Artiles, & A. Ortiz (Eds.), *English language learners with special education needs: Identification, assessment, and instruction,* (pp. 31-50). Washington, D.C.: Center for Applied Linguistics and Delta Systems Company, Inc.

Ortiz, S. (2003, April). *Enhancing outcomes for all children: Comprehensive assessment and nondiscriminatory evaluation of culturally and linguistically diverse children.* Presentation at the annual meeting of National Association of School Psychologists (NASP), Toronto, Canada.

Ortiz, S., & Ochoa, S. H. (2003, November). *Psychoeducational assessment of children from culturally and linguistically diverse backgrounds.* Workshop sponsored by Schoolhouse Educational Services, Minneapolis, MN.

Padron, Y. N., & Waxman, H. C. (1999).Classroom observations of the Five Standards of Effective Teaching in urban classrooms with English language learners. *Teaching and Change, 7*(1), 79-100.

Palincsar, A. S., & Brown, A. (1984). Reciprocal teaching of comprehension-fostering and comprehension-monitoring activities. *Cognition and Instruction, 1*(2), 117-175.

Paquin, N., & Lagroix-Othmer, N. (2002). *Brille, la chenille (Brille, the caterpillar).*

Paradis, J. (2005). Grammatical morphology in children learning English as a second language: Implications of similarities with specific language impairment. *Language, Speech, and Hearing Services in Schools, 36,* 172-187.

Paradis, J., Crago, M., Genesee, F., & Rice, M. (2003). French-English bilingual children with SLI: How do they compare with their monolingual peers? *Journal of Speech, Language, and Hearing Research, 46,* 113 – 127.

Pearson Education. (2008). *AIMSWeb.* Retrieved April 1, 2009 from, http://www.aimsweb.com

Peña, E. D., Iglesias, A., & Lidz, C. S. (2001). Reducing test bias through dynamic assessment of children's word learning ability. *American Journal of Speech-Language Pathology, 10,* 138-154.

Perozzi, J. A., & Sanchez, M. L. C. (1992). The effect of instruction in L1 on receptive acquisition of L2 for bilingual children with language delay. *Language, Speech, and Hearing Services in Schools, 23,* 348-352.

Petzold, A. (2001). Assessing for special education eligibility in the elementary immersion setting. *School Psychology Minnesota, 33*(1), 4.

Petzold, A. (2004, August). *Accurate identification of struggling students in the immersion classroom.* Presentation given at Meeting the Challenges of Immersion Education Summer Institute for Center for Advanced Research on Language Acquisition, University of Minnesota, Minneapolis, MN.

Petzold, A. (2006). Assessment of struggling elementary immersion learners: The St. Paul Public Schools Model. *The ACIE Newsletter, 9*(2), 1-2, 10-11, 13. Available from http://www.carla.umn.edu/immersion/ACIE/vol9/feb2006_bpractices_strugglinglearners.html

Pikulski, J. J. (1997). *Preventing reading problems: Factors common to successful early intervention programs.* Houghton Mifflin. Retrieved on April 1, 2009, from http://www.eduplace.com/rdg/res/prevent.html#1Poehner, M. E., & Lantolf, J. P. (2005). Dynamic assessment in the language classroom. *Language Teaching Research, 9*(3), 233-265.

Polich, E. (1974). *Report on the evaluation of the lower elementary French immersion program through grade 3.* Montreal, Canada: Protestant School Board of Greater Montreal.

Porter, P. (1986). How learners talk to each other: Input and interaction in task-centered discussions. In R. Day (Ed.), *Talking to learn* (pp. 200-224). Rowley, MA: Newbury House.

Public Broadcasting Systems (2008). *Parents guide to reading and language.* Retrieved April 1, 2009, from http://www.pbs.org/parents/readinglanguage/

Punchard, I. (2002). Improving immersion student oral proficiency by fostering the use of extended discourse [Bridge insert]. *The ACIE Newsletter, 6* (1), 1-8. Retrieved April 1, 2009, from http://www.carla.umn.edu/immersion/ACIE/vol6/Bridgev.6.n.1.pdf

Reyes-Wrede, M., & Sala-Healey, R. (2008, October). *Signing strategies for reading.* Presentation at Immersion Education: Pathways to Bilingualism and Beyond; St. Paul, MN.

Rhodes, N.C., & Branaman, L.E. (1999). *Foreign language instruction in the United States: A national survey of elementary and secondary schools.* McHenry, IL, and Washington, DC: Delta Systems and Center for Applied Linguistics.

Rhodes, N. C., & Pufahl, I. (2009). *Foreign language teaching in U.S. schools: Results of a national survey.* (Executive summary). Washington, D.C.: Center for Applied Linguistics. Retrieved March 25, 2010 from http://www.cal.org/projects/Exec%20Summary_111009.pdf.

Rigaud, P. (2005). Attrition in four U.S. elementary immersion schools. *The ACIE Newsletter, 8*(3), 11-15. Retrieved April 1, 2009, from http://www.carla.umn.edu/immersion/ACIE/vol8/May2005_research_attrition.html

Robbins, J., & Chamot, A. U. (2007). Helping struggling students become good language learners. *The NCLRC Language Resource, 11*(7). Retrieved on April 1, 2009, from http://www.nclrc.org/about_teaching/topics/learner_diversity.html#helping_struggling_students

Rousseau, N. (1998). *Description and evaluation of a French immersion learning disabilities program.* Unpublished doctoral dissertation, University of Alberta, Edmonton, Alberta, Canada.

Rousseau, N. (1999). A French immersion learning disabilities program: Perspectives of students, their parents and their teachers. *Mosaic, 6* (3), 16-26.

Roy, N. (1997a). *French immersion support documents and a model for transfer to the English program.* Vancouver School Board, British Columbia: Curriculum Publications.

Roy, N. (1997b). Possible factors influencing student performance in French immersion. Excerpt reprinted from Roy (1997a), *French immersion support documents and a model for transfer to the English program* in *The ACIE Newsletter* (2004, May), 7(3). Retrieved April 1, 2009, from http://www.carla.umn.edu/immersion/acie/vol7/May2004_Student_Performance_Factors.html

Rueda, R., Artiles, A., Salazar, J., & Higareda, I. (2002). An analysis of special education as a response to the diminished academic achievement of Chicano students: An update. In R. Valencia (Ed.), *Chicano school failure and success: Research and policy agendas* (2nd ed.) (pp. 310-332). London: Falmer.

Rulon, K., & McCreary, J. (1986). Negotiation of content: Teacher fronted and small-group interactions. In R. Day (Ed.), *Talking to learn* (pp. 182-199). Cambridge, MA: Newbury House.

Sacramento City Unified School District. (n.d.). *What is differentiated instruction?* Retrieved April 1, 2009, from http://www.scusd.edu/gate_ext_learning/differentiated.htm

Salamone, A. (1993). Immersion teachers: What can we learn from them? In J. W. Oller, Jr. (Ed.), *Methods that work: Ideas for literacy and language teachers* (pp. 129-135). Boston, MA: Heinle & Heinle.

Scarcella, R. C., & Oxford, R. L. (1992). *The tapestry of language learning: The individual in the communicative classroom.* Boston, MA: Heinle & Heinle Publishers.

Scheib, M. (2008). *Accessing foreign language materials as a blind or low vision student* [Electronic version]. Mobility International USA. Retrieved April 1, 2009, from http://www.miusa.org/ncde/tipsheets/foreignlanguageandblind/infoguide/?searchterm=Accessing%20foreign%20language%20materials%20as%20a%20blind%20or%20low%20vision%20student

Schwarz, R. (1997). *Learning disabilities and foreign language learning*. WETA. Retrieved April 8, 2009, from http://www.ldonline.org/article/6065

Scott, B., Vitale, M., & Masten, W. (1998). Implementing instructional adaptations for student with disabilities in inclusive classrooms. *Remedial and Special Education, 19*(2), 106-119.

Semel, E., Wiig, E. H., & Secord,W. A. (2003). *Clinical evaluation of language fundamentals, (fourth edition, Spanish version) (CELF-4)*. Toronto, Canada: The Psychological Corporation/A Harcourt Assessment Company.

Silva- Corvalán, C. (1991). Spanish language attrition in a contact situation with English. In H. W. Seliger & R. M. Vago (Eds.), *First language attrition*, (pp. 151-171). New York: Cambridge University Press.

Snow, C. (1983). Language and literacy: Relationships during the preschool years. *Harvard Educational Review, 53*, 165-189.

Snow, M. (1987). *Immersion teacher handbook*. Los Angeles, CA: Center for Language Education and Research, University of California.

Snow, M. A. (1990). Instructional methodology in immersion foreign language education. In A. Padilla, H. Fairchild, & C. Valadez (Eds.), *Foreign language education: Issues and strategies* (pp. 156-171). Newbury Park, CA: Sage Publications.

Snow, C., & Hoefnagel-Höhle, M. (1977). Age differences in the pronunciation of foreign sounds. *Language and Speech, 20*(4), 357-365.

Sousa, D. A. (2001). *How the brain learns: A classroom teacher's guide* (2nd ed.). Thousand Oaks, CA: Corwin Press.

Sparks, R. (1995). Examining the linguistic coding difference hypothesis to explain individual differences in foreign language learning. *Annals of Dyslexia, 45*, 187-214.

Sparks, R., Artzer, M. Patton, J., Ganschow, L., Miller, K., Hordubay, D., et al. (1998). Benefits of multisensory language instruction for at-risk learners: A comparison study of high school Spanish students. *Annals of Dyslexia, 48*, 239-270.

Sparks, R., Ganschow, L., & Patton, J. (1995). Prediction of performance in first-year foreign language courses: Connections between native and foreign language learning. *Journal of Educational Psychology, 87*, 638-655.

St. Louis Park Public Schools. (n.d.). *Signing strategies: A reading tool in the Spanish immersion classroom*. Retrieved November 4, 2008, from http://www.rschooltoday.com/se3bin/clientschool.cgi?schoolname=school461

Staff Development for Educators. (2008). *Teacher resources*. Retrieved April 1, 2009, from http://www.sde.com/teacher-resources.asp

Stahl, S. A., Jacobson, M. G., Davis, C. E., & Davis, R. L. (1989). Prior knowledge and difficult vocabulary in the comprehension of unfamiliar text. *Reading Research Quarterly, 24*(1), 27-43.

Stanovich, K. (1986). Matthew effects in reading: Some consequences of individual differences in the acquisition of literacy. *Reading Research Quarterly, 21*, 360-407.

Stern, M. (1991). *The French immersion transfer process: Investigation of children transferring from the French immersion program into the regular English program*. Unpublished doctoral dissertation, University of Toronto, Ontario, Canada.

Swain, M. (2001). Integrating language and content teaching through collaborative tasks. *The Canadian Modern Language Review, 58*(1), 44-63.

Swain, M. & Barik, H. C. (1976). A large scale program in French immersion: The Ottawa study through grade three. *ITL: A Review of Applied Linguistics, 33*, 1-25.

Swain, M. & Johnson, R. K. (1997). Immersion education: A category within bilingual education. In R. K. Johnson & M. Swain (Eds.), *Immersion education: International perspectives* (pp. 1-16). NY: Cambridge University Press.

Swain, M. & Lapkin, S. (1982). *Evaluating bilingual education: A Canadian case study*. Clevedon, England: Multilingual Matters.

Swartz, S. L. (n.d.) *Supporting literacy learning for children with autism*. Retrieved April 1, 2009, from http://www.stanswartz.com/SwedenPresentation/supportingliteracy.html

Swartz, S. L., Shook, R. E., & Klein, A. K. (2003). *Guided reading and literacy centers*. Carlsbad, CA: Dominie Press.

Teachernet. (n.d.). Autism Working Group, *Autistic Spectrum Disorders (ASD)—Guidance from the autism working group*. Retrieved on July 1, 2009 from http://www.teachernet.gov.uk/wholeschool/sen/teacherlearningassistant/asd/

Teachers of English to Speakers of Other Languages. (1997). *ESL standards for pre-K-12 students*. Alexandria, VA: Teachers of English to Speakers of Other Languages.

Tharp, R. G., Estrada, P., Dalton, S. S., & Yamauchi, L. A. (2000). *Teaching transformed: Achieving excellence, fairness, inclusion, and harmony*. Boulder, CO: Westview Press.

Theroux, P. (2004). *Enhance learning with technology*. Retrieved April 1, 2009, from http://members.shaw.ca/priscillatheroux/differentiatinglinks.html

Thomas, W., & Collier, V. (1997). *School effectiveness for minority language students*. Washington, DC: National Clearinghouse for Bilingual Education. Retrieved April 1, 2009, from http://www.ncela.gwu.edu/pubs/resource/effectiveness/

Thomas, W., & Collier, V. (2002). *A national study of school effectiveness for minority language students' long-term academic achievement*. Washington, DC and Santa Cruz, CA: National Clearinghouse for Bilingual Education and Center for Research on Education, Diversity, and Excellence.

Thordardottir, E. (2006). Language intervention from a bilingual mindset [Electronic version]. *The ASHA Leader, 11*(10), 6-7, 20-21. Retrieved July 2, 2009, from http://www.asha.org/publications/leader/archives/2006/060815/f060815a.htm

Thordardottir, E., Ellis Weismer, S., & Smith, M. (1997). Vocabulary learning in bilingual and monolingual clinical intervention. *Child Language Teaching and Therapy, 13*(3), 215-227.

Tomlinson, C. A. (2001). *How to differentiate instruction in mixed-ability classrooms*. (2nd ed.) Alexandria, VA: ASCD.

Toppelberg, C. O., Snow, C. E., & Tager-Flusberg, H. (1999). Severe developmental disorders and bilingualism. *Journal of the American Academy of Child & Adolescent Psychiatry, 38*, 1197-1199.

Trites, R. L. (1976). Children with learning difficulties in primary French immersion. *The Canadian Modern Language Review, 33*, 193-207.

Trites, R. L. (1986). *Learning disabilities and prediction of success in primary French immersion: An overview*. Toronto: Ontario Ministry of Education.

Trites, R.L., & Price, M.A. (1977). *Learning disabilities found in association with French immersion programming: A cross-validation*. Ottawa, ON: University of Ottawa Press.

Tucker, B. (2001). *Tucker signing strategies for reading*. Highlands, TX: Aha! Process.

Tucker, B. (2006). *Tucker signing strategies for reading*. Retrieved April 1, 2009, from http://www.tuckersigns.com/index.html

Turnbull, M., Hart, D., & Lapkin, S. (2003). Grade 6 French immersion students' performance on large-scale reading, writing, and mathematics tests: Building explanations. *Alberta Journal of Education, 49*, 6-23.

Turnbull, M., Lapkin, S., & Hart, D. (2001). Grade 3 immersion students' performance in literacy and mathematics: Province-wide results from Ontario (1998-99). *The Canadian Modern Language Review, 58* (1), 9-26.

The University of Kansas Center for Research on Learning. (2009). *Learning strategies curriculum*. Retrieved April 1, 2009, from http://www.ku-crl.org/about/press/learn-strat.shtml

University of Oregon Center on Teaching and Learning. (n.d.) *DIBELS*. Retrieved April 1, 2009, from http://dibels.uoregon.edu/

U.S. Department of Education (n.d.). *Legislation on special education and rehabilitative services*. Retrieved April 1, 2009, from http://www.ed.gov/policy/speced/leg/edpicks.jhtml?src=ln

V.A.K. learning styles. (n.d.). Retrieved April 1, 2009, from https://olt.qut.edu.au/it/ITB116/gen/static/VAK/Index.htm

Vancouver School Board. (2004, May). Possible factors influencing student performance in French immersion. *The ACIE Newsletter, 7*(3), p.13.

Vaughn, S., Gersten, R., & Chard, D. (2000). The underlying message in LD intervention research. *Council for Exceptional Children, 67*, 99-114.

Vygotsky, L.S. (1978). *Mind in society: The development of higher psychological processes*. Cambridge, MA: Harvard University Press.

Wechsler, D. (1974). *Wechsler intelligence scale for children-revised*. New York: Psychological Corporation.

WETA. (2008). *LD Online*. Retrieved April 1, 2009, from http://www.ldonline.org/

WETA. (2008). *IDEA 2004*. Retrieved April 1, 2009, from http://www.ldonline.org/features/idea2004

WETA. (2008). *Parents*. Retrieved April 1, 2009, from http://www.ldonline.org/parents

Wilson, W., & Kamanā, K. (2008, February). Ke Kula 'O Nāwahīokalani'öpu'u: A P-12 university indigenous language revitalization laboratory school. *The ACIE Newsletter, 11*(2), 3-4, 8.

Windsor, J., & Kohnert, K. (2004). In search of common ground-Part I: Lexical performance by linguistically diverse learners. *Journal of Speech, Language, and Hearing Research, 47*, 877-890.

Windsor, J., Kohnert, K., Rowe, A., & Kan, P.F. (2008). Performance on nonlinguistic visual tasks by children with language impairment. *Applied Psycholinguistics, 29*(2), 237-268.

Wire, V. (n.d.). *Autism and foreign language learning*. Retrieved April 1, 2009, from http://www.hilarymccoll.co.uk/autismMFL.html

Wiss, C. A. (1987). Issues in assessment of learning problems in children from French immersion programs: A case study illustration in support of Cummins. *The Canadian Modern Language Review, 42*(2), 302-313.

Wiss, C. (1989). Early French immersion programs may not be suitable for every child. *The Canadian Modern Language Review, 45*(3), 517-529.

Woelber, K. (2003). *Determining eligibility of special education services for immersion students with learning disabilities*. Unpublished master's thesis, Hamline University, St. Paul, Minnesota.

Wong-Fillmore, L. (1983). The language learner as an individual: Implications on research on individual differences for the ESL teacher. In M. Clarke & J. Handscombe (Eds.), *On TESOL '82: Pacific perspectives on language learning and teaching* (pp. 157-173). Washington, D.C.: Teachers of English to Speakers of Other Languages.

Wong-Fillmore, L. (1991). Second language learning in children: A model of language learning in social context. In E. Bialystock (Ed.), *Language processing in bilingual children* (pp. 49-69). Cambridge, UK: Cambridge University Press.

World Health Organization. (1980). *International classification of impairments, disabilities, and handicaps*. Geneva: Author.

Zimmerman, I. L., Steiner, V. G., & Pond, R. E. (2002). *Preschool language scale Spanish (4th ed.)*. San Antonio, TX: Pearson.

Made in the USA
San Bernardino, CA
25 January 2020